MATTHEW

◆

MATTHEW

◆

H. A. IRONSIDE

Revised Edition

Introductory Notes by
John Phillips

LOIZEAUX
Neptune, New Jersey

First Edition, 1948
Revised Edition, 1994

MATTHEW
© 1994 by Loizeaux Brothers

A Publication of Loizeaux Brothers, Inc.
*A Nonprofit Organization Devoted to the Lord's Work
and to the Spread of His Truth.*

Unless otherwise indicated, Scripture quotations are
taken from the King James version of the Bible.

Profile taken from *Exploring the Scriptures*
© 1965, 1970, 1989 by John Phillips.

Library of Congress Cataloging-in-Publication Data

Ironside, H. A. (Henry Allan), 1876-1951.
Matthew/H. A. Ironside. — Rev. ed.
ISBN 0-87213-425-3
1. Bible. N.T. Matthew—Commentaries. I. Title.
BS2575.3.I56   1993
226.2'077—dc20   93-8057

Printed in the United States of America
10 9 8 7 6 5 4 3

CONTENTS

A PROFILE
MATTHEW
BEHOLD THY KING

BY JOHN PHILLIPS

Before being called by Christ to be one of His disciples, Matthew had been a publican (a tax gatherer) for the government of Rome and thus a member of a caste utterly despised by all patriotic Jews. Upon his call, Matthew had thrown a great feast to which he had invited all his former colleagues, and to which he also invited Jesus and His disciples. This was a great way to begin a life dedicated to the Christ of God. Being a Jew himself, Matthew fully understood the Jewish Messianic hope, and his Gospel is designed to convince his own nation that the long-awaited Messiah is none other than Jesus of Nazareth.

There are about thirty sections in Matthew that are peculiar to his Gospel, and most of those sections have some bearing on Matthew's main theme: the King and His kingdom. Words and expressions peculiar to Matthew have the same purpose, such as "the kingdom of heaven" (an expression occurring thirty-two times and not once in any of the other Gospels), "Father in heaven" (occurring fifteen times in Matthew and only twice in Mark), "son of David" (ten times in Matthew), "that it might be fulfilled which was spoken" (nine times in Matthew and in none of the other Gospels), and "that which was spoken" or "it was spoken" (fourteen times in Matthew and nowhere else). Matthew's Gospel is saturated with Old Testament quotations, containing some sixty references to that portion of the Bible. Matthew never lost sight of his audience: Jews trained to believe that when the Messiah came He would conquer all Israel's foes and make

Jerusalem the capital of a Jewish world empire. Such people believed in the Christ but did not believe Jesus was the Christ.

Matthew's material is not always in chronological sequence. He tends to group his material in order to produce a cumulative effect for the point he is making that Jesus is the Messiah of the Jews. For example, beginning in chapter 5, we have the sermon on the mount— what Jesus taught. That is followed by a series of miracles in chapters 8–9 (by no means in the order of occurrence), which show what Jesus wrought. Those miracles are followed in turn by a series of reactions to Jesus, illustrating what people thought. It seems clear that Matthew's material is arranged so that it can be easily remembered—and certainly the contents of his Gospel are more easily remembered than the contents of the other Synoptics.

Matthew had a tendency to group his material so as to produce a cumulative effect. There are five major sections to his Gospel (4:12– 7:29; 8:1–11:1; 11:2–13:53; 13:54–19:2; 19:3–26:2), all ending with words like these: "And it came to pass, when Jesus had finished..." Each section ends with a discourse reflecting the Jewish manner of teaching in ancient days.

Theme of Matthew

The outline of Matthew shows clearly that Jesus is the long-awaited Son of David, King of Israel, and God's promised Messiah.

I. THE KING IS REVEALED (1–9)
   A. His Person (1:1–4:11)
      1. His Ancestry (1:1-17)
      2. His Advent (1:18–2:23)
      3. His Ambassador (3:1-17)
      4. His Adversary (4:1-11)
   B. His Purpose (4:12–7:29)
      1. His Method Revealed (4:12-25)
      2. His Mandate Revealed (5–7)
   C. His Power (8–9)
II. THE KING IS RESISTED (10:1–16:12)
   A. The Resistance Foretold (10)

The King Introduced

The genealogy of Christ given by Matthew is not the same as that given by Luke. Matthew gave the regal line ending in Joseph, the foster father of Jesus, and showed Christ as the Son of David and the Son of Solomon. Luke gave the legal line through Nathan, an elder brother of Solomon (2 Samuel 5:14), ending in Mary, the Lord's mother. The prophet Isaiah, speaking of the death of Jesus long before, challenged the people with the words, "Who shall declare his generation?" (Isaiah 53:8) Matthew proved conclusively that Jesus had every right to the throne of David, for He was indeed "the king of the Jews." At His birth, Gentile wise men paid Him this tribute, and at His death, the Gentile Pilate in the superscription over the cross acknowledged the same thing.

Jesus was introduced to the nation by John the Baptist, His cousin according to the flesh, and the appointed forerunner spoken of in Malachi. Jesus was baptized by John in the Jordan river and was immediately led into the wilderness by the Spirit to be tempted of the devil. The resounding victory the King won over man's ancient foe was but the opening campaign in that bitter struggle which climaxed at Calvary. Returning from this victory, the King selected certain of His disciples and revealed His power over demons and disease.

The sermon on the mount is one of the most revolutionary passages in the Bible. In sweeping statements the King revealed His concept of the kingdom as spiritual, otherworldly, and yet intensely practical. He boldly lifted the law of Moses to a higher plane and, brushing aside all cumbersome traditions and evasive interpretations, faced men with laws of behavior that, humanly speaking, are impossible to obey. Yet He practiced the life He preached, living it out day by day, moment by moment, for thirty-three and a half magnificent years.

The King Resisted

It was not long before the impact of Christ's message produced adverse results. This was not the kind of king the people wanted, nor the kind of kingdom they expected. Resistance began to stiffen despite the marvelous proofs and credentials Jesus gave in His mighty miracles. The leaders, moved with jealousy, began to attack both the person and the work of Christ and were made even fiercer in their opposition by the Lord's withering denunciations of their hypocrisy.

Again and again the Lord warned the disciples that His enemies would triumph temporarily and that they would succeed in having Him crucified. Calmly He announced to them not only His death but His certain resurrection. He spoke of these events more frequently after His unveiling on the mount of transfiguration. In private discourses, public disputes, and prophetic declarations the Lord showed a clear grasp of future events both near and far. The Olivet discourse for example (chapters 24–25) is one of the most concise yet comprehensive prophetic utterances in the Bible.

At last Judas defected to the enemy camp and betrayed the Lord to His foes. A mock trial ensued before both the Jews and the Gentiles, and God's King was crowned with thorns and nailed upon a Roman cross. Three days later He rose in triumph from the tomb, and none of the enemy's lies have been able to halt the spread of the spiritual empire of the risen Christ of God around the globe.

Happy are they who, faced with such a risen, living, reigning, returning King, bow the knee to Him and crown Him Lord of their lives.

INTRODUCTION

While we have no means of knowing just when the Gospel of Matthew was written, or even whether (as some suppose) it first appeared in Hebrew, or was originally written in Greek as it has come down to us, it is very evident that it is placed rightfully at the beginning of the New Testament. This Gospel is very definitely the connecting link between the prophets of old and the new dispensation of grace. The many quotations in it from the books of the prophets are designed to show how our Lord Jesus Christ came as the promised King of Israel, in exact accordance with the numerous predictions that God had inspired His servants to give. Those prophecies were given from Abraham's day to that of Malachi, when prophetic testimony ceased, and was silent for four hundred years, until John the Baptist, the last of the prophets, came declaring, "The time is fulfilled."

Matthew is in a very real sense the Jewish Gospel. This does not mean that it has no message for Christians, but rather that it is designed by the Holy Spirit to present Christ so as to make it clear to honest Jewish inquirers that He is the One of whom Moses and the prophets spoke. In 1:1-17 we have the genealogy of the King, and in 1:18-25 the birth of the King. In 2:1-12 the Gentiles do homage to the King, and in 2:13-23 we see the preservation of the King. Chapter 3 gives the dedication and anointing of the King; while in chapter 4 we have His testing. In chapters 5 to 7 inclusive (the so-called sermon on the mount) the King unfolds the principles of His kingdom. From chapter 8 through 12 we see the King accredited by mighty works of power, but meeting with ever-increasing rejection. In chapters 13 to 20 we behold a new condition—that which was to prevail after the rejected King returned to Heaven, and until He comes again.

The kingdom of Heaven is seen throughout in mystical form. In other words, it is the development of what we generally speak of as Christendom. The culmination as to Israel is seen in chapters 21 to 23, where God's earthly people are seen as set to one side because of their refusal to receive the King when He came to them in exact accordance with their own Scriptures. Chapters 24 and 25 have to do with the second advent of the King. In chapters 26 to 28 we have His death and resurrection, closing with His commission to His disciples to go forth to the nations with the kingdom message.

The genealogy given in Matthew is that of Joseph, the foster father of Jesus, lineal descendant of David and heir to the throne, through whom the throne rights were transmitted to our Lord. His birth occurred in Bethlehem late in 5 B.C. or early in 4 B.C., while the visit of the wise men took place possibly some two months afterward, and this was followed almost immediately by the flight into Egypt.

We need not be surprised to find that everything in connection with the advent of the King was of a miraculous character when we realize that He was truly *Immanuel*, "God with us," as predicted in Isaiah 7:14. When God came down to earth, how could it be otherwise than that certain natural laws should be suspended in order that He might enter into our world in a manner becoming to His majesty and power? So we see Him taking our humanity as born of a virgin mother, His coming made known in some supernatural way to the wise men from the East, and His life preserved by divine arrangement so that the malice of Herod could not reach Him and destroy Him. The beauty and simplicity of the narrative fills us with admiration and moves our hearts to worship and thanksgiving for God's unspeakable Gift.

While it is of great importance that we observe and take into account the special dispensational place of this Gospel, we shall lose much if we fail to realize that it *is* gospel, and not law. For the gospel is God's message concerning His Son, and here the Son is presented in His kingly aspect that we may learn to reverence Him as such and bow in subjection at His feet.

CHAPTER ONE
THE BIRTH OF THE KING

Genealogy of the King (Matthew 1:1-17)

The Gospel of Matthew begins with the genealogy of our Lord from Abraham to Joseph. But this was not the bloodline. It was the royal line, however, and carried with it the throne rights. As Son of Abraham, our Lord is the promised seed in whom all nations of the world shall be blessed (Genesis 22:18). As Son of David, He is the King who is to reign in righteousness upon David's throne (Isaiah 9:6-7). His actual descent from David was through His mother Mary, who was the daughter of Heli. She was married to Joseph before her holy child was born, thus giving Him legal, full title to the throne, though the curse on Jeconiah (Jeremiah 22:30) would have precluded His occupancy of it had He actually been the son of Joseph.

Matthew 1:17 epitomizes the genealogy, dividing it into three groups of fourteen generations each. In order to do this, certain names are omitted and in the last instance Mary's name has to be counted to make fourteen, unless, as others have suggested, we are to consider the birth of Jesus as the thirteenth and the second coming of Christ as the fourteenth.

Others have drawn attention to the inclusion of the names of five women in this list, all of whom no Jewish chronologist would naturally have desired to recognize. These are Tamar, whose shameful story is recorded in Genesis 38; Rahab the harlot, a Gentile who, though a woman of evil character, became the wife of an Israelite prince; Ruth the Moabitess, also a stranger from among the Gentiles, who entered this royal line only through her levirate marriage to

Boaz, her first husband's near kinsman; Bathsheba, definitely mentioned as "her that had been the wife of Urias," thus bringing to mind David's terrible failure; and last of all, the sweetest of all, Mary the virgin of Nazareth, the one whose fair name has been impugned by unbelieving Jews because she became the mother of Jesus apart from the natural order.

What a list is this! How it reveals the grace that is in the heart of God, who in His sovereignty chose to bring these five women into the line of promise. The names of unchaste Tamar, Rahab, and Bathsheba tell us of mercy that goes out to the most sinful and depraved. The name of Ruth, loyal and devoted, yet a stranger, speaks of grace acting in spite of the ban upon the Moabites (Deuteronomy 23:3-6). When we think of Mary the virgin mother, we adore the God who gave us His holy and blessed Son through her as the human instrument.

Birth of the King *(Matthew 1:18-25)*

"Before they came together." The Scriptures are clear about the virgin birth of Jesus. His mother Mary was engaged to Joseph, but had not yet been married to him when he learned that she was to become a mother through direct operation of the Holy Spirit and altogether apart from natural generation. "Minded to put her away privily." If Mary was not a virgin, the penalty for her condition according to the law was death. Joseph thought to save her from this. "Fear not to take unto thee Mary thy wife." The wonderful mystery of the incarnation was revealed to Joseph by angelic ministry.

"Thou shalt call his name JESUS." *Jesus* from the Greek and *Joshua* from the Hebrew are one name, and the meaning is "Jehovah the Savior." "That it might be fulfilled." This is a distinctive phrase in this Gospel, used often because the object of the inspired writer is to show that Jesus is the Messiah promised in the prophets. "They shall call his name Emmanuel...God with us." Isaiah made this prediction nearly seven centuries before its fulfillment (Isaiah 7:14). The name given is an intimation of the mysterious union of the divine and the human in the virgin's Son.

"Took unto him his wife." He married her notwithstanding her condition, that she might have the place in Israel of a wedded wife before she became a mother. "He called his name JESUS." Obedient to the last detail, by calling the child "Jesus," Joseph evidenced the reality of his own faith.

The name "Jesus," as intimated above, is simply the Anglicized form of the Greek *Iesous*, which is the equivalent of the Hebrew *Joshua*—"the salvation of Jehovah." Many had borne that name before the Savior came into the world, and even in its Greek form it was not uncommon. We read of a "Jesus, which is called Justus" in Colossians 4:11. But throughout all the centuries since the incarnation, death, and resurrection of our blessed Lord, that name has stood out as distinct from every other. To Christians it is the name above every name at which every knee shall bow. Having taken it here on earth, He will keep this name "Jesus" for all the ages to come. The two shining ones who announced His future coming (Acts 1:10-11) spoke of Him as "This same Jesus." In Revelation 22:16 He says, "I Jesus have sent mine angel to testify unto you these things in the churches." In response to His last message from Heaven, "Surely I come quickly," the seer replied, "Even so, come, Lord Jesus" (Revelation 22:20)! By this name we shall know Him throughout a blissful eternity, provided we know Him now on earth as our very own Savior, Jesus, who has redeemed us to God by His blood.

CHAPTER TWO
THE PRESERVATION OF THE KING

Visit of the Magi (Matthew 2:1-12)

The circumstances connected with the nativity of our Lord in David's city, Bethlehem, were given in considerable detail by Luke. Matthew told us only that He was born in that city in the days of Herod the king. This establishes the date of His birth as several years earlier than the commonly accepted record. He was born around 4 B.C. The question of His birthdate, however, is one to which chronologists have given much thought and study, and inasmuch as they are still in disagreement as to the exact date, we need not discuss it here.

It was prophesied of the Messiah that He would bring blessing to the nations as well as to Israel. Aged Simeon epitomized these promises when he declared of Jesus that He would be "a light to lighten the Gentiles, and the glory of thy people Israel" (Luke 2:32). The incident now before us is an earnest or foretaste of this.

Many non-Scriptural ideas and legends have been linked with the visit of these wise men from the East. Contrary to the pictures we see generally, they are not called kings, but magi—that is, wise men who devoted themselves to the study of ancient lore. Undoubtedly they were somewhat acquainted with certain prophecies, possibly those of Balaam (who was of the East) and of Daniel, whose book was written partly in the Hebrew and partly in the Chaldee languages. We need to remember also that the entire Old Testament had been translated into Greek some two centuries earlier. This translation, known as the Septuagint (LXX), was available to scholars throughout the world and was studied, undoubtedly, by many Gentile students of sacred

lore. We have no authority for saying there were only three magi.
This may have been deduced from the fact that three kinds of
offerings are mentioned (Matthew 2:11). It is probable that an
attempt to see in their visit the fulfillment of Psalm 72:10 is responsible for the idea that they were oriental kings. But Psalm 72 is yet to
be fulfilled at Christ's second coming.

The wise men had learned of the birth of the promised King by
divine revelation, or else had worked out the great time prophecy of
Daniel 9 so that they felt assured He was present in Israel. Guided by
a star they came inquiring as to the place in which He might be found.
Their question, "Where is he that is born King of the Jews?" proved
most distracting to the aged wretch who sat on the throne at that
time—one of the most wicked kings that ever reigned. He called a
meeting of the chief priests and scribes, and sought from them the
answer to the inquiry of the eastern visitors. Without hesitation they
pointed him to the prophecy of Micah 5:2 where, quoting from the
Septuagint, they read, "Thou Bethlehem, in the land of Juda, art not
the least among the princes of Juda: for out of thee shall come a
Governor, that shall rule my people Israel." They knew the Scripture;
yet subsequent events proved they were unprepared to welcome Him
of whom those sacred records spoke.

Herod, determined in his heart to destroy the infant King—if
indeed He had appeared already—conferred with the magi as to when
the mysterious star had first appeared; and then bade them go on to
Bethlehem. If they found the baby, they were to return and report to
him so that he too might do Him honor. Actually his intention was the
very opposite.

Led by the star that was seen again as they left Jerusalem, they had
no difficulty in locating the house where the holy family resided at
this time. It is evidently a mistake to suppose that Mary and Joseph,
with the child, were still in the stable where the shepherds found
them. They were now in a more convenient dwelling. Doubtless
some weeks or even months had elapsed since the birth of Jesus.

Beholding Him the wise men prostrated themselves before Him
and presented their well-selected gifts: gold, speaking of the divine
nature and righteousness; frankincense, suggesting the fragrance of
His perfect human life; and myrrh, pointing forward to His sacrificial

death. Mary's thoughts may well have been exalted as she beheld these eastern sages thus doing homage to her sacred Son. Joseph is not mentioned. He may not have been present during the visit of the strangers. "Being warned of God in a dream" not to return to Herod, the wise men departed to their homes by a different route.

Preservation of the King (Matthew 2:13-15)

From His earliest infancy the holy child Jesus was in a very special way under divine protection, for though He was God manifest in the flesh, He was not exempt from human suffering. Angels watched over His early years like a heavenly bodyguard. They announced His birth, even as Gabriel had predicted His incarnation. They were sent of God to explain the mystery of Mary's condition to Joseph; and then they instructed him as to each step he was to take in order to guard his sacred charge from the vengeance of Herod and others who might seek to put Him to death before the appointed time. The angels were created by the eternal Word, the Son, who in the fullness of time became man for our salvation. It was their joy to herald His coming into the world and to watch over and minister to Him in His humiliation down here. Upon the departure of the magi it was an angel who spoke to Joseph in a dream (which in itself reminds us how God often has revealed His will to men, as in Job 33:14-17). Joseph was commanded to "take the young child and his mother, and flee into Egypt," there to abide until further instruction came, in order to protect the child from the wrath of Herod. Herod was determined not to permit anyone to live who might contest the rights of his family to the throne.

According to the bidding of the angel Joseph "arose . . . and departed into Egypt." There God was to provide a place of refuge where the holy baby would be permitted to develop in peace and security. The family, with Jesus, remained in Egypt until word came that Herod had died, "that it might be fulfilled which was spoken of the Lord by the prophet, saying, Out of Egypt have I called my son." These words were spoken by Jehovah through Hosea (11:1) and referred primarily to Israel as a nation. Now they were to be fulfilled a second time in Him who came to redeem Israel. He, like the family

of Jacob, went down into Egypt and was brought out of it in God's due
time.

Vengeance of Herod *(Matthew 2:16-23)*

Herod's reaction to the refusal of the wise men to bring him word
again was terrible. In his rage and fury, he ordered the massacre of
all the innocent children two years of age and under who were in
Bethlehem, hoping thereby to destroy Him who was born to be King
of the Jews.

"Then was fulfilled that which was spoken by Jeremy the prophet."
"Jeremy" is a translation of the Greek form of *Jeremiah.* The
prophecy referred to is found in Jeremiah 31:15. "In Rama was there
a voice heard . . . Rachel weeping for her children." Primarily, these
words seem to refer to the distress of the mothers in Judah when their
sons went into captivity. But the passage is cited as fitting perfectly
with the grief of those mothers of Bethlehem whose infants were so
ruthlessly slaughtered. Often in Scripture we find these twofold
applications.

"When Herod was dead, behold, an angel of the Lord appeareth."
In due time the word came through a heavenly visitant speaking to
Joseph in a dream as before, "Saying, Arise, and . . . go into the land
of Israel." The way was now clear for the young child Jesus and His
mother to return to their own land. Herod had passed away and now
had to answer to God for his life of crime and cruelty. Joseph "arose
. . . and came into the land of Israel." Joseph's obedience to each
message of the angel is noteworthy. Without raising any questions,
he complied immediately with every commandment that was given
him in this supernatural way. We know very little of the life and
experience of this man who was chosen to be the foster father of
Jesus, but what little we are told makes us realize that he was one who
was very sensitive to the word of the Lord. He furnishes us with a
most precious example of implicit obedience to the will of God, even
under most perplexing and difficult circumstances.

"When he heard that Archelaus did reign in Judaea . . . he was
afraid." Herod had murdered most of his own offspring, but Archelaus
was permitted to live, and to him Herod willed his kingdom. Joseph

feared Archelaus might be as vicious as his ungodly father, so he hesitated about actually putting his little family into his power. But again God directed him by appearing to him in a dream and warning him not to settle in Judea but to turn aside "into the parts of Galilee."

"He came and dwelt in a city called Nazareth." From Luke's Gospel we learn that Mary was living in Nazareth when Gabriel first appeared to her (Luke 1:26). Joseph also dwelt there, and it was from this city that the two journeyed to Bethlehem where Jesus was born (Luke 2:4). They returned, therefore, to their own former hometown, and there Jesus grew from childhood to manhood. Because of His residence there He was called a Nazarene, a name intimately connected with the Hebrew word *Netzer* meaning "branch," as in Zechariah 6:12 and other Scriptures. In a secondary sense it might mean "a separated one," a Nazarite as in Numbers 6:2, for Jesus was the true Nazarite, separated to God from His birth. The city of Nazareth evidently took its name from this word *Netzer*, possibly because of some special tree or sprout found in that vicinity. Therefore, it was easy to link the name "Nazarene" with the prophecies concerning Jesus as the branch, or sprout of the Lord (Isaiah 4:2), the branch out of David's roots (Isaiah 11:1). But as applied to Jesus by His enemies, it was a term of reproach—a term, however, which the early Christians readily appropriated and gloried in (Acts 24:5).

CHAPTER THREE

THE INTRODUCTION OF THE KING

John Prepares the Crowds *(Matthew 3:1-6)*

Our Lord told us that of those born of women none was greater than John the Baptist. He stands out pre-eminently as a devoted man of God, true to principles and unyielding in his stand against iniquity even in high places (Matthew 14:4). However, his greatness consisted in the fact that he was chosen of God to herald the coming of Christ as Israel's Messiah and the world's Redeemer (John 1:29-31). John formally opened to Christ the door into the sheepfold (John 10:2-3) by baptizing and acknowledging Him as the anointed of God. Time can never dim the luster that belongs to him as the forerunner of the Christ. John was permitted to see and know the One of whom he prophesied—a privilege denied to all the earlier prophets.

Luke gave the date of the beginning of John's ministry as the fifteenth year of Tiberias Caesar, which most authorities identify with A.D. 26. His special ministry was the calling of the people of Israel to repentance. He "came...in the way of righteousness," (Matthew 21:32) to emphasize God's holy and just demands on His creatures and to insist that only the self-judged sinner is fit for the presence of the Lord. Such a ministry is needed greatly today when men have lost, in large measure, the sense of the sinfulness of sin. It is useless to preach the gospel of the grace of God to men who have no realization of their need of that grace. Only when the soul is awakened to see its uncleanness and unrighteousness in the eyes of a holy God will there be the cry, "God be merciful to me a sinner."

"In those days came John the Baptist, preaching in the wilderness of Judea, And saying, Repent ye: for the kingdom of heaven is at hand." The wilderness of Judea is the region east and south of Jerusalem, including the lower Jordan valley, and the western side of the Dead Sea. John's message was a call to self-judgment. He urged the people to take sides with God against themselves.

In Isaiah 40 we find the prophecy that was fulfilled in John the Baptist. His message was, "Prepare ye the way of the Lord." Israel had waited expectantly for centuries for the Messiah, but they were not ready to receive Him: they needed that preparation of heart which comes from honestly facing one's sins before God.

Both John's raiment and his food are mentioned in Matthew. Elijah-like, he appeared in wilderness garb and subsisted on wilderness fare. He was a man of the great open places, whose manner of living added to the force of his words. It is considered debatable by some whether he actually ate locusts, or whether the term used refers to the carob-pod of the locust tree. But inasmuch as locusts are eaten today and have been used as food (very much like dried shrimp) from time immemorial, it seems most likely that John actually used them in his diet. On one occasion Jesus called attention to John's abstemiousness (Matthew 11:18; Luke 7:33).

As John proclaimed the need of repentance, his hearers came to him from all parts of the land "and were baptized of him in Jordan, confessing their sins." Baptism in itself was not an act of merit. It was meant to imply that the baptized person admitted that his just desert was judgment because of his sins. Thus those who were baptized condemned themselves and justified God (Luke 7:29). It is clear that John did not preach that his baptism freed men from their sins (John 1:29). He pointed the people to Jesus as the only One through whom they could obtain remission of sin.

John Calls Religious Leaders to Repentance (Matthew 3:7-12)

When haughty religious professors who gave no evidence of repentance came with the rest seeking baptism, John rebuked them sternly, saying, "O generation of vipers, who hath warned you to flee from the wrath to come?" Strong language was used because of the hypocrisy of these religious formalists, who by their hidden wickedness proclaimed themselves children of the evil one. The Pharisees were the orthodox party in Israel, and the Sadducees were the heterodox group (Acts 23:8); but both alike rested on their own fancied righteousness and therefore saw no need to repent (Romans 10:3). John demanded evidence of repentance before he was willing to administer the sacred rite of baptism. While good works have no value so far as procuring salvation is concerned, the truly repentant one shows by a new life the reality of his profession by turning to God and away from his iniquities.

These religious professors were ready to reply indignantly that they were children of Abraham, and so needed no repentance. John realized what was going through their minds and exclaimed, "Think not to say within yourselves, We have Abraham to our father: for I say unto you, that God is able of these stones to raise up children unto Abraham." It is a common thing for unspiritual religionists to rest upon and glory in the piety of their forefathers. But unless that same faith of our forefathers is found in us, our glorying is vain. God, who made man from the dust of the earth, could raise up children of faith from stones if He so willed. John added, "And now also the ax is laid unto the root of the trees: therefore every tree which bringeth not forth good fruit is hewn down, and cast into the fire." Too often in our day the ax is laid to the fruit of the tree. But it is the root that is wrong. There must be a new man if there would be fruit for God. To lay the ax to the root of the tree implies the utter condemnation of the natural man and suggests the positive need of new birth.

Continuing his indictment, John explained that the outward symbol was only for those who professed sincere repentance toward God, and who cast themselves on His mercy as needy, helpless sinners. When Christ came He would baptize with (or in) the Holy Spirit and fire.

"Whose fan is in his hand, and he will throughly purge his floor, and gather his wheat into the garner; but he will burn up the chaff with unquenchable fire." The wheat represents the children of the kingdom (Matthew 13:38). They are the ones who were to be baptized in the Holy Spirit. The chaff represents the evil-doers who will be baptized in the fire of judgment. Nothing could emphasize our Lord's deity more than John's declaration regarding Him and this twofold baptism. Imagine a creature baptizing in the Holy Spirit. Only One who is Himself divine could do this. And on Pentecost Peter declared unhesitatingly that it was God who sent the Spirit (Acts 2:33). He it is who will consign the impenitent to the fire of everlasting punishment (Matthew 25:41). This is not to be confused with the cleansing efficacy of the Holy Spirit, nor with the tongues "like as of fire" that appeared at Pentecost. "He will burn up the chaff with unquenchable fire" is placed in direct contrast to gathering the "wheat into the garner."

John Baptizes Jesus (Matthew 3:13-17)

The day arrived at last for the manifestation of the King. Jesus appeared in the throng, and stepped forward to undergo the rite to which so many confessed sinners had submitted. He who was to take the sinner's place came to be baptized of John, that He might thereby be identified with sinners for whom He was to lay down His life. "But John forbad him, saying, I have need to be baptized of thee, and comest thou to me?" To the Baptist it seemed inappropriate that the sinless One should submit to a baptism of repentance for the remission of sins. He felt his own need rather to be baptized of Jesus.

"And Jesus answering said unto him, Suffer it to be so now: for thus it becometh us to fulfil all righteousness. Then he suffered him." It is as though Jesus said, "I wish to submit to this as a pledge that I have come to fulfill every righteous demand of the throne of God on behalf of sinful men." It was our Lord's public dedication to the work of the cross for which He had come into the world. It is a very shallow interpretation indeed that makes the act of baptism the fulfilling of righteousness. In other words, it was not in order that He might set us a good example that Jesus was baptized, but rather that He might identify Himself with sinners. He was the One who was to make Himself responsible to satisfy every righteous claim for those who acknowledged that they were justly under the curse of the violated law, and so with no righteousness of their own. They were like debtors giving their notes to God. Jesus endorsed those notes, guaranteeing full payment. The settlement was made on the cross.

In the last two verses of this chapter we learn how God expressed His approval of the Son in a remarkable manner. Immediately following our Lord's open dedication of Himself, "the heavens were opened" above Him, and in visible manifestation the Holy Spirit anointed Him for the great work He had come to undertake to the glory of God and for the salvation of a lost world. It is to this anointing that Peter referred in Acts 10:38, and of which Jesus Himself spoke in John 6:27. He was anointed as prophet, priest, and king, and sealed by the same Spirit as the holy One of God, who alone could meet the need of a dying world.

Here in Matthew's Gospel it is His anointing as the King to which our attention is directed particularly. Mark emphasized His prophetic office, and John presented Him as our great high priest, but this was after finishing the work the Father gave Him to do.

Finally, in audible tones the Father declared His delight in His Son. He who had in His baptism offered Himself to God to become a sacrifice for sin was thus attested to be Himself the sinless One, for the sin offering must be most holy (Leviticus 6:25). There was in Him no taint of sin, no inbred evil such as all of Adam's fallen sons possess. He could say, "I do always those things that please him" (John 8:29). Thus the Father ever found His joy in contemplating the perfection of His Son. He would have us delight in Him too.

CHAPTER FOUR
THE TESTING OF THE KING

Jesus Is Tempted (Matthew 4:1-11)

Before the Lord Jesus presented Himself to Israel as the promised King He had to pass through a period of testing, which He did for forty days. Jesus met Satan, the strong man armed, and bound him before He began His public ministry and went forth to spoil Satan's goods.

Why was Jesus tempted? And being tempted, was there a possibility that He might have sinned, and so jeopardized or annulled the whole plan of redemption? These are questions asked often and it behooves us to be able to give Scriptural answers concerning them.

If we would be clear in our thinking as to this, we must remember that while our Lord was, and is, both human and divine, He is not two persons, but one. Personally He is God the eternal Son who took humanity into union with His deity in order to redeem sinful men. He has therefore two natures, the divine and the human, but He remains just one person. Therefore as man here on earth He could not act apart from His deity. Those who maintain that He might have sinned may well ask themselves, "What then would have been the result?" To say that as man He might have failed in His mission is to admit the amazing and blasphemous suggestion that His holy divine nature could become separated from a defiled human nature and so prove the incarnation a farce and a mockery. But if we realize that He who was both God and man in one person was tempted, not to see if He would (or could) sin, but to prove that He was the sinless One, all is clear. The temptation was real, but it was all from without, as Adam's was in the beginning. But Adam was only an innocent man;

whereas Jesus, the last Adam, was the Lord from Heaven, who had become man without ceasing to be God, in order that He might be our kinsman-redeemer (Leviticus 25:48).

The temptation and His attitude toward it proved that He was not a sinful man, either in nature or in act, and He could therefore take our penalty upon Himself. He could bear the curse of the broken law for others because He was not under that curse Himself. Scripture tells us definitely that He "knew no sin" (2 Corinthians 5:21); He "did no sin" (1 Peter 2:22); "in him is no sin" (1 John 3:5). He could say, "The prince of this world cometh, and hath nothing in me" (John 14:30). There was no lurking traitor within to answer to the voice of the enemy without. There was no sin within to tempt Him. (A literal rendering of Hebrews 4:15b is, "He was tempted as we are sin apart."). From the moment of His birth He was holy, not merely innocent (Luke 1:35).

The temptation of Jesus took place, if we may trust tradition, on mount Quarantania, west of the Jordan, across from Jericho, a very forbidding and desolate wilderness. It followed His baptism almost immediately, in the early part of A.D. 27, shortly before the Passover.

As the perfect man, Jesus was ever subject to the Spirit's control. Mark tells us the Spirit drove Him into the wilderness (Mark 1:12). He was impelled to go, for it was imperative that His holiness be demonstrated from the very beginning of His ministry. Temptation is really testing. He was tested by Satan, that evil personality who is the foe of God and man. It was he who tested the first Adam and found him wanting. Now he must be overcome by the last Adam, the second man (1 Corinthians 15:45,47).

Jesus fasted for the full period of testing—forty days. It was not until all this was over that He is said to have become hungry. Then, in the hour of nature's weakness came the tempter, endeavoring to overcome Him. The tests were threefold: the appeal to the body, the soul, and the spirit. They involved the desires of the flesh, the lust of the eyes, and the pride of life (the ostentation or vainglory of living). The order of the temptation is different in Matthew and in Luke. Matthew evidently gives the three points in their historical order, taking them exactly as they occurred. Luke gives the moral order, in accordance with 1 John 2:16. Thus the first appeal was to appetite, the desire of the flesh, the physical; the next to the esthetic nature, the desire of the eyes, the soul; and the last appeal was to the spiritual nature, the pride of life, or the vainglory of living. The Lord Jesus was impervious to every suggestion of evil.

These are the same temptations in character that the serpent brought to bear on Eve in Eden. She saw that the fruit of the tree was good for food (the lust of the flesh), pleasant to the eyes (the lust of the eyes), and to be desired to make one wise (the pride of life). She succumbed on every point and when Adam collaborated with her in disobedience to God, the old creation fell. They were tested in a garden of delight, a most beautiful environment. Jesus was tempted in a dry, thirsty wilderness among the wild beasts, but stood firm as a rock against all Satan's wiles and blandishments. Thus He manifested Himself as King of righteousness, and so the suited One to be crowned King of peace (Hebrews 7:1-2). He who triumphed over the enemy after being tested in all points like as we, apart from sin, is now our great high priest, appearing in Heaven on our behalf, ready to assist us in every hour of weakness and temptation.

"And when the tempter came to him, he said, If thou be the Son of God, command that these stones be made bread." Every test was a direct assault on the truth of His divine-human personality. There might seem to be nothing inherently wrong for Jesus to satisfy His hunger by making bread from stones, but as man He had taken the place of dependence on the living Father (John 6:57). Therefore He acted only in obedience to the Father's will, and He could not entertain any suggestion coming from another and an opposing source. He would not act on the enemy's advice, even to relieve His hunger.

"But he answered and said, It is written, Man shall not live by bread alone, but by every word that proceedeth out of the mouth of God." Jesus met each temptation with a definite word from God—a quotation from the holy Scriptures. In this instance He quoted Deuteronomy 8:3 where Moses reminded Israel that the spiritual nourishment found in the Word of God is far more important than material food. When God provides food for His children He does not give them stones for bread, nor make bread out of stones; but when we get out of the place of dependence on the Father, we are very likely to break our teeth on hard stony bread, which we thought would be better than that which comes from God.

"Then the devil taketh him up into the holy city, and setteth him on a pinnacle of the temple." Whether the devil actually did this or it was only in vision we are not told, nor is it important that we should know. The point is that even the sanctuary may be a place of temptation, for pride of grace is one of the greatest snares to which we are exposed. From that elevated place Jesus saw the throngs gathered in the courts below. Satan was about to use this as a reason why He should display His power.

In tempting Christ, Satan quoted only a part of Psalm 91:11-12. He omitted the most pertinent portion—"To keep thee in all thy ways." It was no part of the holy ways of the Son of God to leap spectacularly from the temple heights in order to astonish the worshiping multitudes below as they beheld Him suspended in the air above them, sustained by angel hands. This would have been a presumptuous use of the promise. When Satan quotes Scripture, look closely at the text and be sure nothing vital is omitted, for it is possible to back up the gravest error with a text from the Bible used out of context.

"Jesus said unto him, It is written again, Thou shalt not tempt the Lord thy God." Where God commands, faith can act upon His words, knowing—as Augustine said—"God's commands are God's enablings." But to expose oneself to danger needlessly is to tempt God, and this is contrary to the principle of faith.

"Again, the devil taketh him up into an exceeding high mountain, and showeth him all the kingdoms of the world, and the glory of them." These things belonged to Christ, the heir of all things; but Satan has usurped the inheritance. He attempted to present to Jesus what might be called a shortcut to world-dominion.

"And saith unto him, All these things will I give thee, if thou wilt fall down and worship me." Actually, they were Satan's to give only by God's permissive will, for "the most High ruleth in the kingdom of men, and giveth it to whomsoever he will" (Daniel 4:25). Satan had robbed Adam of the authority given him and reigned as usurper in the hearts of wicked men. But he had no undisputed title to the kingdoms of the world, which he offered to give to Jesus if He would worship him, thereby obtaining the kingdom without the cross.

"Then saith Jesus unto him, Get thee hence, Satan: for it is written, Thou shalt worship the Lord thy God, and him only shalt thou serve." By another "saying" of God the foe was vanquished. Jesus did not dispute Satan's word as to his sovereignty of the kingdoms of the world. It is not by debate the victory is won, but by the Word itself.

"Then the devil leaveth him, and, behold, angels came and ministered unto him." What a glorious consummation to the temptation! The defeated, foul fiend fled away. Holy messengers from the court of Heaven came with gladness to minister to their Creator, who in grace had taken the creature's place. When we think of angels ministering to Jesus as they did in the wilderness and in Gethsemane, we realize how truly human He had become, in that He who had created those glorious beings should now be served by them.

God's King must reign in righteousness. The sinner's substitute must be as an unblemished lamb—with no defect outwardly or inwardly. Therefore the Lord as a man must be subjected to the most searching tests to demonstrate His fitness for the great work He came to do. Had the temptation brought to light any evidence of inbred sin or moral corruption of any kind, it would have been the proof that Jesus was not the holy One of God, destined to bring in everlasting righteousness and to make propitiation for iniquity. But nowhere was the perfection of Jesus demonstrated more clearly than when Satan made every effort to find some defect in His character, some form of self-seeking in His heart. The King was tested and proved to be all that God the Father had declared at His baptism—the One in whom He had found all His delight.

We read in Hebrews 2:18 that our Lord Jesus "suffered being tempted." We suffer as we resist temptation, and so are kept from sinning against God (1 Peter 4:1). In this we see the great contrast between Christ as the holy One, and ourselves as sinners with a nature that delights in evil. When born of God we are made partakers of the divine nature, and so we too hate iniquity.

Having been tried and proved to be perfect in all His ways, the King then began His public ministry, accredited by mighty signs and wonders, which should have made it clear to all Israel that He was in very truth the promised Messiah.

Jesus Begins His Ministry (Matthew 4:12-17)

The quotation from Isaiah in Matthew 4:15-16 differs from that which we find in our Old Testament because it is taken from the Septuagint, the Greek translation in common use at that time, instead of from the original Hebrew (see Isaiah 9:1-2).

As He went from place to place Jesus preached, saying, "Repent: for the kingdom of heaven is at hand." This message was the same as that of John the Baptist. "The kingdom of heaven," as we have seen, is a term used only in this Gospel. It speaks of Heaven's rule over earth. This was now ready to be set up if there had been readiness on the part of Israel to receive it. But it could be set up only on a foundation of national repentance; and for this the people were not prepared. They would not receive the King; consequently they lost the kingdom, as the sequel shows. Before that kingdom would be restored to Israel (Acts 1:6) God was to make known another program, which for the time being was hidden from human understanding.

Jesus Calls His First Disciples (Matthew 4:18-25)

Peter and Andrew had been attracted already to Jesus (John 1:40-42). Now they left all to follow Him, little realizing what was in store for them, both of joy and sorrow. James and John also were to be numbered among the King's closest friends, to bear witness to Israel. James was to die a martyr's death early in the new age. John was destined to outlive all the rest of the chosen twelve.

Matthew 4:23-25 epitomizes the nature and scope of the ministry of Jesus. Everywhere Jesus and His disciples went He brought blessing and salvation to those who sought His favor. Many followed Him from place to place, doubtless expecting that at any moment He might declare His royal authority and, overthrowing the Roman power, bring deliverance to Israel. But before this could be done there was another and far greater work that had to be accomplished—the settlement of the sin question: for this He had come into the world. The King must be the victim before He could take His great power and reign. And so, although for the moment the crowds applauded and the common people heard Him gladly, He moved on with even tread to the place called Calvary.

CHAPTER FIVE

THE PRINCIPLES OF THE KINGDOM

PART ONE

In the so-called sermon on the mount our Lord was not preaching the gospel, but He was revealing the principles of His kingdom, which should guide the lives of all who profess to be His disciples. In other words, this sermon states the law of the kingdom. The observance of this law must characterize the loyal subjects of the kingdom as they wait for the day when the King Himself will be revealed. Throughout, the sermon recognizes the existence of definite opposition to His rule, but those who acknowledge His authority in their lives are called on to exhibit the same meek and lowly spirit that was seen in Him during the days of His humiliation here on earth.

For the natural man this sermon is not the way of life, but rather a source of condemnation; for it sets a standard so high and holy that no unsaved person can by any means attain to it. He who attempts it will soon realize his utter helplessness, if he is honest and conscientious. He must look elsewhere in the Scriptures for the gospel, which is the power of God unto salvation to all who believe (Romans 1:16). The keenest intellects of earth have recognized in the sermon on the mount the highest of ethical teaching, and have praised its holy precepts even when conscious of their inability to measure up to its standards. So far as the unsaved are concerned, therefore, the teaching given here becomes indeed, as C. I. Scofield well said, "Law raised to its nth power." Just as the righteous requirements of the law are "fulfilled in us [the believers], who walk not after the flesh, but after the Spirit" (Romans 8:4), so the principles laid down in this sermon will demonstrate themselves in the lives of all who seek to walk as Christ walked.

It is not for us to relegate all these laws or principles to the Jewish remnant in the last days or to disciples before the cross, though fully applicable to both. But we discern here "wholesome words, even the words of our Lord Jesus Christ" (1 Timothy 6:3) which we dare not refuse to obey. Those who refuse to obey are described as "proud, knowing nothing, but doting about questions and strifes of words, whereof cometh envy, strife, railings, evil surmisings" (1 Timothy 6:4) We need to remember that, though a heavenly people, we have earthly responsibilities, and these are defined for us in this greatest of all sermons having to do with human conduct.

The Beatitudes (Matthew 5:1-12)

"Blessed are the poor in spirit." These are the men and women who recognize the fact that they have no spiritual assets. They confess their lost condition and so rely upon divine grace.

"Blessed are they that mourn." The very sorrows men are called to pass through prove a means of blessing if they know the "God of all comfort" (2 Corinthians 1:3) who binds up broken hearts (Psalm 34:18). God makes our griefs become the means of our growth in grace when we trust His love and rest in the realization that all things work together for the good of His own (Romans 8:28).

"Blessed are the meek." The world admires the pushing, self-assertive man. Jesus Christ was meek and lowly in heart. Those who partake of His spirit are the ones who get the most out of life after all. It is they who "inherit the earth," for they see in all nature the evidences of the Father's love and care.

"Blessed are they which do hunger and thirst after righteousness." Such hunger and thirst—such deep, earnest desire—gives evidence of the new life. These desires are not given to mock us. Satisfaction is the promised portion of all who thus yearn after God, in whom alone righteousness is found.

"Blessed are the merciful." To those who show mercy, mercy will be extended. This is a law of the kingdom. The hard, implacable man, who deals in stern justice alone, will be dealt with in the same way when failure comes into his own life.

"Blessed are the pure in heart." Purity is singleness of purpose. The pure in heart are those who put God's glory above all else. To such He reveals Himself. They see His face when others discern only His providential dealings.

"Blessed are the peacemakers." Strife and division are works of the flesh (Galatians 5:19-21). Sowing discord among brethren is one of the things that the Lord hates (Proverbs 6:16-19). We are commanded to follow after the things that make for peace (Romans 14:19). In doing this we display the divine nature, as children of Him who is the God of peace (Romans 15:33).

"Blessed are they which are persecuted for righteousness' sake." This intimates clearly that the instruction set forth here is intended not, as many have insisted, for the millennial kingdom of Christ when there will be no persecution for the sake of righteousness. Rather, this instruction is intended for the disciples of Christ during the time of His rejection, when His followers are exposed to the hatred of a godless world.

"Blessed are ye, when men shall revile you . . . and shall say all manner of evil against you falsely, for my sake." We all shrink from false accusation, but we may find comfort as we remember that our Lord Himself was not exempt from this. There is blessing as we go through these experiences in fellowship with Him, not even attempting to justify ourselves, but leaving it to Him to clear us in His own way and time.

"Rejoice, and be exceeding glad," instead of giving way to depression of spirit, "for great is your reward in heaven." God is taking note of all that His people suffer at the hands, or by the lips, of a godless world or false brethren. He will make up for it all in His own way when we see His face. His prophets in every age have been called upon to endure similar treatment, but He has observed it all and will reward according to the lovingkindness of His heart.

In the next section we have Christ's disciples presented through various symbols, all speaking of the importance of faithfulness to the trust He has committed to us.

Salt and Light (Matthew 5:13-16)

"Ye are the salt of the earth." Salt preserves from corruption. The disciples of our Lord are left in the world to witness against its iniquity and to set an example of righteousness. Savorless salt, like an inconsistent Christian, is good for nothing.

"Ye are the light of the world." Christ so designated Himself as long as He was in this world (John 9:5). In His absence His disciples are to witness for Him as lights in this dark world (Philippians 2:15). The light reveals the evils that are hidden in the darkness (Ephesians 5:13).

"On a candlestick . . . it giveth light unto all that are in the house." One who professes to be a follower of Christ, but who hides his light under a bushel—that is, obscures his testimony by an overoccupation with the affairs of this life—makes no real impression for good on his community. But one who lives consistently and is out-and-out for Christ shines as a lamp on a stand, enlightening the whole house.

"Let your light so shine before men, that they may see your good works." Mere profession is not enough. The life should speak for God. As we live Christ before men, we let our light shine. Thus they recognize our good works and see in them an evidence of sincerity. So they glorify God by recognizing the reality of His work in the souls of those who are faithful in their witness and behavior. We need to remember that we do not let our light shine by mere profession, but as it was said of our Lord Himself, "the life was the light of men" (John 1:4). So it is a devoted, faithful life that gives light to others.

Next, we see how our Lord applied the precepts of the law, neither ignoring them nor in any way belittling them, but showing that there is a deeper meaning in them than is seen on the surface. The law, rightly applied, makes manifest man's utter helplessness and inability to keep its holy precepts in his natural state.

The Law Fulfilled (Matthew 5:17-20)

"I am not come to destroy, but to fulfil." This our Lord did in three ways: by His perfect obedience He magnified the law and made it honorable (Isaiah 42:21); by His death He met all its claims against the lawbreakers, and so He became the end of the law for righteousness to all who believe (Romans 10:4); by His Spirit He enables believers to fulfil the righteous requirements of the law (Romans 8:4).

"One jot or one tittle." The jot is the *yodh*, the smallest letter of the Hebrew alphabet. The tittle is a little mark indicating a slight change in the meaning of a letter. Our Lord's words indicate the perfection of holy Scripture.

"Whosoever . . . shall break one of these least commandments." Anyone who ignores the divine authority of God's revealed will by loosening the moral effect of His commands, so as to make men careless of their obligations to Him, shall be esteemed as of no worth in His kingdom.

"Except your righteousness shall exceed." The scribes and Pharisees were extreme legalists and trusted in their own righteousness, but had not submitted to the righteousness of God (Romans 10:3). The righteousness God accepts is of a higher character. This higher righteousness is suggested in the verses that follow.

Murder *(Matthew 5:21-26)*

The law forbade murder. Jesus shows that unreasonable anger is, in itself, a violation of the spirit of the commandment, "Thou shalt not kill." It is as a result of such a condition of mind that murder is committed. To use vile invectives against another is the manifestation of the hatred which causes men to kill, and therefore places one in danger even of hellfire.

To profess to be a worshiper of God while willfully wronging another or cherishing malice in the heart is obnoxious to God. Let him who comes to His altar with a gift first seek out the brother he has wronged and then draw near to sacrifice.

Nor should one permit a spirit of antagonism toward another to continue if it is within his power to come to agreement. Sin never dies of old age, but becomes worse as time goes on. Many a one has suffered severely because of what might easily have been cleared up if he had given heed to these words (see Luke 12:58-59).

Adultery and Divorce (Matthew 5:27-32)

In these verses Jesus shows us that an unchaste look, a leering, concentrated lascivious gaze upon a woman is actually, in God's eyes, a violation of the seventh commandment. With such a standard who can plead "Not guilty!" How important then is the admonition to put to death any offending member lest one be betrayed into greater sin, which, if unrepented of, brings eternal judgment in Hell.

We have next an absolutely authoritative declaration concerning the marriage relationship. Of old, because of the hardness of men's hearts, God permitted certain things that are forbidden to the disciples of Jesus (Matthew 19:8). Matthew 5:31-32 and 19:9 make clear that marriage, which is in God's intention for life, is dissolved by the grave sin of fornication on the part of either husband or wife. This leaves the innocent party free to marry again, but as 1 Corinthians 7 intimates, "only in the Lord." It is absurd to say, as some have done, that fornication here refers only to immoral behavior before marriage and discovered only afterward (as in Deuteronomy 24:1), but has no reference to the same sin committed after marriage. This would be to make violation of the marriage vows a lesser offence than sexual sin indulged in while single. The clear sense of the passage is evident. The adulterous husband or wife breaks the tie. A divorce in the courts legalizes the separation, and the innocent one is as free before God as though never married at all.

Oaths (Matthew 5:33-37)

Judged by the high standard for communication found in these verses, how much of our conversation is unworthy of those who profess to be subject to the Lord. What careless speech and foolish bywords professed Christians indulge in, just as though Jesus had never spoken regarding this matter.

Loving Our Enemies (Matthew 5:38-48)

The balance of the chapter may be considered as one whole section, revealing the evidence of grace in the lives of the disciples of Christ.

"An eye for an eye." This is pure law—absolute righteousness (Exodus 21:24). Judged by that standard, every man's case is hopeless.

"Resist not evil." God has dealt with His children in grace. Therefore He expects them to exhibit the same grace toward others.

"Let him have thy cloke also." This was far above what the law demanded. When the grace of Christ controls the heart one can suffer the loss of all things without resentment.

"Go with him twain." Ordinary etiquette in those days demanded that one go a mile to direct or guide a bewildered or belated traveler. Grace goes the second mile.

"Turn not thou away." The disciple of Christ is to be like his Master—willing to communicate. He may not be in a position to give all that is asked of him, or to lend all that one might want, but he is to be ready to comply, so far as possible, with requests for aid and assistance.

"It hath been said, Thou shalt love thy neighbour and hate thine enemy." The Scriptures of the Old Testament plainly commanded the former, but it was rabbinical tradition that added the latter of these sayings, possibly basing it on such passages as Deuteronomy 23:6 and some of the imprecatory Psalms (Psalm 137:9).

"But I say unto you." Speaking as the sent One of the Father, the Lord Jesus Christ corrected the faulty position of the rabbis and set forth His perfect law of love, even for one's enemies. By doing them good and praying for them, we overcome the evil in a Christlike way. No matter how badly others treat us, we are to seek to help them. We are to bless them that curse us, to be kind even though they express hatred, to pray for them even when they persecute and seek to injure us. This is the grace of God in action, as seen in the lives of surrendered believers who are dominated by the Spirit of Christ. Does this seem too high a standard for sinful man to attain? It is! But a regenerated man can do what is impossible for the natural man.

"That ye may be the children of your Father which is in heaven." As we obey our Lord's commands given here, we reveal the fact that we are children of the heavenly Father, who showers His mercies on just and unjust alike and would have us imitate Him. It is the divine nature, of which each believer is a partaker (2 Peter 1:4), that enables him to approximate the character portrayed in this searching discourse.

"If ye love them which love you, what reward have ye?" Even the most blatant worldling loves his own, and can appreciate those who show appreciation of him. But those who follow the Lord are to love all men, even those who by bitter opposition would make life miserable if they could.

"If ye salute your brethren only . . . do not even the publicans so?" It is a small thing if Christ's disciples show only the same interest in others that men evidence who are engaged in the most despicable callings. Publicans were detested by the Jews. They were taxgatherers in Israel who bought their offices from the Roman government and "farmed the taxes." They extorted everything possible from their own countrymen, fattening upon the proceeds after turning over only what was obligatory to the assessor appointed by the state. Yet these gave recognition to their own brethren.

"Perfect, even as your Father . . . is perfect." This is perfection in the sense of the complete absence of partiality, thus imitating Him who is no respecter of persons (Acts 10:34), but who lavishes His favors on just and unjust alike.

God's choicest blessings are for those who demonstrate the same spirit of reverence for Him and meekness and compassion for others, which were seen in all their fullness in our blessed Lord as He walked this earth in the days of His flesh (Hebrews 5:7). That spirit, which is beyond the reach of the natural man, is fulfilled in those who have received a new life and nature through trusting in Christ as their Savior. No adverse circumstances can disturb the serenity of those who know the Lord and who acknowledge His authority over their lives.

Surely every right-thinking person must admit that the righteousness inculcated by our Lord in this matchless discourse (which has won the admiration of intelligent people everywhere) is a standard far beyond that to which the natural man can attain. It is only when one has been born again that he can live on this high plane. When men talk of the sermon on the mount being religion enough for them, they only show how little they understand the meaning of our Master's words. He portrays a supernatural life that can be lived only by supernatural power—the power that the Holy Spirit gives to him who believes the gospel.

CHAPTER SIX

THE PRINCIPLES OF THE KINGDOM

PART TWO

Giving to the Poor *(Matthew 6:1-4)*

"Do not your righteousness...to be seen of men" (Matthew 6:1, RV). Particularly in view here is righteousness in the sense of fulfilling our obligations to minister to human need. All should be done without ostentation.

"They have their reward." When the applause of men has been sought and obtained, we need not expect further reward when we stand before the judgment seat of Christ.

"When thou doest alms." Nothing is more objectionable than advertised charity. It is extremely humiliating to the one who receives, and hurtful to the soul of him who gives.

"Thy Father which seeth in secret." God's eye is upon all His children, and He will value aright all that is done for His glory (2 Chronicles 16:9). To do good secretly, knowing that one has the Lord's approval and that he is imparting happiness to others in their distress, should be reward enough to the true child of God. But God, who takes note of all that is done in His name, will not fail to recognize it when we see Him as He is.

Prayer *(Matthew 6:5-15)*

In these verses we have our Lord's own teaching in regard to prayer. To ignore this, as though it were not in keeping with the truth of the present dispensation of the grace of God, would result in robbing our own souls of some of the most precious and important instruction that we have in all the Word of God. Think of the privilege of sitting at the feet of the great intercessor Himself and hearing Him tell us how to pray! It is indeed a priceless opportunity not to be despised or passed on to disciples of some other age. We need to remind ourselves anew that inasmuch as we are blessed with all spiritual blessings in the heavenlies in Christ Jesus, there is nothing in Scripture of a moral or spiritual character that is not part of our heritage.

We are first warned against mere formality in prayer and pretended piety, rather than concern for the glory of God. He demands reality. There were those of the Pharisees who looked on prayer as having a certain degree of merit in itself (even as Mohammedans, Romanists, and others do now). Formal prayers were recited in public places, and the longer the prayer the more intense was the impression made on those who stood by. They were inclined to judge a man's piety by the length of his devotions. Jesus warned His disciples against such an abuse of prayer. He did not forbid their praying in public places. In 1 Timothy 2:8 this is definitely implied. But He did inveigh against praying to be seen of men, or engaging in any other religious exercise for ostentation. For the individual the proper place for prayer is in the closet, the hidden room alone with God, where no human eye beholds nor human ear hears. God, who sees in secret, will hear and answer according to His own will.

Nor is it necessary to weary the Lord with words (Malachi 2:17). Vain repetitions, the continued repeating of meaningless or empty phrases, is expressly forbidden. How incongruous are the ejaculations of the rosary in the light of this Scripture! We are not heard for our "much speaking." He who knows all our needs better than we know them ourselves would have us lay them before Him in childlike simplicity, not as though He needed to be made willing to aid by our constant pleading (Matthew 6: 8). It is true that elsewhere our Lord speaks of importunate prayer, but that is not to be confounded with empty repetitions of certain pious phrases.

In Matthew 6: 9-13 we have the beautiful and suggestive outline that is commonly called the Lord's prayer. This title is a misnomer, except in the sense that it is His because He gave it. But actually it is "the disciples' prayer." Jesus Himself could not pray it, for it includes a request for the forgiveness of sins, and He was ever the sinless One. There does not seem to be any valid reason for supposing that He meant it to be repeated frequently, or as part of a service of prayer or worship, as it is commonly used today. No mention is made of its use in the early Christian assemblies of the book of Acts, nor is it even referred to in the Epistles. It would seem that the Lord gave it as an outline or pattern of prayer; thus suggesting the manner in which God should be addressed and the petitions we are entitled to present to Him. While there is no expression in this prayer that is a contradiction of subsequent Scripture, it is limited in a marked degree. Now that the Holy Spirit has come to guide us in our supplications, it would seem needlessly formal to be bound to use the exact words we have here when we come to God either in public or in private devotions.

Let us note the order of the requests:

"Our Father which art in heaven, Hallowed be thy name." This is an expression of worship and adoration on the part of those in acknowledged relationship with God. He is known as Father, which therefore applies only to those who are born again.

"Thy kingdom come" looks on to the second advent of Christ when the kingdom of God will be established in power over all this world.

"Thy will be done in earth, as it is in heaven." In Heaven no one seeks to circumvent the will of God. Here on earth self-will has caused untold misery. When men learn to do God's will in this world as saints and angels delight to do it in Heaven, the golden age will have come indeed.

"Give us this day our daily bread." This is the expression of dependence on the living Father for every day's necessities. We never are able to be sure of tomorrow except as God provides for our needs.

"Forgive us our debts, as we forgive our debtors." In the Epistles we are told to forgive as we have been forgiven (Ephesians 4:32; Colossians 3:13). This is to be the measure of our forgiveness.

In the government of God as Father over His own children, our forgiveness of daily offences depends upon our attitude toward those who offend us. If we refuse to forgive our erring brethren, God will not grant us that restorative forgiveness for which we plead when conscious of sin and failure. A Father's forgiveness of an erring child takes into account the attitude of the failed one toward other members of the family. This, of course, has nothing to do with that eternal forgiveness that the believing sinner receives when he comes to Christ.

"Lead us not into temptation, but deliver us from evil" (or the evil one). This is the recognition of our own acknowledged weakness, a cry to God to preserve us from being placed in circumstances where we might be overpowered by the voice of the tempter (see Luke 11:2-4).

The last part of verse 13 is not found in the best manuscripts and is omitted in most revisions. It seems to have been added after it became customary to use this prayer in a ritualistic service.

Fasting (Matthew 6:16-18)

In these verses the Lord reverts to what had been said before in verses 1-4. All dissimulation or hypocrisy is sternly rebuked. To seek to establish a reputation for piety by a melancholy demeanor is utterly foreign to the straightforwardness that should ever characterize those who profess subjection to Him. Jesus was guileless in all His ways, and He calls for absolute honesty in the behavior of His disciples. Let him who is abstaining from food or other things in order to have more time with God, cultivate a cheerful manner as becomes one who enjoys communion with the Father.

Storing Treasures (Matthew 6:19-24)

The right attitude toward temporal possessions is inculcated in these verses. All treasures are to be held in subjection to God and used as He directs. He who is in touch with eternal realities can well afford to hold earthly possessions with a loose hand. Worldly wealth soon passes away and leaves him who has nothing else poor indeed. But those who lay up heavenly treasure by spending and being spent for God, while numbered perchance among the poor of this world, will be rich in faith. When life is ended here they will find endless treasure held in reserve above. The more we distribute for the blessing of others as guided by the Lord, the more wealth we lay up in Heaven.

We are so constituted that our hearts will be set on that place in which our riches are laid up. The worldling has everything here, but will be poor for eternity. The heavenly-minded believer may be poor indeed in this world's goods but rich toward God.

What we need to be concerned about, therefore, is a single eye for the glory of God, an eye that discerns His will in order that we may walk in it. If we turn away to paths of self-will, we go into willful darkness and will soon lose our way. We must choose for ourselves whether we will serve God or mammon (riches). We cannot serve both. The love of one crowds out love for the other (see Luke 11:34-36).

Worry (Matthew 6:25-34)

It is the will of God that His children should live without worry or anxiety. When Jesus said, "Take no thought," He did not mean that His disciples should be careless or improvident. But they are forbidden to be anxious, to become distressed and perplexed as they face the future. He who has saved and cared for us thus far can be depended on to undertake and provide for us to the end. Our Lord directs attention to the fowls of the air that are fed by the heavenly Father, and to the flowers of the field clothed in beauty by a beneficent Creator. We cannot even increase our stature by anxious thought. Why, then, give way to worry as to how we shall meet future exigencies? The God who clothes the grass of the field has promised to clothe His children. Why, then, be of little faith?

The nations of the world make the pursuit of these temporal things the main object of life. We are not to imitate them in this, but rather to be concerned first of all with pleasing God, and ordering our behavior in accordance with the righteous principles of His kingdom. Jesus sums up our entire responsibility when He says, "Seek ye first the kingdom of God." It is not "Seek *for* the kingdom" but "Put the interests of God's kingdom first in your life." The message is for those who are already disciples of Christ. As such, we are to fulfill its righteousness—that is, the things that are obligatory on us as subjects of our blessed Lord. If we put the kingdom first, we may have the assurance that all needed temporal mercies will be provided.

And so Matthew 6 closes with the exhortation to leave tomorrow with God while seeking to please Him today. When tomorrow comes He will provide all needed grace for whatever problems we have to face. Today is ours to glorify Him.

Intent of the Sermon

Because so many earnest believers, in seeking to avoid the extreme of legalism, come dangerously close to the extreme of antinomianism, let us revert for a few moments to some questions referred to already in chapter 5. Two questions are frequently asked. The first is, *Was the sermon on the mount intended for Christians?* No one can rightly be called a Christian until united to Christ by the Holy Spirit in the present dispensation of the grace of God (Ephesians 3:2). The disciples were first called Christians at Antioch (Acts 11:26), but they *were* disciples, as all Christians are. During our Lord's earthly ministry those who received His word became His disciples. To them He set forth the principles of the kingdom He had come to announce. These principles are in no way opposed to the fuller revelation given to the church later on. As mentioned before, just as the righteousness of the law is "fulfilled in us, who walk not after the flesh, but after the Spirit" (Romans 8:4), so the higher righteousness of this wonderful sermon will characterize those who are regenerated and controlled by the Holy Spirit.

The second question is, *Does this sermon show men the way of salvation?* No; it was not intended to do so. It sets forth the behavior that should be seen in those who are saved. If men are seeking salvation by human effort then this sermon can only condemn them, for it presents a standard of righteousness even higher than the law of Moses, and thus exposes the hopelessness of the sinner to attain to it. But he who confesses his sinfulness and in faith turns to Christ and obeys the instruction given here, builds on a rock that cannot be shaken.

CHAPTER SEVEN
THE PRINCIPLES OF THE KINGDOM
Part Three

Judging Our Brother (Matthew 7:1-6)

In the first five verses of this section the Lord exposes that almost unconscious hypocrisy, so common to us all, which leads us to judge our fellows so severely, while overlooking or excusing our own sins as though they were of little moment.

"Judge not." There are circumstances when the people of God are commanded to judge when dealing with offenders against the Christian standard of morals, even to excluding them from church fellowship (1 Corinthians 5:3-5,12-13). But we are not to attempt to sit in judgment on the hidden motives. We are so easily prejudiced and our snap judgments are wrong so often. We cannot read the heart or discern the thoughts. This is God's prerogative alone. If we disobey this command we need not be surprised if others pass judgment on us in a similar way.

"With what measure ye mete." We will be measured ourselves by the same stringent rule that we apply to other men.

"The mote...the beam." There is a fine irony here that is very striking. These two words stand out in vivid contrast. The word translated "mote" signified originally a bit of dry twig or straw, such as the wind often carries into the human eye, thus causing blurred vision and tears until it is ejected. The word translated "beam" really means a stick of timber, but was used colloquially in the Greek speech of our Lord's days on earth as a synonym for a splinter, which, though small in itself, seems a veritable beam because of the pain it causes. In one of the papyrus notes found in Egypt some years back, a youth wrote to his mother telling of the suffering he had endured because a "beam" had been driven into his thumb underneath the nail. This makes clear our Lord's meaning. No one is fit to rebuke another when there is something in his own life that is worse than that which he detects in the other.

"How wilt thou say to thy brother..." Even the world says, "Consistency, thou art a jewel." One cannot expect to correct a fault in another if he has an even more glaring one in his own life.

"Thou hypocrite." The original word translated *hypocrite* was used by the Greeks to designate an actor. It means literally "a second face," as Greek actors wore masks to represent the characters portrayed. We speak of being "two-faced." God demands reality. Our Lord insists on this. No shallow, empty religiousness will do for Him. We cannot know Him as our Father who loves to meet our needs in His grace and mercy, unless we are honest in seeking His face. To judge others superciliously, while living in sin ourselves, is abominable in His sight. If we are honestly seeking to know Him and ready to do His will, He will guide us into the narrow way of unselfish devotion to God and to the interests of those for whom Christ died. This is indeed the way to life.

"Neither cast ye your pearls before swine." It is folly to endeavor to present the deeper and more precious things of the divine revelation to men who have no desire for holiness.

Praying Earnestly (Matthew 7:7-12)

"Ask...seek...knock." In these words our Lord stresses the importance of prevailing prayer, which is not just a casual or thoughtless repeating of certain words. We are bidden to ask—that is, to make our requests known to God (Philippians 4:6-7). If a prayer is not answered at once we are to seek further by endeavoring to learn more clearly the mind of God in the matter, that we may pray with enlightened intelligence (Isaiah 26:9). Then we are to knock with the importunity that implies sincerity and faith. Such importunity brings the answer (Luke 11:5-10). God does answer prayer. This is one evidence of the supernaturalism of what is commonly called "revealed religion," as distinguished from mere human philosophy. The word *religion,* is too broad a term for Christianity itself, but is used here because it is a convenient expression to designate man's relationship to God as revealed in both the Old and New Testaments. In all past dispensations, as well as in the present one, God has been revealed as the hearer and answerer of prayer (Psalm 65:2; Isaiah 56:7; Matthew 21:13). He invites us to come to Him with our petitions, and promises to give according to our needs (Philippians 4:19).

"Every one that asketh receiveth." When God's conditions are complied with, the answer is sure—not for some, but for all who approach Him in prayer in accordance with His revealed will. It is not necessarily true that we always receive exactly what we ask. God reserves to Himself the right to answer as His wisdom dictates. But He never ignores the cries of His children.

"Will he give him a stone?" A stone might bear an outward resemblance to a loaf of bread, but it cannot be eaten. Earthly fathers are considerate of their children's needs and do not ordinarily mock them by ignoring their requests for food, or by giving something they cannot use when they plead for sustenance.

"A fish...a serpent." One is food to strengthen and build up; the other is poisonous, dealing death. No one with a real father's heart gives that which is harmful to a child, but rather that which will be for good.

Human parenthood is only a feeble picture of the father-heart of God, who delights in giving to His children that which is for their good. In the family, the father should be an example of the love and forethought of the heavenly Father, who delights to bless His children by giving them what will be for their lasting profit. Prayer is the appointed means whereby these mercies are received.

"Whatsoever ye would that men should do to you, do ye even so to them." This is indeed the golden rule. It is linked with prayer, for no one can pray aright who is not characterized by active benevolence to his fellows (1 John 3:17-22). This is not the gospel; it is the fruit of the gospel. People often speak glibly of the golden rule, as though the keeping of it were a comparatively small matter, or as though it involved the whole of Christianity. How frequently we hear the assertion, "The golden rule is good enough for me. It is all the religion anyone needs." But who, judged by this standard of unselfish living, would ever pass muster before God's holy tribunal? It is but another way of insisting on the demand of the law, "Thou shalt love thy neighbour as thyself." No one save our blessed Lord has ever fully lived this out. Consequently, the golden rule but adds to our condemnation, and emphasizes the need of salvation by grace. Only as Christ is received and dwells in us by His Spirit can we come up to this high and holy standard.

It has been said frequently by those who would disparage the Lord Jesus and His teaching, that the golden rule was in no sense original with Him, but was simply an adaptation of what others had taught before Him. Confucius is said to have proclaimed this some hundreds of years before Christ. But there is a vast difference between the positive instruction of the Lord Jesus Christ, commanding His disciples to do to others as they would have others do to them, and the negative teaching of the Chinese sage, who said, "Do not do to others what you would not like them to do to you." The one is the manifestation of divine love; the other is but ordinary human advice (see Luke 6:31).

Following the Narrow Way (Matthew 7:13-14)

The broad and narrow ways are placed in vivid contrast. The first is the road followed by all who ignore the grace of God revealed in Christ and its claims on mankind. The other is the path of devotion to Him who "came not to be ministered unto, but to minister, and to give his life a ransom for many" (Matthew 20:28). Note that the narrow way leads to life, not merely to Heaven at the end of life.

"Wide is the gate, and broad is the way, that leadeth to destruction." This is the way of self-will, of disobedience to God's Word. All are on the broad way who refuse to own their needy condition and who ignore the claims of Christ. It is entered by a wide gate, for all men naturally choose this road.

"Strait is the gate, and narrow is the way...unto life." There is no real life apart from the knowledge of Christ (1 John 5:12). It is as we yield our wills to Him that we enter the strait gate and pass into the narrow way. This way leads to life—life in its richest, fullest sense—to be embraced in measure here on earth but enjoyed in all its fullness in a blest eternity.

Warning against False Prophets *(Matthew 7:15-23)*

"False prophets . . . in sheep's clothing, but inwardly . . . ravening wolves." The metaphor is a very striking one. It suggests a prowling wolf with the fleece of a sheep drawn over its body as it roams about the outskirts of the flock waiting for an opportunity to pounce upon an unsuspecting lamb or sheep. In like manner teachers of falsehood do not come out in their true colors at first, but seek to hide their actual identity and intentions in order that they may draw away disciples after them (Acts 20:30). The only safe way is to test teachers by the Word itself, and particularly by the doctrine of Christ, as in John's second Epistle.

"Ye shall know them by their fruits." This is the test for any system of doctrine, and for those who propagate it. That which is of God will result in fruit for His glory.

"Every good tree...a corrupt tree." The two are put in vivid contrast, picturing men and women who are born of God and those who are still unregenerated. This is a parable from nature, designed to impress on our minds that we, like trees, are either good or bad, and our behavior will betray or indicate our true character. Goodness and badness are used here, as throughout the book of Proverbs, in a relative sense (Proverbs 12:2; 13:22; 14:14). Actually there is none good until changed by regeneration (Romans 3:12). The testimony of the lips indicates the state of the heart.

"Evil fruit...good fruit." A heart in rebellion against God cannot produce in the life that which brings honor to Him. Neither can one who is subject to God's will go on in sin, bringing discredit on His holy name.

"Hewn down, and cast into the fire." Though God has long patience, even with wicked men (James 5:7; 2 Peter 3:9), the day draws closer when judgment must fall on those who persist in their unrepentant course. This was what John the Baptist also proclaimed (Matthew 3:10).

"By their fruits ye shall know them." Whatever the professions men may make, it is the life that tells (1 Thessalonians 1:5; 2:10). Good men delight in purity and righteousness. Evil men grovel in that which is sinful and corrupt. Where grace operates in the soul, the good fruit of the Spirit (Galatians 5:22-23) will be manifest in the life. That which is really of God will produce godliness on the part of its recipients.

"Not every one that saith...Lord, Lord, shall enter into the kingdom of heaven." Mere lip profession is of no avail if the heart and life are not subject to the Word of God. We are not saved by our works, but good works are the test of reality. He who is born of God will delight in obedience to the Father's will (Ephesians 2:8-10).

"In thy name done many wonderful works?" There may be much of outward show and apparently successful service coupled with a Christless profession. In the day of manifestation, nothing will avail but a personal faith in Christ whom we profess as our Lord.

To none will He say in that day, "I used to know you, but I know you no more." His word to the lost will be, "I never knew you." Of all His own He says, "My sheep hear my voice, and I know them" (John 10:27).

Building Wisely (Matthew 7:24-27)

In bringing His great discourse to an end the Lord presented in a most graphic and solemn way the eternal results of our attitude toward His message. He who hears and heeds the words of Christ makes it evident that he is a genuine believer. He builds his house upon the rock that is Christ Himself. No storm of adverse circumstances, no assaults of the prince of the power of the air, can avail to destroy the house that is based upon the Rock of ages.

He who hears with the outward ear, but takes no heed to obey the truth, is as one building on sinking sand. When the testing time comes, the one who has built his hopes for eternity on anything short of Christ Himself will come to disaster. Because Jesus is Lord, He calls for unqualified obedience to His Word. He speaks as the King and sets forth with clearness and conciseness the principles upon which His kingdom is founded, so utterly opposed to the selfish policies of earthly rulers and nations. To own Him as Lord and obey His Word is to build a house that will stand in "the wreck of matter and the crash of worlds." To fail to heed His voice means both temporal and eternal loss.

Christ is presented in many Scriptures as the foundation on which the church is built. He is also the rock on which each individual believer is established. He who trusts in Him builds on a sure foundation (Isaiah 28:16; Romans 9:33) which will never fail. To build our hopes on any other person, system, or fancied meritorious behavior, is to erect our house on shifting sands. In the day of judgment, all who have relied on anything save Christ and His finished work will find themselves lost and hopeless for eternity.

Christ's Authority As a Teacher (Matthew 7:28-29)

Although He had addressed Himself primarily to His immediate disciples, the throngs drew near to listen, and as the great discourse reached its dramatic conclusion they were amazed at the clarity and profundity of His teaching. Never had such words as these been heard in Israel. There was something so definitely authoritative about them that the hearers were deeply moved.

Ordinarily the scribes and other teachers in Israel based everything they taught on the authority of noted rabbis who had preceded them. But Jesus spoke directly as giving the last and final word on every subject He set forth. This was what astonished His hearers. This sermon was like a plumb line, testing all their pretention to righteousness. Did they face it honestly before God and recognize their sinfulness and need of a Savior? We are not told, but we may be sure that many went to their homes pondering the great truths that had been set before them.

Conclusion

Did Jesus set aside or belittle the moral law? He did not. He referred to what was said of old as that which was divine and authoritative. But He added to or explained it in its deepest spiritual meaning, so that men would understand its true application. Moral principles are unchanging. They are the same in every dispensation. But the child of God today is lifted above mere legal obedience through love for Christ and the controlling influence of the Holy Spirit.

Christ's kingdom, as far as its outward aspect is concerned, is now in abeyance. He has gone "into a far country," even Heaven itself, to receive a kingdom, and to return (Luke 19:12). At His second advent the kingdoms of this world will become the kingdom of our God and of His Christ (Revelation 11:15). But while He is personally absent, though present by the Spirit, yet unseen to mortal eyes, all who are born again are in the kingdom of God. Though in the midst of a rebellious world, Christians are responsible to maintain allegiance to the One whom that world rejects. They must be loyal to the true King, even though a false usurper, Satan, is acknowledged by unsaved men as the prince of this world (John 12:31; 14:30). Loyalty to earth's rightful King necessarily involves obedience to His words (1 Timothy 6:3-5). Through obedience Christ's disciples know the reality of the kingdom, which is not meat and drink (temporal things), but righteousness and peace and joy in the Holy Ghost (Romans 14:17).

It was concerning this aspect of the kingdom that our Lord instructed His disciples during the forty days between His resurrection and ascension (Acts 1:2-3). This was the burden of the apostles' message, as they called on men to acknowledge the lordship of Christ (Acts 2:36; 20:25). And this was the theme of Paul's preaching to the very end (Acts 28:31). The risen Christ is Lord of all, and He gives remission of sins to all who believe on His name. Those thus brought into this new place before God, saved by pure grace, are now called upon to admit His lordship in all things. They are left in this world to witness for Him and to make known His grace to the lost. They are to seek the good of all men. In doing this, they will be misunderstood often, and will be subject to cruel persecutions and vindictive treatment. But they are not to retaliate in kind. By manifestation of the Spirit of Christ they are to overcome evil with good (Romans 12:21), showing themselves to be law-abiding citizens, ever seeking the blessing of their fellowmen.

When our Lord returns and the kingdom of God is fully displayed on earth, the principles proclaimed in this sermon will prevail everywhere, for then righteousness and praise will be made to spring forth among all nations (Isaiah 61:11). That will be the time of earth's regeneration (Matthew 19:28). When the individual is regenerated (Titus 3:5), even now he is given power to walk before God in holiness and righteousness (1 John 3:7-10).

The more we meditate upon Jesus' sermon the more we will realize how far short we come of rising to the heights of unselfish devotion to Christ. As the Holy Spirit brings these instructions home in power to our hearts, we will find ourselves searched more and more deeply by His solemn utterances. He who desires truth in the inward parts (Psalm 51:6) was speaking through His Son in a manner calculated to lay bare all the hidden springs of character. He wants every honest soul to realize how much he needs to grow in grace and in the knowledge of Christ, in order that he may represent Him aright in this world where He is still the rejected One.

CHAPTER EIGHT

THE WORKS OF THE KING

PART ONE

Jesus Cleanses the Leper (Matthew 8:1-4)

Having listened to the instruction of the King as He proclaimed the laws of His kingdom, we are now called on to consider His works. We may think of these as His royal credentials, proving Him to be in very truth the promised Messiah who was to bring healing and plenty to Israel, reigning in righteousness and peace (Psalm 72:7). John wrote of the first miracle performed by the Lord Jesus Christ at the wedding in Cana; he said that in doing it He "manifested forth his glory" (John 2:11). This was true of all the marvelous signs He performed. Each one spoke in some special way of the mystery of the incarnation, "that God was in Christ, reconciling the world unto himself" (2 Corinthians 5:19).

In all His works of power Jesus Christ was but revealing His personal glory. They were the evidences of His messiahship, for He wrought them all, not merely of His own volition as the eternal God veiled in humanity, but as the obedient Son, controlled by the Holy Spirit (Acts 10:38). He chose in all things to be subject to the Father, and by the Spirit the Father accomplished all His works in and through the Son (John 5:17-19). For the time being, during "the days of His flesh," Jesus Christ was the active servant of the godhead here on earth and as such we need not wonder at the mighty deeds that characterized His ministry. It would have been far stranger had it been otherwise. It would be difficult to imagine that God, who came down to earth and took our flesh-and-blood humanity into union with

His deity, could go through the world unmoved by human suffering and do nothing to relieve it. Jesus was greater than anything He ever did. When He acted in power, performing what we, with our limited understanding, call miracles, He was but doing that which was perfectly in keeping with His divine-human personality.

Let us consider first the cleansing of the leper. Had Israel been right with God, disease would have had no place among them (Exodus 15:26). Every sick person in Palestine was a sad testimony to the fallen condition of the favored nation. Everywhere Jesus went He found men and women suffering from illnesses of various kinds. Each one pictured the consequences of sin in one form or another.

Leprosy speaks of the uncleanness and loathsomeness of sin. It is a constitutional disease that produced fearful havoc in the bodies of its victims, even as sin works havoc in the souls of those who are under its power. A man was not a leper because he was disfigured by horrible ulcers and painful sores. These things were but the witness to the disease that was working within. Even so, one is not a sinner because he sins; he sins because he is a sinner.

Here we read of a poor leper who came to the Lord Jesus and worshipped or did homage to Him, pleading for deliverance, though uncertain as to the readiness of Jesus to grant it. He said, "Lord, if thou wilt, thou canst make me clean." At once the answer came, as Jesus reached forth His hand and touched him: "I will; be thou clean." Immediately the man was freed from his uncleanness. The Lord then commanded him to go to the priest at the temple and offer the gift that Moses commanded, as recorded in Leviticus 14. This was for a testimony to the priest that God was working in Israel.

Jesus Heals the Centurion's Servant (Matthew 8:5-13)

Here we find a Roman centurion who had come to know the God of Israel. His servant was sick of the palsy. In this paralyzed man we have a picture of the helplessness of the sinner. And such was the condition of all of us until grace saved us. It was while we were yet without strength that Christ's death availed for us.

Yearning over his helpless servant, the centurion came pleading that Jesus might heal the sick man. The response of Jesus was immediate. "I will come and heal him," He said. But the centurion protested, declaring that he was not worthy to be so honored. "Speak the word only," he said, "and my servant shall be healed." The people said of the centurion, "He is worthy" (Luke 7:4); but he said, "I am not worthy," for he knew his own heart too well to claim any personal merit.

His was a sublime manifestation of implicit faith in the power of the Lord. Even as he, an officer in the Roman army, could speak with authority to those in subjection to him, he was sure Jesus could command the sickness to depart and He would be obeyed. Such confidence rejoiced the heart of Jesus. In Israel He had not found such trustfulness. He saw in this an earnest of the great Gentile harvest yet to be gathered in, when believing sinners out of all nations would join with Abraham, Isaac, and Jacob in giving glory to God. But many of "the children of the kingdom"—those who by national birth were the seed of Abraham but lacked Abraham's faith—would be rejected and would go into the outer darkness, to be shut out of the joys of the kingdom for which they had waited so long. For them there would be weeping and gnashing of teeth: the one speaking of the grief they would suffer, and the other speaking of the resentfulness of their hearts, indicating that they would remain unrepentant.

The Lord then gave a message of assurance to the centurion, bidding him go his way, for as he had believed so it was done to him. He returned to find his servant healed, for "Where the word of a king is, there is power" (Ecclesiastes 8:4), and God's anointed King was in the midst of Israel.

Jesus Heals Many (Matthew 8:14-17)

In this section we have an illustration of the restlessness of sin which is like a fever in the soul, but which responds at once to the healing touch of the Savior. Peter was a married man, and the mother of his wife seems to have formed part of the family group. This lady was stricken with a fever and was tossing upon her couch in distress; but when Jesus came, all was changed. He touched her hand, and there was healing in that touch of power. Disease fled before it, for He was the Lord of life.

The restored woman at once sought to show her gratitude by service. When Jesus rebukes the fever of sin, service becomes a joy, and life a glad experience.

In all these instances of healing we see the proof that our Lord Jesus is the all-sufficient One, in whom are infinite resources to meet every emergency. Nothing ever takes Him by surprise, and no need is too great to bring to His attention. His life on earth was the manifestation of divine love and compassion, giving to men an altogether new understanding of the goodness of God and His care for His children. And what He was on earth, He is in the glory: "Jesus Christ the same yesterday, and today, and for ever" (Hebrews 13:8). He does not always exert His power in the same manner, but nothing ever alters His concern for His own. His was unlimited power. No case was too hard for Him. Unlike some who have founded religious cults upon the effort to relieve physical ailments, He made no distinction between cases brought to Him for relief. No matter what the disease or form of infirmity, He healed them all. In this way He demonstrated His creatorial power, and His compassion for mankind.

No doubt it was because the news of these remarkable healings had gotten around that the people came from all the nearby districts, seeking deliverance from their many ailments. No one applied to Him in vain. His heart was filled with compassion. He delivered all who came, no matter what the illness might be that was causing pain and suffering.

"Spoken by Esaias." The prediction of Isaiah 53:4 was literally fulfilled in Jesus' daily ministry as He bore away the sicknesses and carried the infirmities of the people in His deep sympathies. It is a mistake to suppose that this prophecy refers to His atoning work on the cross. It was here on earth, as He moved among suffering humanity, that He bore our infirmities, and took from men their diseases and pains. There is no such thought in Scripture that Christ made an atonement for sickness, as He did for sin. Sickness is a judicial result of sin and does not call for atonement. It is true, however, that as a result of the work of the cross, the believer's body will be redeemed and glorified when the Lord returns for His people. Then "this corruptible must put on incorruption, and this mortal must put on immortality" (1 Corinthians 15:53). Until then our bodies are just as subject to sickness and death as those of the unsaved.

Jesus Explains the Cost of Discipleship (Matthew 8:18-22)

Having accomplished so many mighty works in Capernaum and its vicinity, "he gave commandment to depart." His was a ministry not to a favored few but to all who were distressed. So He passed on to other needy groups.

As they walked toward the seashore to take the boat that was to carry them to the country of Gadara and the region of Decapolis, He evidently discoursed with those who thronged about Him concerning discipleship. As a result two men spoke up expressing their interest.

First a scribe glibly said, "Master, I will follow thee." He little realized what following the Master would really mean. He was moved by enthusiastic admiration of Jesus, but had no conception of the rejection He was to undergo. Jesus would have no man make a sudden decision without counting the cost, for he who would follow Christ must be prepared to tread His path of loneliness and rejection. He who had created all things was homeless in His own world and among His own people. To follow Him was to share His sorrows.

Then a young man said, "Suffer me first to go and bury my father." We need not suppose that the father was dead, but the young man pleaded the claims of natural ties as an excuse for not at once following Jesus. Note our Lord's reply to this man: "Let the dead bury their dead." That is, let those who are dead spiritually attend to the disposal of the remains of the physically dead. The paramount thing in life is to follow Him. To speak of following Jesus on our own terms is to fail to realize that He is Lord of all. Are we seeking to make a bargain with Him, or have we yielded ourselves unreservedly to His authority?

Jesus Demonstrates His Power over Creation (Matthew 8:23-27)

Jesus wanted to cross the sea to the eastern side, His disciples accompanying Him, to go from Capernaum to Gadara. Capernaum was on the northwest shore.

"A great tempest." Was it the prince of the power of the air who sought thus to destroy Him before His hour was come? No storm could sink the ship in which He sailed.

Although the sea of Galilee is but a small body, yet because of its position deep down between high hills, it is subject to sudden storms of great intensity, caused by shifting air and heavy winds coming through the passes with tremendous velocity. These storms come up very quickly and often with scarcely any warning.

"Lord, save us: we perish." Fear engendered by unbelief led the disciples to cry out. Faith would have enabled them to rest in the fact of His presence with them. In another Gospel we are told that Jesus said to His disciples, "Let us pass over unto the other side" (Mark 4:35). This should have been the ground of their confidence. He did not bid them enter the ship to be drowned in the lake, but to go with Him to the other side. Had they remembered these words, their faith would not have failed.

First He rebuked their unbelief. Then He rebuked the elements. Mark told us that He gave a direct command to the boisterous winds and waves—literally, "Peace, be muzzled," as one might address an angry dog. Immediately the elements were calmed and the raging storm ceased. The winds and the sea recognized the voice of their Master when Jesus rebuked them, for He who had been sleeping in physical weariness was the Creator of the universe.

"What manner of man is this!" As yet they did not understand the mystery of the incarnation. It was as He worked in power among them that their understanding was opened to know who He really was. Awed and relieved, they looked upon their Master in amazement, wondering at the manifestation of authority they had witnessed. Realizing they were in the presence of One whom even the winds and waves obeyed, they marveled as they considered His mysterious power and personality.

Jesus Delivers the Demon-possessed (Matthew 8:28-34)

In the country of the Gadarenes a remarkable series of incidents occurred that demonstrated our Lord's power over demons, but failed to impress the people of that community at the time. Later the attitude of many of them was changed through the testimony of the man out of whom the legion of demons was cast.

Only Matthew mentioned two demoniacs. Mark 5:2 and Luke 8:27 speak of but one. There is, of course, no contradiction here. There were two of these poor unfortunates, both of whom were freed by the Lord Jesus from the awful curse that had separated them from society and driven them out among the tombs. But there was one whose experience was particularly noticeable and whose healing made a very deep impression upon the Gadarenes, or Gergesenes, as they were called by Matthew.

While there is a great mystery about demon possession, it is evident that demons are fallen spirits under Satan's domination. They have not yet been confined in Hell, but are able to control men and women to their ruin. They knew Jesus at once and recognized Him as the Judge who is to pronounce their final doom. From Him they shrank and recoiled with horror.

Is demon possession possible today? Unquestionably it is. There are many authentic cases of this terrible affliction related by servants of Christ who have come in contact with it. Particularly is this true in pagan lands where Satan holds supreme sway. When the gospel comes in, the powers of Hell rally to fight against the message of the cross. There are many instances of the casting out of demons and the complete deliverance of those who have been under their power.

In accordance with Mosaic law swine were considered unclean beasts not fit for food (Leviticus 11:7). They were apparently tended by degraded Jews who sought gain by selling them to the Gentiles. Tending swine became the occupation of the prodigal (Luke 15:15). According to the law, such a calling was absolutely illegal in the land of Israel.

It would seem that demons seek embodiment in some way. If driven from the men whom they controlled, they pleaded to be allowed to take possession of the bodies of unclean swine. It was a well-merited judgment upon the unprincipled owners of swine when their stock in trade was destroyed. It is not necessary to be able to explain the incident in Matthew 8:28-34, nor just what part the evil spirits had in it. What the passage emphasizes is the enormous capacity of mankind for evil. Two thousand swine (Mark 5:13) could not contain the demons who had found domiciles in two degraded men!

The swineherds hastened in surprise and terror back to the town, where they related the strange things that had occurred, dwelling on the deliverance of the demoniacs and the destruction of the swine. Angered because of pecuniary loss, and doubtless fearful of further ill effects if the Lord Jesus came to know more of their wickedness, the men of Gadara begged Him to leave at once. It was a pitiable thing to refuse the One who might have brought them untold blessing, but to the Gadarenes their swine were of far greater value than the souls of men.

Matthew did not mention that one of the healed demoniacs besought Jesus that he might be with Him; but the Lord had another plan for him. It was to bear witness to his friends at home of the mighty power of the Christ, who had set him free (Mark 5:19). This is the privilege and responsibility of all who are saved. If we know the Lord Jesus for ourselves, are we witnessing faithfully to others, that they too may experience His salvation? Mark and Luke gave us the information concerning the demoniac who became the disciple of Jesus, and told us of the way this man spread abroad the good news of the blessing Christ had brought to him. He carried the message throughout all Decapolis, the ten cities on the eastern side of the sea of Galilee (Mark 5:20). When Jesus returned to that district some time afterward He received a welcome that was in marked contrast to the opposition formerly encountered (Mark 6:53-56).

Conclusion

"Do you not have difficulty about the miracles?" one scientist asked another. The first was confessedly an agnostic. His friend had been but lately led to confess his personal faith in the Lord Jesus Christ. "Not since I know Jesus as the Son of God," was the answer. "From the moment I was enabled to believe in Him as the supreme miracle—God become man for my redemption—it was easy to accept every other miracle that Scripture tells us He performed. Knowing Him, nothing He is said to have done is incredible."

As we reflect on the various miracles recorded in this chapter and those that follow, our hearts may well be stirred to worship and praise while we dwell upon the compassion of Jesus for poor, afflicted humanity. He "went about doing good" (Acts 10:38). Never do we read of Him as working a miracle simply to excite the astonishment of those who followed Him. All His miracles were directly intended to relieve human suffering or to minister to the needs of mankind.

In the miracles we see God speaking and acting in His Son. God finds delight in ministering to the needs of His creatures, and in delivering them from the distressing circumstances that fill their souls with fear, and in freeing them from the enthrallment of Satan, whatever form it may take. Because Jesus is God manifest in the flesh, His works are the works of God, and ever reveal the divine interest in and attitude toward men.

We need to learn to confide in Him more fully, and as we do, we shall know by practical experience how real and how definite is His concern for those who trust His love and count upon the exercise of His power. Jesus is the exact expression of the divine character (Hebrews 1:3, literal rendering), and in His activities of grace we see God's heart revealed.

CHAPTER NINE

THE WORKS OF THE KING

PART TWO

Healing of the Palsied Man (Matthew 9:1-8)

The events recorded here and in the previous chapter did not follow one another in chronological sequence, but they are grouped together according to their moral order as testimonies to prove that Jesus Christ was the Messiah. They probably all occurred in the second year of His public ministry.

Upon returning from Galilee to the northwestern shore of the sea of Galilee, Jesus went to Capernaum where He healed a palsied man. Mark and Luke wrote that this miracle took place not in the open country, but in a house. Four friends assisting the sick man found it impossible to press through the crowd that thronged the door, so they went up onto the roof and opening up the tiles, or displacing the thatch, they let the palsied man down by cords to the feet of Jesus.

"Jesus seeing their faith." It is evident that not only the palsied man but also the friends who brought him had fullest confidence that Jesus would grant healing in accordance with their plea. He responded at once, but in a way they had not expected, by saying, "Son, be of good cheer; thy sins be forgiven thee." Thus He met the greater need first.

To certain of the scribes nearby this was blasphemy of the worst kind. A man was claiming for himself a divine prerogative. None but God could forgive sin. Who then was Jesus that He should presume to use such language?

He knew their thoughts and reproved them by asking, "Whether is easier, to say, Thy sins be forgiven thee; or to say, Arise, and walk?"

So far as they were concerned one would be as impossible as the other.

Men are ever prone to consider physical ills as of greater importance than the sinfulness of their hearts, and so are far more concerned about bodily health than they are about being right with God. But our Lord placed the emphasis upon the state of the soul. He would have men realize the corruption of their hearts (Matthew 15:19) and their need of deliverance from the guilt and power of sin (John 8:34), that they might enter into a life of communion with God and be assured of His eternal favor (John 14:23). To Him physical illness was the evidence that sin is in the world. He was not content to deal only with the effect, but He ever sought to reach the cause.

But in order that they might know that the Son of man has power on earth to forgive sins He turned to the palsied man and commanded him to arise, take up his bed and walk. As the Lord's critics looked on in wonder and amazement, the formerly helpless one sprang to his feet and walked off to his own house, healed and forgiven. The assembled multitude rejoiced and glorified God for so marvelous a display of His grace and power. This was what Jesus desired. He delighted to have men give honor to the Father, who was working in and through His Son.

Calling of Matthew (Matthew 9:9-13)

Matthew, also called Levi (Mark 2:14), was the tax collector of the port of Capernaum. Evidently he had heard and seen the Lord Jesus before. Now the time for decision had come. Obedient to the call of the Savior, he arranged immediately to close up his business and become a disciple of Christ in fulltime service. The Lord Jesus Christ and His disciples were invited to Matthew's house where he gave a farewell dinner to his former associates before launching forth upon his new career. Later, under the Spirit's inspiration, he became the author of this Gospel.

"Why eateth your Master with publicans and sinners?" The legalist can never understand the grace of God to the undeserving and utterly lost. Accustomed to think of human merit as commending men to the Lord, they were shocked to think of Jesus Christ as fellowshiping with sinners. Our Lord used an illustration that every-one could understand in answering the objection of these self-righteous critics. He said it is sick people who need a doctor, and He was the great physician who had come to minister to sin-sick souls.

"I will have mercy, and not sacrifice." Jesus directed the attention of these legalists to a declaration made by Jehovah in Hosea 6:6. It is far more to God to see mercy extended to the needy than to receive sacrifices and offerings. So Jesus had come not "to call the right-eous"—that is, those who supposed they had no need of mercy—"but sinners to repentance."

Defending His Disciples (Matthew 9:14-17)

These verses bring before us the drastic distinction between the principle of law, which we are told elsewhere prevailed until John the Baptist (Luke 16:16), and the grace and truth that came by Jesus Christ (John 1:17).

"Then came to him the disciples of John" with a question as to fasting. It is evident that many who had been baptized by John had not fully committed themselves to Jesus but were waiting for clearer proof that He was the promised Messiah. They were troubled because the abstinence taught by John, which was considered meritorious by the Pharisees, was not practiced by the disciples of Jesus.

In reply He made it clear that as long as He was with them in per-son there was no call for fasting. But in the coming day (as yet not understood by them) when He would be removed from them, fasting might well be in order. The bridegroom's presence calls for joy and gladness. His absence would impress upon His followers the neces-sity of self-abnegation.

"No man putteth a piece of new cloth unto an old garment." Jesus had not come to add something to the legal dispensation but to supersede it with that which was entirely new. To attempt to amal-gamate the two principles of law and grace would annul the true meaning of both (see Romans 11:6).

The new wine of grace was not to be poured into the skin-bottles of legalism. Such an attempt would only destroy both. It is all-important that we realize this, for we see in Christendom today many teachers of the law who try to impose legal principles upon those who are saved by grace. As Paul said, these teachers are without understanding as to what they affirm (1 Timothy 1:5-7).

Raising the Dead (Matthew 9:18-26)

Two miracles are interwoven in these verses. Both are designed to reveal the power and compassion of the King who was in the midst of Israel though unrecognized by the great majority.

"There came a certain ruler." The name of this man was Jairus (Mark 5:22). He was a leader in the local synagogue at Capernaum. He evidently believed in the claims of Jesus Christ and so asked Him to come to his help. His little daughter was, as he put it, "even now dead"; that is, she was so ill he realized she was at the point of death unless there was divine intervention. Moved with tender compassion, the Savior at once started to the home of the ruler, and we are told that "so did his disciples."

"A woman...touched the hem of his garment." Afflicted with a constitutional disease, her very life ebbing away, this woman pressed through the crowd and touched the border of the Lord's robe. That blue fringe was worn by all pious Israelites, in obedience to the Mosaic law (Numbers 15:38-41; Deuteronomy 22:12), and marked them out as the subjects of the holy One. She was confident that if she just touched Jesus' garment she would be healed immediately.

"Daughter, be of good comfort; thy faith hath made thee whole." The Lord recognized her faith and gave the assurance that because of this, all was as she had hoped. She was made perfectly whole.

In the meantime, the daughter of Jairus had apparently gotten beyond all hope of recovery. Life had left her body, and the visit of Jesus seemed now to be useless. Already preparations were being made for the burial, and the hired mourners were beginning their lamentations. The coming of the Lord Jesus Christ was to change all this, for He gives the oil of joy for mourning (Isaiah 61:3).

"The maid is not dead, but sleepeth." Was the little girl just in a coma, or was she actually dead? The consensus of opinion among most Christian scholars is that this was the sleep of death. However, the Greek word translated here as "sleep" is different from that which is found in other passages where sleep and death are used synonymously. This difference has led some to conclude that she was simply in a state of suspended animation. At any rate, she was dead as far as human power to help is concerned.

"He . . . took her by the hand, and the maid arose." Elsewhere we are told that He tenderly commanded her to arise, and as He took her hand she responded and came back to life, and was given food (Mark 5:41-43; Luke 8:54-55).

The story went from one to another and the people spoke with amazement of the wonderful event that had transpired. It was a testimony to the power of Jesus Christ, the great prophet who had risen up in the land.

Healing of the Blind and the Mute (Matthew 9:27-34)

Two other instances recorded in this section demonstrated the messiahship of Jesus. However, instead of convincing the stern, self-righteous Pharisees, these works of power only gave occasion for the blasphemous charge that Jesus Himself was in league with Beelzebub, the prince of the demons.

Recognizing Jesus as the promised Son of David, two blind men implored mercy. Testing their faith, Jesus asked, "Believe ye that I am able to do this?" Upon receiving an affirmative answer, He touched their eyes and replied, "According to your faith be it unto you."

They immediately looked at Him with eyes that saw His blessed face. Their blindness was gone. We can understand how ready they would be to proclaim abroad the fame of Him who had healed them. But He instructed them, "See that no man know it." He did not desire to be known as simply a wonder-worker. So exuberant were they that they could not contain themselves, but went throughout the district spreading the story of that which Jesus had done on their behalf.

We may wonder why Jesus bade them refrain from all this. The reason doubtless was that He desired people to be impressed by His message rather than His works. He was while on earth the express image of the divine person (Hebrews 1:3)—that is, the exact expression of the character of God. The compassion He demonstrated for distressed mankind shows the heart of God as He looks on the sorrow and suffering that sin has brought into the world. Wherever the Lord went He delivered men from these evidences of Satanic malice. His miracles witnessed to the truth of His deity and bore testimony to His messiahship. Faith in the miracles saved no one, however. But faith in Him who performed them was then, as it is now, the means of salvation from sin and deliverance from its effects.

In the healing of the mute we see demonstrated again the authority of Jesus over demons. Let us remember that in the Gospel where we have *devils* in the plural, it should always be *demons*.

A man was brought to Jesus possessed with a dumb demon, or a demon who so controlled the vocal powers of the poor abject wretch as to make speech impossible. Jesus immediately cast out the demon, and to the joy and delight of his friends, and the amazement of the multitudes, he who had been dumb spoke. The people cried, "It was never so seen in Israel."

But the haughty religious leaders, determined to resist and refuse any and all evidence that Jesus was the Messiah, declared, "He casteth out [demons] through the prince of the [demons]." It was an ominous sign of that which the Lord of glory was to face: utter rejection by those who should have received Him. For the time being He did not rebuke these blasphemers but went on quietly with His great ministry.

Praying for More Laborers *(Matthew 9:35-38)*

These cities and villages into which Jesus went were all in Galilee. With His disciples He passed from town to town, teaching in the synagogues, preaching the gospel of the kingdom, and healing diseases of every kind. This term, "the gospel of the kingdom," is an important one. It was the proclamation of the good news that God was about to set up His kingdom in this world. The kingdom was offered to Israel by God, but only on condition of their repentance and acceptance of the King. As we know, they failed in this and the kingdom was taken from them and given to others who were ready to meet the proper requirements. There is, of course, a difference between "the gospel of the kingdom" and the gospel of the grace of God; yet they are not to be distinguished as two gospels, for we are told distinctly in Galatians 1:9 that to preach any other gospel than that which Paul himself carried through the world was to incur the curse of God. The gospel is God's message concerning His Son. It takes on different aspects at different times, but it is all the gospel of Christ.

In Matthew Christ is presented as the King; the emphasis is on His royalty rather than His redemptive work. Yet the latter is not ignored, for at the very beginning of this Gospel the angels' declaration was, "He shall save his people from their sins" (Matthew 1:21). And we shall see more of His redemptive work in a later chapter. The different aspects of the gospel are to be distinguished, but they all have to do with the presentation of the Christ of God as the only remedy for the world's great need.

The heart of our blessed Lord was deeply moved as He looked on the multitudes with no one in Israel to guide them aright. They were like unshepherded sheep until He, the Good Shepherd, came to feed and care for them.

He directed the attention of His disciples to the great harvestfields filled with precious souls needing to know the truth concerning Himself. Into this harvestfield they were to go forth and reap. He bid them pray the Lord of the harvest to send laborers to gather in the ripened grain. Read in connection with the Lord's words at the well of Sychar, as recorded by John, we understand something of the deep concern that Jesus ever has for the salvation of lost men and women.

> Say not ye, There are yet four months, and then cometh harvest? Behold, I say unto you, Lift up your eyes, and look on the fields; for they are white already to harvest. And he that reapeth receiveth wages, and gathereth fruit unto life eternal: that both he that soweth and he that reapeth may rejoice together. And herein is that saying true, One soweth, and another reapeth (John 4:35-37).

These words may well be taken to our own hearts. He would have us look on the fields and go out to sow and reap and pray, that many

more may be raised up to carry on the great work of world evan-
gelization (see Luke 10:1-2).

Conclusion

Both this and the preceding chapter present the credentials of the
King. His works of power attested His Messianic claims. All His
miracles were performed not for self-glorification, however, nor to
have men hail Him as "some great one" (Acts 8:9), but to alleviate the
ills of suffering humanity. It had been predicted long before that
God's anointed King would open the eyes of the blind, unstop the ears
of the deaf, cause the lame to leap as an hart, and enable the tongue
of the dumb to sing (Isaiah 35:5-6). All this the Lord Jesus did, and
more, ministering to needy people out of the loving compassion of
His heart. Peter reminded Cornelius that "God anointed Jesus of
Nazareth with the Holy Ghost and with power: who went about doing
good, and healing all that were oppressed of the devil; for God was
with him" (Acts 10:38).

Yet we need to remember that this ministry was confined, with
very few exceptions, to the lost sheep of the house of Israel (Matthew
10:6) as a testimony to the chosen nation that their long-looked-for
King was in their midst (Zephaniah 3:15). But though they witnessed
so many evidences of His divine authority, the leaders of the people
steadfastly resisted His claims and spurned His testimony (John
7:48). Though the common people heard Him gladly (Mark 12:37),
even among these there were many who believed only in a superficial
way because they saw the miracles that He did (John 2:23). Faith
must be in Christ Himself, not in the signs and wonders He performs.
To recognize in Him a great teacher, prophet, or miracle-worker is
not the same as receiving Him as Savior and owning Him as Lord of
one's life.

CHAPTER TEN

THE KING'S COURIERS

The King Sends Out His Couriers (Matthew 10:1-15)

The calling of the twelve apostles was the initial act of a new and wider ministry. The twelve were disciples before they became apostles. Jesus had been training them for some time, and they were recognized as His disciples or pupils. They were learners in the school of Christ before they were commissioned as apostles and sent out two by two as couriers of the King, to proclaim that the long-awaited kingdom of Heaven was near. Their commission is given in this tenth chapter. It differs considerably from that given in Matthew 28:16-20, after the King had been rejected, and when He was about to return to the Father. This earlier commission had to do with their ministry to Israel only. The later one embraced all nations.

As the King's messengers to the chosen nation they were to count on the loyal subjects of the King to provide hospitality and to further them on their way. They were to go without purse or scrip or other provision, as though for a long journey. If received in peace, they were to preach the gospel of the kingdom and heal the sick, as empowered by the Lord. If rejected, they were to declare that judgment was about to fall, and were to proceed on their way to other towns and villages. The Lord Jesus forewarned them of the ill-treatment that awaited them in some places, but declared that the heavenly Father would watch over them.

After the cross all this was changed, and they were commissioned to go into all the world and to make disciples of all nations. This commission has never been revoked and is in force today, though it has never yet been fully carried out. If we do not see this distinction we are likely to become confused, for very opposite instructions are found in the Gospels as to the responsibility of the messengers in each instance. It is true that the great majority in Israel had no heart to respond to the message, but the circumstances were quite different. God had foreseen the rejection of His Son, and His sacrificial death was the very foundation of the divine plan of blessing for the world, but that did not lessen Israel's responsibility, as Peter later declared (Acts 2:23).

It was fitting that the offer of the kingdom should first be extended to the Israelites, for they were by natural birth the children of the kingdom. It was to them that the promises had been given. They looked forward for centuries to the coming of the King and the unveiling of His dominion over all the earth, with Israel as the chosen nation through whom blessing would come to all the rest of the world (Isaiah 60:1-16). When they refused to bow to the message as given by the Lord and His apostles, the kingdom was taken from them and given to another people (Matthew 21:43).

"When he had called unto him his twelve disciples, he gave them power [authority]." These twelve had been with Him for some time. Now He separated them from others of His followers, setting them apart as His authoritative messengers. In Matthew 10:2 they are designated for the first time as "apostles"—that is, "sent ones," or missionaries. Jesus had found them in various walks of life, and had summoned them to be His companions in preparation for the great work with which He was to entrust them. All except Judas Iscariot— that is, the man of Kerioth—proved faithful to their trust.

"Go not into the way of the Gentiles." The King must first be presented to Israel and the kingdom offered to them. It was not until Israel had rejected both that the gospel was sent out into all the world and to all nations (Matthew 28:19-20; Mark 16:15; Luke 24: 46-47; Acts 1:8).

The twelve were to seek out "the lost sheep of the house of Israel," giving Israel an opportunity to repent of their sins and to receive their King, and so be prepared to enter His kingdom. Their message or proclamation was a brief one: "The kingdom of heaven is at hand." The nation had been waiting long for this kingdom. Now it was presented for their acceptance or rejection.

"Freely ye have received, freely give." Miraculous powers were granted to the King's couriers in order to accredit their proclamation. But they were not to misuse these powers for their own enrichment. They were to give of what had been given them, not seeking any return for themselves.

The Lord sent the twelve without silver or gold for their expenses, or extra garments to wear. They were the King's representatives, going to His own people, and so had a right to expect to be cared for by the faithful in Israel who were waiting for the King. As they went from city to city and village to village they were to inquire in each place who in it was worthy—that is, who was esteemed as a man of piety and righteous life, waiting for Israel's redemption. In his house they were to seek hospitality. If such was refused, they were to pass on and shake off the dust from their sandals as a testimony against that house. Those who received them would find blessing. Those who rejected them would be exposed to judgment—a judgment so severe that what fell on Sodom and Gomorrah of old would seem mild in comparison. This was because of the fact that light increases responsibility. They had privileges such as the people of the cities of the plain never knew, and their guilt was therefore far greater if they refused to receive the King and dishonored His apostles.

The King Warns of Coming Persecution (Matthew 10:16-23)

The afflictions Jesus described in these verses go far beyond what the messengers experienced during the short time of their Galilean ministry. It seems clear that the Lord's words were intended to prepare them for what they would be called on to face after the Lord's crucifixion and resurrection, when they continued to witness first to Israel, then to Gentiles. On the other hand we need to remember that the Scriptures indicate a future witnessing to Israel by a faithful group of Jewish believers, the wise (or *maskilim*) of Daniel 12, in the tribulation period between the rapture of the church and the revelation of the Son of man at His second advent. During that dark hour of antichrist's rule these verses will be the guide and comfort of the witnesses who will then go forth to herald the return of the once-rejected King.

"I send you forth as sheep in the midst of wolves." Jesus would not have His followers under any illusion as to what was involved in representing Him among a people who in the past had slain the prophets and spurned their entreaties to return unto the Lord. The disciples were going to face hostile foes where they might have expected to find cordial friends. Under such circumstances how much they needed the wisdom that comes down from above.

When arrested and summoned before civil or ecclesiastical courts, they need not be anxious or perplexed as to how they should defend themselves. "In that same hour" it would be given them what they should speak through the Spirit of the Father speaking in them. The expression "the Spirit of your Father" is an unusual one, and does not necessarily imply the full truth of the indwelling Comforter, who was not to come until after Jesus was glorified. Therefore, the Lord used this rather ambiguous term, but one that would still be applicable when the new dispensation of the Spirit came (see Luke 12:11-12).

They were to be prepared for family misunderstandings and household feuds engendered by faithfulness to Christ. So bitterly is the world opposed to its rightful King that those who are loyal to Him will be hated for His name's sake, and so they could expect suffering and persecution such as would turn shallow and unreal souls aside. But salvation is assured to the one who endures to the end. This does not imply that we are saved by our own faithfulness or devotedness. All is of grace. But where there is a genuine work of God in the soul there will be final perseverance, whether in the days of the great tribulation yet to come or in this present evil age.

Nevertheless the disciple of Christ is not to court persecution or needlessly expose himself in a foolhardy way to danger. If persecuted in one city he is to flee to another, even as Paul did when he left Thessalonica for Berea on account of persecution. Later he fled from Berea to Corinth and Athens when the Jews sought to stir up the people of Berea against him.

The last part of Matthew 10:23 is, as noticed already, difficult to apply unless we see that in the coming hour of tribulation there will be a noble band of witnesses acting upon this same commission. The calling of the church has come in parenthetically for the present. When this special work of God is completed, the church will be translated to Heaven and the interrupted kingdom-testimony will be continued.

The King Promises Care and Comfort (Matthew 10:24-33)

In these verses the Lord tells of the Father's care over all those who are content to be identified with Him in the day of His rejection.

"The disciple is not above his master." A disciple is a learner. Humility becomes one in that position. Christ's servants and disciples are responsible to obey His Word. Why should they expect better treatment than that accorded their Master?

"They have called the master of the house Beelzebub." According to Jewish thought, Beelzebub (a Philistine word probably) was the chief of the demons. There were those who blasphemously applied this name to Jesus.

"Nothing covered, that shall not be revealed." This is a solemn consideration. All hidden motives and actions will be brought into light in the day when God will judge the secrets of men (Romans 2:16).

"Preach ye upon the housetops." That which they had learned of Jesus in secret, in hours of wonderful fellowship with the prince of teachers, the disciples were to proclaim boldly in public places.

"Not able to kill the soul." The death of the body does not result in the death of the soul. After the body dies, the soul lives on to be reunited to the body in the resurrection and, in the case of the impenitent, cast into Hell. In Scripture the terms "mortal" and "immortal" are connected with the body (Romans 8:11; 1 Corinthians 15:53). But this does not deny the fact that the soul lives after the body dies; and this is what is commonly meant when men speak of the immortality of the soul. Our Lord's words in Matthew 10:28 are clear and definite as to this. There is that in man which disease cannot affect, which the assassin's weapon cannot destroy. Man cannot kill the soul. God will deal with the soul of man in His own infinite righteousness.

"Two sparrows sold for a farthing." A farthing was an infinitesimal coin; yet two sparrows, dressed and spitted, were sold in the markets for this amount. They were used as food by the poorest of the people. Nevertheless, God took note of every sparrow's fall. Nothing is too insignificant for God to note, and His care extends to the minutest detail of our lives. God cares for all His creatures, but man has a special place in His heart and is valued above all other animate beings.

"Confess me before men." Christ claims absolute authority over our lives. We are to acknowledge Him openly before others, and He will confess our unworthy names in the day when we are to appear before God. If we refuse to own Christ now as Savior and Lord, He will deny us in the day of judgment.

The King Warns of Conflict (Matthew 10:34-39)

"Not to send peace, but a sword." This seems like a strange statement in view of the angels' message at His birth (Luke 2:14). But He foresaw His rejection and knew that the conflict between good and evil must go on until His return. His servants must be prepared to fight valiantly against iniquity.

"To set a man at variance against his father." The claims of Christ are paramount to all others. His disciples must be prepared to encounter opposition even in their own homes and on the part of their nearest kindred. This was true not only as a result of the mission of the twelve in that day, but also it has been sadly fulfilled throughout all the centuries since.

"Not worthy of me." If Jesus were less than God, how preposterous would be such claims as He makes here! He demands the supreme place in our hearts. We are to put love for Him before love to father or mother, or son or daughter.

"Followeth after me." To take the cross is to acknowledge our identification with Him as the rejected One. A man carrying a cross was a man devoted to death. And we are called to die daily (1 Corinthians 15:31) in order that He may be glorified in us.

"He that loseth his life for my sake shall find it." To live for self is to fail to recognize the purpose of our creation. But if we give up all that men of the world value for His name's sake, we gain eternally. Elsewhere the Lord Jesus Christ said, "Except a corn of wheat fall into the ground and die, it abideth alone: but if it die, it bringeth forth much fruit" (John 12:24). These words form an admirable commentary on His teaching regarding saving and losing one's life. The corn of wheat saved rather than planted is really lost. That which is lost by planting is saved in the coming harvest.

The King Rewards Acceptance of His Couriers (Matthew 10:40-42)

A reward is in store for all who receive Christ's messengers and aid them in their witness. It is encouraging to note how completely the Lord identifies His representatives with Himself. To receive one sent by Him is the same as to receive Him, and vice versa. To welcome a prophet as one speaking for God means to share in the prophet's reward. The same principle is true in connection with the reception of a righteous man. What is done for the servant is appreciated by the Master. Even a cup of cold water given to one of Christ's little ones will not go unrewarded. He esteems all that is done for them as done unto Him. Who that knows Him would not serve such a gracious Lord with gladness of heart?

Obedience is the test of devotion. If we truly love our Lord, we will be glad to yield all we are and have to Him for service. He has entrusted us who are saved with the message of His gospel. This does not mean that we are all called to be preachers or missionaries, but we are asked to confess Him before men that others may be drawn to Him as we have been. We will find life at its richest and best if we yield to His call, no matter how great the cost may seem to be. A life laid down for His glory is a life saved. A life given to the service of sin or self is a wasted life. No sacrifice should be too great for Him who gave Himself for us.

CHAPTER ELEVEN
THE GRACE OF THE KING

Jesus Speaks of John the Baptist (Matthew 11:1-15)

After commissioning the twelve and sending them out to preach the gospel of the kingdom Jesus went alone to minister in other cities. Two of John the Baptist's disciples came to inquire of the Lord whether He was indeed the coming One or whether they should look for another. The Lord Jesus answered by demonstrating His power over disease and demons, and took occasion to give due recognition to John and his message.

We need not speculate whether doubts had entered the mind of His forerunner John, or whether he simply sent his troubled disciples to the Lord with their questions so that Christ Himself could reassure them and confirm their faith. John was in prison at this time because of his faithfulness in reproving Herod for his wickedness in taking as his paramour Herodias, the wife of his brother Philip. John's day of popularity was over. As he languished in the gloomy fortress of Machaerus (if tradition be correct) he may have wondered if in some way he had misunderstood the testimony regarding Jesus.

In answer to the questions, Jesus reminded John's disciples that all the credentials of the King were manifested in power. The mighty miracles He did were to attest His claims: the blind were made to see and the lame to walk; lepers were cleansed; the deaf were made to hear; even the dead were raised up. What greater signs could be looked for? To the poor the glad tidings of the kingdom were proclaimed. But it was a time of testing. There was no outward pomp or show such as might be naturally expected in connection with the advent of a king. Therefore faith in God and His Word was important. Jesus declared, "Blessed is he, whosoever shall not be offended [or scandalized] in me." It took real faith to see in the meek and lowly Jesus of Nazareth the royal Son of David, destined to rule all nations with the iron rod of righteousness.

After the departure of John's disciples, Jesus spoke in highest terms of the Baptist and his testimony. What was it that had attracted the throngs to him? He had no outward show of magnificence or grandeur. John did not appear in gorgeous robes or other costly array such as might have been found on royal attendants in kings' palaces. He came, Elijah-like, in poor clothing, subsisting upon the simplest food. Yet of all born of women up to that time, he was the greatest because he was given the honor of introducing the Messiah to Israel. But great as his privileges were, the simplest and poorest member of the kingdom of Heaven is greater by far. For though John pointed to the open door, it was not given to him to enter into the new condition of things which the kingdom suggests. He closed one epoch; Jesus opened another. "All the prophets and the law prophesied until John." He fulfilled Malachi's prophecy that Elijah was to come before the great and dreadful day of the Lord.

Having said this, Jesus exclaimed, "He that hath ears to hear, let him hear." It is so easy to hear with the outward ear but fail to receive the truth in the heart.

Jesus Condemns the Lack of Response (Matthew 11:16-19)

The Lord brings out in vivid contrast the difference between John's ministry and His own, but shows that there was very little response to either. As He continued His gracious ministry it became increasingly evident that by far the great majority of Israel was in no mood to receive His message. The leaders and the people generally refused to acknowledge Him as the anointed One sent by God to deliver them from their bondage, not only to the Roman authority but to sin and Satan. If we did not know something of the hardness of our own hearts until subdued by divine grace, it would seem incredible that men could resist clear and evident proof of the messiahship of the Lord Jesus.

"Children sitting in the markets." Jesus likens the people to whom the message had come to irresponsible children who could make a play of the happiest or the saddest experience of life, but had little realization of the importance of either.

"Ye have not danced...ye have not lamented." Whether a wedding or a funeral it was all the same. There was no response to either. Neither the glad note of the gospel nor the solemn call to repentance seemed to have any effect on the great majority of the people.

"John came neither eating nor drinking." John was an ascetic, a man of the wilderness, who denied himself all ordinary comforts. But they declared he was a demoniac.

"A man gluttonous, and a winebibber." Jesus was a man of the people. He moved freely among them and participated in their feasts. But His very geniality was misinterpreted. They accused Him of pampering His appetites.

Christ is revealed to men only when they bow before God in repentance. It has been remarked often that the same sun which softens the wax hardens the clay. So it is with the preaching of the gospel. Some respond to it with gratitude and enjoy its blessings; others turn from it in unbelief and so are hardened in their sins. "To the one," said Paul, "we are the savour of death unto death; and to the other the savour of life unto life" (2 Corinthians 2:16). It was so when the prince of all preachers was here. There were those, chiefly among the poor and the outwardly sinful and degraded, who received the message eagerly and found life and healing. But the proud, self-righteous religionists, who did not feel their need of God's grace, spurned the message and the messenger, even blasphemously declaring that the Lord Himself was an agent of Beelzebub, the prince of the demons.

Jesus Condemns Unrepentant Cities (Matthew 11:20-24)

In this section the cities that had enjoyed the greatest privileges were rebuked by Jesus because the majority of their people persisted in their unbelief. The cities that had heard His words and seen His works of power refused to change their careless attitude, and so continued in their sins. We may well be amazed at the impenitence and hardness of heart of the residents of the cities where Jesus had done so many of His mighty works, but have our own hearts been any more ready to receive the truth?

"Woe unto thee, Chorazin [and] Bethsaida." These were cities situated near the northern end of the sea of Galilee, the one a little to the west, and the other on the shore. Chorazin is today an almost unidentifiable ruin; Bethsaida is a very poor little village.

"It shall be more tolerable for Tyre and Sidon." These were Phoenician cities noted for their wickedness and destroyed centuries before. But their people are still awaiting the day of judgment. Note that there will be degrees of punishment according to the measure of light received and rejected.

Capernaum was blessed above all other cities of Galilee, for the Lord performed more mighty works there than in any other place. In this sense it was indeed exalted. But it was condemned to utter ruin, because it knew not the time of its visitation.

Sodom had become a synonym for the vilest and most unnatural sin. But the people of Capernaum were guiltier because they had much greater light and far more privileges, yet they persisted in their sins.

Jesus Offers Rest for the Weary (Matthew 11:25-30)

With what relief of mind we turn to the closing verses of this chapter! Though spurned by so many to whom His heart went out in pity and compassion, our Lord was not soured, as we might have been. Ungrateful people responded to His love and grace with coldness and ill-treatment, but He accepted it all as from His Father's hand, and continued to offer deliverance and blessing to all who would come to Him.

"I thank thee, O Father." At the very time when our Lord was experiencing the bitterness of man's indifference and opposition, He turned in worship and praise to the Father, rejoicing that though the great ones in Israel rejected Him, the humble received His words. His prayer is the language of complete subjection to the Father's will. As the dependent man on earth, He was wholly resigned to that which the Father had foreseen.

"No man knoweth the Son, but the Father." The mystery of the incarnation, God and man in one person, is insoluble and past human comprehension. But the Father may be known "to whomsoever the Son will reveal him." The fatherhood of God, unknown by human wisdom, is revealed by the Son. He has made God known to those who receive His words, as the Father of all the redeemed.

"Come unto me...and I will give you rest." Surely, none but God revealed in the flesh could rightly use such language as this. The best man earth ever knew could make no such declaration. All others who speak as directed by the Spirit of God point men from themselves to Christ for rest of conscience and peace of mind. Jesus alone could make this offer to the burdened and heavy-laden. He has proved His deity times without number by His ability to fulfill this promise.

All who are truly subject to Him find rest of heart in the midst of the cares of life as they learn of Him, the meek and lowly One. A yoke is designed to curb the will and bring one under control. He who exchanges sin's heavy burden for the glorious yoke of subjection to the Lord finds it blessed indeed to serve so good a Master.

"My yoke is easy, and my burden is light." Many shrink from submitting to His yoke, fearing it may involve greater sacrifices than they are ready to make. But all who acknowledge His authority and blend their wills with His find they enter a rest such as the weary of this world never know.

The Two Rests. The rest that the Lord Jesus gives freely to all who come to Him is rest of conscience in regard to sin. The distressed soul, burdened with a sense of guilt, comes to Him and finds peace when he trusts Him as the great sin-bearer. The second rest is rest of heart. Adverse circumstances may rise up to alarm and fill the heart with fear and anxiety, but he who takes Christ's yoke and learns of Him is able to be calm in the midst of the storm. He finds perfect rest as he trusts all to Him who rules over the waterfloods and is Lord of all the elements.

These two rests are the same as the two aspects of peace presented in the Epistles. Rest of conscience is the equivalent of peace with God that is the portion of all who are justified by faith (Romans 5:1). Rest of soul is the same as the peace of God that passes all understanding (Philippians 4:6-7), and is enjoyed by all who learn to commit everything to the Lord.

CHAPTER TWELVE
THE KING'S AUTHORITY DENIED

Jesus Teaches concerning the Sabbath (Matthew 12:1-8)

The events recorded in Matthew 12 bring us to the close of the first great division of this Gospel in which the King and the kingdom were presented to Israel and deliberately rejected by the leaders of the nation.

In the first eight verses we have a most interesting and instructive incident recorded. Here Jesus declares Himself to be Lord of the sabbath, again attesting to His deity. The sabbath was Jehovah's witness to His power in creation (Exodus 20:10-11) and to the redemption of Israel from Egyptian bondage (Deuteronomy 5:14-15). It was distinctively "the sabbath of Jehovah." The Jehovah of the Old Testament is the Jesus of the New, and He is Lord of the sabbath, as of all else.

Walking quietly in the country, the Lord and His disciples passed through a cornfield. The hungry disciples began to pluck the ears of corn and to eat. This was quite in keeping with the provision made in the law, for in Deuteronomy 23:25 we read, "When thou comest into the standing corn of thy neighbour, then thou mayest pluck the ears with thine hand; but thou shalt not move a sickle unto thy neighbour's standing corn." This incident occurred on the sabbath day however, and the Pharisees immediately took exception to it, exclaiming, "Behold, thy disciples do that which is not lawful to do upon the sabbath day." There was absolutely no prohibition in the law of Moses in regard to this, but in the traditions of the elders there were many added laws and regulations that made it at times almost impossible for the ordinary man to know whether he was violating one of them or not. Among these rules was the prohibition to gather fruit or grain of any kind on the sabbath day. Even to rub it out in the hand as the disciples were doing seemed to these Pharisees a violation of that which they regarded as sacred.

The Lord defended His followers, however, by pointing out that the meeting of man's need means far more to God than the obedience to legal restrictions. He cited the case of David and his men who were hungry. They asked the high priest if they might be permitted to eat the shewbread that had been taken from the holy table before the Lord. Under ordinary circumstances it was not lawful for anyone but the priests themselves to eat this bread. But when God's anointed king was rejected and his followers were in distress, their need was paramount to any legal prohibition.

The Lord also reminded His critics that the priests in the temple work on the sabbath day and, therefore, might be said to profane it, but they were blameless in so doing.

He then added the remarkable declaration: "In this place is one greater than the temple." How little the Pharisees understood His words. Everything in that temple, as far as it was arranged according to the Word of God, spoke of Jesus and His redemptive work. But though He had come in person to what He called His Father's house, people failed to realize who it was who walked among them. His words were not simply an announcement of His deity, however. Rightly understood this declaration should have made it clear to the Pharisees that man himself means more to God than any building, no matter how holy, and more than any rules and regulations, no matter how well-authenticated. Hosea 6:6 says, "I desired mercy, and not sacrifice; and the knowledge of God more than burnt offerings." Had the critics but pondered these words of the prophet Hosea they would have understood the value God gives to man and would not have condemned the disciples for doing that which in itself was perfectly innocent.

"The Son of man is Lord even of the sabbath day." This remarkable assertion of Jesus can mean nothing less than that He claimed to be God incarnate. No mere human would have the right to use such language as this. Jesus was the One to whom all the sabbaths of the law pointed, and He had absolute authority over them.

Jesus Heals on the Sabbath (Matthew 12:9-21)

Entering into a village synagogue Jesus saw a man with a withered hand. A test question arose among those who were gathered there. They asked, "Is it lawful to heal on the sabbath days?" In the Gospels of Mark and Luke we read that Jesus turned the question back to those who posed it. For them to say no would indicate that they were utterly indifferent to human sufferings; to reply in the affirmative would be to accuse themselves. So they did not answer. (see Mark 3:4; Luke 6:9).

Jesus then asked another question—one that would go home to many of them. Possibly they had rescued sheep on the sabbath on numerous occasions. Sheep to them constituted property, and property must be cared for even on the sabbath day.

Without waiting for an answer, Jesus replied to His own questions by pointing out that a man is much better than a sheep, and it is always lawful to do good on the sabbath day. He turned to the man who was expectantly looking toward Him, and commanded him to stretch out his hand. In an instant new life came into that withered hand and it was restored whole like the other. One would think that surely this miracle would have convinced even the most prejudiced Pharisees that God's King was with them. But so bigoted were they that they went out and held a council against Him, endeavoring to devise some means by which they might destroy Him.

Jesus knew what was in their minds, and therefore withdrew Himself and went elsewhere. Great multitudes of the common people followed after Him. Many of them were sick, and we are told that He healed them all. But He charged them not to spread abroad the report of His marvelous power. He had not come, as we have noticed in an earlier chapter, to create astonishment in the minds of men by His wonder-working ability. He had come to reveal that meekness and lowliness which the prophet Isaiah predicted would be seen in Messiah when He appeared. The quotation given in Matthew 12:18-21 is from Isaiah 42:1-4.

Jesus Confirms His Authority Is from God (Matthew 12:22-30)

A crisis is reached in connection with the King's presentation of Himself to Israel. He had given evidence after evidence of His messiahship, but those who should have been the first to recognize Him were determined not to do so. Now once more He demonstrated His power over the unseen world by casting out a demon who had made the wretched man in whom he resided to be both blind and dumb. When Jesus cast out the evil spirit, the man both spoke and saw. The crowds that thronged about the Lord were amazed and cried out, "Is not this the son of David?" They saw in the miracle the proof that Jesus was the King of David's line who had come to redeem Israel. But they were silenced by the Pharisees who exclaimed, "This fellow doth not cast out devils, but by Beelzebub the prince of the devils." This was the second time that the leaders of the nation deliberately rejected Jesus by ascribing all His works of power to Beelzebub. Only in this way could they account for the great miracles Jesus performed and refuse to see in them His credentials as the promised King. It was evident now that there would be no repentance. These religious leaders were bent upon the destruction of Him whom the people had just acclaimed "the Son of David."

Jesus knew the thoughts of the Pharisees and did not need any man to tell Him what was in their minds. He observed that "if Satan cast out Satan, he is divided against himself; how shall then his kingdom stand?"

Jesus continued, "If I by Beelzebub cast out devils, by whom do your children cast them out?" He was referring to the disciples, who had also been empowered by the Lord to cast out demons. Afraid of offending the relatives of the disciples, the Pharisees did not want to say of the disciples what had been said of Jesus.

It was clear that Jesus was either revealing the mighty power of God, or deceiving the people by Satanic influence. They must decide which they would believe. He challenged them to recognize the true condition of affairs by saying, "If I cast out devils by the Spirit of God [which of course He did], then the kingdom of God is come unto you." It was this that Jesus wanted the people to understand: the King was there and the little group of His disciples were His acknowledged subjects. Thus the kingdom in embryo was actually in the midst of the Israelites. Would they receive it, or spurn the privilege of entering into it?

No one could enter a strong man's house and spoil his goods unless he were able to overcome the owner. Jesus had met the strong man, Satan, in the wilderness and overcome him. Ever since He had gone about through the land of Israel spoiling his goods. Now the time had come for those who heard Him to take a definite stand. They must be either for Him or against Him; neutrality would not do. Those who were not with Him, who did not proclaim themselves on His side, were really against Him; for all who would not gather with Him were but scattering abroad.

Jesus Warns of the Unpardonable Sin (Matthew 12:31-37)

Matthew 12:31-32 has troubled many people. If rightly understood, these verses ought to trouble no one except those who are determined to refuse the testimony of the Holy Spirit concerning the person of the Lord Jesus Christ. The sin of which Jesus spoke was a dispensational sin, and definitely cannot be committed, at least in exactly the same way, by individuals today. Jesus had come in the power of the Holy Spirit, presenting Himself to Israel as their rightful King. His mighty works, as we have seen, accredited His testimony. The only way in which men could refuse to own His grace and yet recognize His power was by attributing all His mighty works to the devil. Those who did this gave evidence that they had sinned until their consciences were seared as with a hot iron. They had gone beyond the redemption point, not because God would not have been merciful to them if they had repented, but because they had so persisted in their sin that there was on their part no evidence of nor desire for repentance. Had they simply spoken against the Son of man, Jesus said they would have been forgiven. But He solemnly added, "Whosoever speaketh against the Holy Ghost, it shall not be forgiven him, neither in this world [age], neither in the world [age] to come."

Jesus was not intimating, as the Roman Catholics tell us, that there is forgiveness for some in another world, though they leave this world with sin still upon their souls. The Lord was speaking of two ages:

the age that was just closing, and the age to come, which is, properly speaking, the millennium. The present age was hidden at that time in the mind of God. Yet we can apply His words to our own day also, for those who deliberately refuse the testimony of the Holy Ghost concerning Christ could not be forgiven in the Jewish age, nor in this or any other age to follow.

Many dear souls have tormented themselves, or have been tormented by the devil, with the awful thought that they are guilty of the sin here described. Yet deep in their hearts they fully recognize the deity of the Lord Jesus and have no thought of attributing to the devil the power that Jesus displayed.

In Matthew 12:33-37 Jesus used perhaps the strongest language recorded of Him, as He addressed these hypocritical religious leaders who determined to persist in their rejection of Him, no matter what the cost. He calls for a clean-cut distinction between evil and good. Every tree is known by its fruit. His life of holiness was the testimony to the reality of His claim. Their evil lives were the evidence of their corrupt hearts.

"O generation of vipers"! These hypocrites were the brood of the serpent, and they manifested the nature of that old serpent, the devil, in their attitude toward Christ. Out of the abundance of their hearts their mouths spoke.

Thus our words indicate the condition of the inward man. A good man, made good by grace, speaks from the treasure of his heart words that are good. An inherently evil man reveals his wickedness by the words that fall from his lips. In the day of judgment God will deal with men according to what they themselves have spoken. Account will have to be given for every word, and by these words we will be either justified or condemned.

Jesus Condemns the Jews' Unbelief (Matthew 12:38-45)

A number of the scribes and Pharisees added insult to injury, we might say, by coming to the Lord and asking for a sign, which He refused to give. He directed their attention to events of the past which would only make their condemnation the greater in the day when they would have to give an account to God.

One would think that their own self-respect would have kept the scribes and Pharisees from asking for another sign, after they had seen so many and rejected them all. In answer to their demand Jesus replied that it was an evil and adulterous generation that was seeking a sign. No sign should be given to such a generation except the sign of the prophet Jonah. Jesus also referred to His resurrection from the dead that was soon to take place, but as we know failed to convince these men of the folly and wickedness of their course.

Whatever others may say, Jesus had no doubts regarding the authenticity of the records of the book of Jonah, and He was God incarnate, who knew all things. He said that Jonah was three days and three nights in the belly of the sea-monster. Through this experience Jonah became a sign of the Son of man who was to be three days and three nights in the heart of the earth—that is, the grave. Moreover, our Lord authenticated the repentance of Nineveh. He declared that in the judgment the Ninevites would condemn the generation who refused His testimony, because the Ninevites had repented at the preaching of Jonah, and He was greater far than Jonah.

Jesus brought forth also another witness from the Old Testament, the Queen of Sheba, whom He calls the queen of the south. She came from the uttermost parts of the earth to hear the wisdom of Solomon, because she had learned that he could reveal to her precious things concerning the name of the Lord, which her soul longed to understand. She did not consider a journey of perhaps a thousand miles too great in order to hear the wisdom of Solomon. But these deniers of the truth were unmoved, though Solomon's Lord Himself was in their midst. When at last they shall stand trembling in their sins before the bar of God, the queen of the south will appear to upbraid them because of their willful rejection of light. She followed the gleam from the very ends of the earth in order that that light might be hers forevermore.

Jesus then told a remarkable parable of unbelieving Israel's past, present, and future state. The unclean spirit in the parable is the spirit of idolatry that was cast out of the nation of the Jews as a result of the Babylonian captivity. Since their return from Babylon they had been like an empty house swept and garnished. They were free from idolatry; but on the other hand, they had not received the Lord

Himself to dwell among them. In a coming day this evil spirit of idolatry will take with himself seven other spirits even more wicked than he, and they will enter and dwell in the apostate nation. This will result in the recognition of the antichrist, the willfull king, as the messiah, and so their last state will be worse than the first. The wicked generation that rejected Jesus will still be evident in that hour of tribulation.

Jesus Introduces a New Family (Matthew 12:46-50)

Whether His mother failed in measure to comprehend the mystery of her Son we cannot say, but we do know that His brothers did not believe in Him until after His resurrection. They interrupted His preaching by sending one to announce their presence, evidently with the suggestion that He should cease ministering and come to them. But He stretched forth His hand toward those who were ready to learn from Him and said, "Behold my mother and my brethren!" And He added that all who did the will of the Father in Heaven are His brother, sister, and mother. It was the renunciation of all fleshly ties. The break with Israel was practically complete. He was looking forward to an altogether new order of things.

CHAPTER THIRTEEN
THE MYSTERIES OF THE KINGDOM

Parable of the Sower (Matthew 13:1-9)

In Matthew 13 our Lord used seven parables to describe the condition that He saw the kingdom would take on earth as a result of His rejection. This series of parables is divided into four that were spoken in the open air by the seaside, and three that were given to the disciples only after they had entered into the house. The first of this series is not a likeness of the kingdom, as in the case of the other six. When the Lord explained the parable of the sower to His disciples, He said it was given to them to know the mysteries of the kingdom of Heaven, thus equating the sowing of the Word with the spreading of the kingdom in its secret or mystical form through the world. Therefore in this parable we see the seed of the kingdom sown in the earth and the results.

In verse 1 the Lord's action (He "went out of the house, and sat by the sea side") seems to be parabolic. This, in itself, appears to indicate the break with Israel after His countrymen rejected Him. Multitudes gathered about Him, however, pressing closely to the water. He entered into a ship, probably Peter's fishing boat which Luke 5:3 tells us was once used as a pulpit, and addressed the multitudes standing on the shore. The hills at this particular locality rise gently from the shore, thus making a natural open-air arena or theater, where the voice would carry easily to great throngs standing on the shore or sitting on the hillside.

"Behold a sower went forth to sow." The sower in the first instance was the Lord Himself. He went from place to place sowing the seed of the Word of God. It should be a matter of encouragement to all those who engage in the same blessed occupation that even when the divine preacher Himself was ministering the Word, fruit resulted from the Word that was sown in only one out of four hearts; and even then the amount of fruit produced varied.

In verses 4-7 we read of three types of non-productive soil. The first soil was the trampled wayside where the fowls of the air devoured the seed almost as rapidly as it was strewn. Then there was the stony ground where the seed appeared to take root; green sprouts came up, but only to be parched by the sun, to the disappointment of the sower. Other seed fell among thorns, which soon choked the tender shoots so that there was no fruit whatever.

That which fell into good ground took root, sprang up, and became fruitful—some producing a hundred times, some sixty times, and some thirty times what was planted.

This was the parable. For the moment the Lord made no application, but left it for His hearers to weigh His words as He exclaimed, "Who hath ears to hear, let him hear."

Parable of the Sower Explained (Matthew 13:10-23)

When opportunity arose and the multitudes had gone, the disciples came to Jesus asking for an explanation of the parable. To those who trusted Him and set value upon His words, the Lord was always ready to explain anything that seemed difficult for them to apprehend. In response to the question, "Why speakest thou unto them in parables?" Jesus replied at once, "It is given unto you to know the mysteries of the kingdom of heaven, but to them it is not given." The word *mysteries* as here used does not necessarily mean something mysterious and difficult to understand, but rather secrets that are revealed only to initiates. The Lord was ever ready to take into His confidence earnest seekers after the truth. He used the parabolic form for a double purpose. He desired to test His hearers as to whether they really wanted to know the mind of God or not, and also to illumine His discourses. Where people already had faith and had accepted His testimony, He was prepared to give more. But where there was no real confidence in His message they would become more bewildered by the parabolic form of instruction than if He had spoken in plain language.

Some have quibbled over this, as though it indicated on the part of the Lord Jesus a deliberate intention to blind the eyes and close the ears of those who listened to His words. It was really the very opposite. Those who were anxious to know the truth came to Him as the disciples did, asking for an explanation of what was beyond their comprehension. Those who were indifferent turned carelessly away and became even more unconcerned because of not understanding the meaning of His illustrations. Jesus quoted from Isaiah 6:9-10 in which this very method of teaching was predicted. It was never God's desire to harden anyone's heart or to close anyone's eyes against the truth, but it is a principle that runs throughout the Word of God that the truth either softens or hardens. The very same gospel message that breaks down honest hearts and leads to repentance, hardens the hearts of the dishonest and confirms them in their path of disobedience.

Jesus pronounced a blessing on the apostles because they had eyes to see and ears to hear. Theirs was a place of peculiar privilege. Throughout the centuries that had gone many prophets and righteous men had looked forward in faith to Messiah's coming. They had longed to see and hear what the followers of Jesus were then seeing and hearing, but this had been denied them (see Luke 10:23-24).

The Lord then proceeded to explain the parable. "When any one heareth the word of the kingdom," He said, "and understandeth it not, then cometh the wicked one, and catcheth away that which was sown in his heart." This is the explanation of the seed scattered on the wayside, only to be devoured by the fowls of the air. Note that the message is called distinctly "the word of the kingdom," making it clear that it is by sowing the Word that the kingdom makes its way through the world. Satan and his emissaries are ever busy trying to annul the effect of gospel preaching. It is their sinister aim to fill the hearts and minds of the hearers with prejudice and unreasonable opposition so that they do not fairly weigh the message as it comes from the preacher's lips; thus there is no favorable response whatever. The Word heard only with the outer ear is soon forgotten.

In vivid contrast to these utterly indifferent hearers we have next the stony-ground hearers. These represent those exuberant people who are ever ready to take up with almost any kind of religious propaganda. They listen to the proclamation of the gospel and its clearness without any depth of conviction or evidence of repentance. They profess faith in the Word, apparently receiving it joyfully, but because there is no root in them, nothing but empty profession, they soon fall away, particularly when they find that the Christian way of life entails tribulation and persecution.

The thorny-ground hearers have never counted the cost of faith in Christ. They are not characterized by the single eye but are double-minded, occupied with the cares of this world and seeking after wealth. The temporal responsibilities connected with these pursuits choke the Word, and so there is no fruit.

In contrast to all these others we have the good-ground hearers, whose soil has been prepared by the plowshare of conviction. The Word falling into an honest heart is received in faith, and the message is understood as the Holy Spirit opens it up. The result is that the soul is born again, and the life becomes fruitful for God. There are degrees of fruitfulness, however. All do not give the same evidence of devotion to Christ and appreciation of the truth; and so the Lord speaks of those who bring forth an hundredfold, others sixtyfold, and others only thirtyfold.

Parable of the Tares (Matthew 13:24-30)

This second parable is definitely said to be a likeness of the kingdom of Heaven. In this parable the kingdom of Heaven is not Heaven itself; neither is it, as used in this part of Matthew's Gospel, to be confused with the coming glorious kingdom of our God and His Christ when all the world will be subjected to Jesus as King. The parable of the tares speaks of a mixed condition of things, such as has prevailed in Christendom ever since the beginning of the present age. Tares, which are the children of the evil one, are mingled with the wheat, the children of God, thus depicting the Satanic imitation seen in the church today.

This parable is also explained farther on in the chapter. We now need only to take note of the fact that the Lord was portraying a state of things in which false converts and true believers would be found together. The great difference between the two is that those who are genuine bring forth fruit; whereas the others are without fruit, and even are hurtful rather than helpful. The tares themselves are actually poisonous weeds. "His enemy," Jesus said, "came and sowed tares." That enemy, we know, is the devil. But when the servants of the householder came asking if they should root up the tares, the answer was in the negative. Not until the time of harvest would the great separation take place.

Parable of the Mustard Seed (Matthew 13:31-32)

We are not to understand from our Lord's words that the mustard seed is the most infinitesimal of all seeds in the entire vegetable kingdom, but it is the least of the seeds of the garden herbs; yet when it is grown it becomes the greatest of all the herbs, towering over the rest, so that it forms a place of shelter. The parable was not explained so far as the record goes, but it is easy to understand it in the light of other Scripture passages. It speaks of the development of the king-dom of Heaven into a great world power. Such dominions were frequently likened to large trees with spreading branches, as in the case of Babylon (Daniel 4), Assyria (Ezekiel 31:3), and other similar powers. So that which began as a field of wheat developed in the course of centuries into the mustard tree. The professing church of God became a power to be reckoned with among the nations, but its branches sheltered all kinds of false professors and evil teachers. The birds of the air, lodging in the branches of the mustard tree, represent the hosts of evil. It is a most graphic picture of what Christendom became throughout the course of centuries when the false church seemed to dominate the world.

Parable of the Leaven (Matthew 13:33-35)

This is the fourth parable spoken by the Lord as He sat by the seaside. Perhaps of all the teachings of the Lord nothing has been more misunderstood than the parable of the leaven. The general idea among Christians is that the woman here represents the church; the three measures of meal, the world; the leaven, the gospel through which the whole world will eventually be converted. Nothing could be more contrary to the teaching of the Word of God than this. It is a solemn fact that after nearly twenty centuries of gospel preaching there are more unbelievers in the world today than there were when Christ commissioned the apostles to go and evangelize the nations. Scripture nowhere warrants us to expect to see a converted world before the coming again of our Lord Jesus Christ.

In order to understand this parable one needs to inquire as to the meaning of leaven. Throughout the Word of God leaven is always used in an evil sense. The people of Israel were to put all leaven out of their houses during the Passover season, and the apostle Paul explained this when he said, "Christ our passover is sacrificed for us: Therefore let us keep the feast, not with old leaven, neither with the leaven of malice and wickedness; but with the unleavened bread of sincerity and truth" (1 Corinthians 5:7-8). Leaven, then, speaks of malice and wickedness, and the Christian is to put these out of his life. The Lord Jesus warned His disciples to beware of the leaven of the Pharisees, which is hypocrisy and self-righteousness; the leaven of the Sadducees, which is false doctrine and materialism; and the leaven of Herod, which is worldliness and political corruption. In Leviticus 2 we have the meal offering, in which there was to be no leaven. This offering represents our Lord Jesus Christ's humanity which was absolutely without sin.

In the parable the woman is surreptitiously hiding the leaven in the meal offering. The three measures of meal certainly do not represent the world, but rather the truth of God concerning His Son. The woman is not the church, but the false church—that woman Jezebel of whom we read in Revelation 2:20, who calls herself a prophetess and teaches the servants of God unholy principles that are subversive of the faith. Therefore in this parable we see the false church inserting the leaven of corrupt teaching into the food of God's people. Is not this exactly what has been taking place during the past almost two millennia of church history? "The mystery of iniquity" began to work in apostolic days, and it has spread throughout the centuries until today there is practically no great doctrine of Scripture that has not been perverted by false teachers.

With this fourth parable the Lord ended what we might call His public ministry for that occasion. He had opened up secrets that God had kept hidden until that time, even as it had been declared by Him prophetically in Psalm 78:2.

Parable of the Tares Explained (Matthew 13:36-43)

Dismissing the outdoor gathering Jesus entered the house, followed by His disciples. In this place of seclusion the apostles came to Him a second time asking for further explanation. He delivered three more parables and explained that of the wheat and the tares.

He explained that He Himself was the sower of the good seed. The field is not the church, but rather that world out of which the church was eventually to be gathered. It is important that we remember this because of what follows. "The good seed," Jesus said, "are the children of the kingdom; but the tares are the children of the wicked one." Here we have the result of the sowing: those who believe the gospel message are the wheat; those who accept the teachings of Satan are the tares, for the enemy that sowed the evil seed is the devil himself. He has ever been busy sowing the tares wherever servants of God have sown the good seed. But Christ's servants are not to attempt to destroy the tares during this age. Our understanding is too limited. We might make the fatal mistake that Rome made of rooting up the good in order to destroy the bad. At the end of the age—it is not the end of the world He has in mind but the end of the present age—"The Son of man shall send forth his angels, and they shall gather out of his kingdom all things that offend, and them which do iniquity; and shall cast them into a furnace of fire." Notice that the Son of man will send forth *His* angels. What a definite proof of His deity we have here! He is both Son of God and Son of man in one blessed, adorable person. The angels are His, and they do His bidding.

Then observe the mixed condition that prevails in the kingdom down to the end of the age. The angels gather out of His kingdom all things that cause scandal. There will be false professors mingled with the true in the world, down to the end of the age. "Then shall the right-eous shine forth as the sun in the kingdom of their Father." This is the heavenly side of the kingdom into which the Lord will gather His own in that day. Again the challenge comes, "Who hath ears to hear, let him hear."

Parables of the Treasure, Pearl, and Net (Matthew 13:44-53)

In the fifth parable the treasure is not Christ, but Israel. The sinner is not seeking Christ, but the blessed Lord is coming from Heaven to earth to find His own people who were of inestimable value to Him. In order to redeem Israel to Himself Christ died upon the cross, but they were not yet ready to receive Him as their King, so the treasure was hidden in the field, and would remain hidden until He returned.

From of old, Israel was recognized as God's special treasure (Exodus 19:5). The Lord Himself is represented by the man who found and hid this treasure. At Calvary He sold all that He had and bought the field, which is the world (Matthew 13:38). Israel was purchased with the world but remains hidden among the nations during the present age. When Israel turns to the Lord, they will be revealed as Jehovah's peculiar treasure (Malachi 3:17, RV), and through them blessing will come to all the Gentile nations.

"The kingdom of heaven," is likened next "unto a merchant man, seeking goodly pearls." Again the seeker is Christ, who came from the throne of glory to this poor world, seeking for jewels to adorn His crown forever.

"One pearl of great price." This is the church, which is of supreme value in His eyes. He gave Himself for the church. At the cross He "sold all that he had, and bought it." There He literally impoverished Himself to purchase the church as His own choice pearl (Ephesians 5:25; 2 Corinthians 8:9). Many think of salvation as the pearl and the sinner as the merchantman, but that is to invert completely the message of the gospel.

"The kingdom of heaven is like unto a net." It is literally a dragnet. This parable illustrates the present work of the professing church when vast numbers of both saved and lost are gathered in from the waters of the nations (Revelation 17:15) and are numbered among the professors of faith in Christ.

"Gathered the good into vessels, but cast the bad away." When the dragnet is full it is drawn to shore, and the good and bad fishes are separated from each other.

"So shall it be at the end of the world [age]." It is not the end of the world that is in view, but the consummation of the present age of grace, immediately preceding the ushering in of the age of the kingdom in full manifestation.

"Wailing and gnashing of teeth." Judgment does not necessarily produce repentance. When the final separation takes place the false professors will be cast away in judgment, which results in wailing because of their suffering, and gnashing of teeth because of their hatred against God and His Christ (Psalm 35:16; Lamentations 2:16).

Having presented this remarkable panorama of parables covering the entire present age, and reaching into the tribulation period, thus viewing its consummation at the second coming of the Lord, Jesus questioned His disciples as to how much they had really apprehended. Though they declared they had understood these things, it is evident they but feebly entered into them. But a groundwork had been laid in their hearts and minds on which they could later build. So the Lord likened them unto scribes instructed unto the kingdom of Heaven, who in days to come would be able to bring forth out of their treasure things new and old. With this Jesus closed that particular period of ministry and returned to Nazareth.

The Prophet Without Honor (Matthew 13:54-58)

"Whence...this wisdom, and these mighty works?" Even in His own country—that is, in the city of Nazareth—there were few who responded to the message of the kingdom. They heard His teaching and saw His miracles with amazement, but failed to recognize Him as the Messiah (see Luke 4:16-24).

"Is not this the carpenter's son?" The answer is no. He is the eternal Son of God, born of a virgin, but brought up under the fostering care of Joseph, from whom He learned the trade of the carpenter.

"Whence then hath this man all these things?" They were frankly puzzled. Jesus was so different from others of His townspeople. His wisdom and power were inexplicable from a merely human standpoint. Without scholastic training, He was more profound than the scribes.

"They were offended in him." They were stumbled by His lowliness and took offense when He intimated that their very familiarity with Him in past days, when they knew Him as a simple artisan, blinded their eyes to the fact that He was God's mouthpiece.

"Because of their unbelief." Even God Himself is restricted by man's unbelief. He who does for faith "exceeding abundantly above all that we ask or think" (Ephesians 3:20), may be hindered in His working by stony-hearted opposition and unbelief.

The one great truth that this chapter in the life of our Lord demonstrates clearly is that unbelief on the one hand, or faith on the other, are not dependent on intellect or logic. The secret of both is the state of the conscience. Where one is determined to go contrary to what he knows to be right, he will continue in unbelief and refuse to submit to the authority of the Lord Jesus Christ. When one repents of his sins and honestly seeks deliverance from them, he will have no difficulty in believing the record God has given of His Son (1 John 5:11). It may be safely said, without fear of successful contradiction, that if one claims to have intellectual difficulties about believing the Bible, it is because he is living in some sin which the Bible condemns and from which he does not wish to be delivered. Unjudged sin is responsible for lack of faith in God.

This chapter brings to us a new revelation in connection with the kingdom. We saw in the preceding chapter how the leaders of the people of Israel crossed the deadline, and refused the offered kingdom by deliberately discrediting all the credentials of the King. They attributed His power (which they could not deny) to Beelzebub, and so committed the sin against the Holy Spirit for which there could be no forgiveness, either in that age or in the age to come. This resulted eventually in the setting aside for the time being of Israel nationally, and the introduction of a new order of things that God had foreseen from eternity. In its fullness this new order involved the revelation of the mystery of the church as one body called out from Jews and Gentiles, but the time had not yet come to unfold this mystery. Preliminary to that time, Jesus could speak of other mysteries that had been kept secret from the foundation of the world, the mysteries of the kingdom of Heaven.

Conclusion

In concluding let us notice the distinction between the kingdoms of God and of Heaven. We are told that God's kingdom rules over all (Psalm 22:28; 103:19) and is from age to age (Daniel 4:3). The expression *the kingdom of God* is never found in the Old Testament. The kingdom of God takes on different forms at different times. During the present age it is designated in Matthew's Gospel, and there only, as "the kingdom of heaven." From Matthew 13 on, the expression refers specifically, not to the final establishment of the kingdom of God over all the earth, but to the mystical form in which that kingdom was to be revealed between Christ's ascension to Heaven and His second advent.

In Matthew, the King is seen as rejected by men and having returned to Heaven, from which place He directs His saints on earth. These saints disseminate the Word of the kingdom, causing a vast throng of mankind to acknowledge Him, at least outwardly, as earth's rightful King. When He returns He will come in power and glory to root out of His kingdom all offenses and destroy all who work iniquity. He will gather out of His kingdom all who are unreal. Those who are genuine will have their part either in the heavenly or the earthly sphere of the kingdom of the Son of man, which will be the aspect taken by the kingdom of God in the millennial age.

In the parables of Matthew 13 our Lord set forth the condition that He saw the kingdom would take on earth as a result of His rejection. This was all foreknown to God and provision was made for it. Christ, refused by the leaders of the nation of Israel made propitiation for sin by His sacrificial death upon the cross (Acts 2:23; 1 John 4:10), and then, as the rejected man, left this world, ascending to Heaven, where He sits exalted at God's right hand. The kingdom of the prophets is in abeyance until His promised return to build again the tabernacle of David, which has fallen down (Acts 15:16). But during His personal absence the Holy Spirit has come in a new way as the

Comforter, to enable His servants to preach the Word in convicting power (John 16:7-11). Wherever the gospel is carried, it is the seed of the kingdom (Luke 8:11). As a result we see in the world today a great body of people who recognize in the Lord Jesus earth's rightful King, and give Him heart allegiance. There are millions more who give Him lip-service and in an outward way own His authority, though their hearts are far from Him. These together constitute the kingdom in its mystical form (Matthew 13:11).

The kingdom promised to Israel by the prophets depended upon the reception of the King by the chosen nation. In rejecting Him they lost their opportunity, and so the kingdom was taken from them (Matthew 21:43). When they turn to the Lord, He will appear in glory, and all things that are written concerning the kingdom will be fulfilled. In the meantime, as the Word of the kingdom is proclaimed, there will arise a mixed group who profess to recognize the authority of the Lord Jesus. This group constitute the kingdom in mystery. It is a wider sphere than the church, inasmuch as it includes both true and false professors. The separation of the two groups will take place at the end of the age, after which the kingdom of the Son of man will be established over all the earth.

Men often speak of "building the kingdom." This is an expression in common use, but never found in Scripture. We are commissioned to preach the gospel to every creature, and when men believe the message they become members of the church, the body of Christ. As such they are in the kingdom of Heaven also, but our primary object is to lead them to recognize Jesus as Savior and Lord.

No one can enter the kingdom of God in reality except by new birth. Many profess allegiance to the absent King but have never yielded their hearts to Him. These are in the sphere of the kingdom, but are not actually of it. Let us be sure our faith and profession are real.

CHAPTER FOURTEEN
THE KING'S AUTHORITY OVER ALL NATURE

John the Baptist Is Beheaded (Matthew 14:1-14)

Herod was as corrupt as any of his ancestors—a monster of iniquity living in unblushing adultery with one who was lawfully the wife of his own brother. At first he was somewhat interested in John the Baptist and his proclamation of the nearness of the kingdom of Heaven. But he became indignant when his own vices were denounced by the fearless desert preacher, and sought to silence him by shutting him up in prison. Eventually Herod made John a martyr by an act of judicial murder. When Herod heard of the wonder-working power of Jesus, he was filled with terror. Superstitious as most immoral creatures are, Herod's uneasy conscience suggested that the stern prophet of the wilderness, whom he had delivered over to an undeserved death, must have come back from the grave. But there was no sign of self-judgment or confession of his horrid iniquity.

Herodias was the direct cause of the death of John. Her hatred of the man who dared to condemn openly the grossness of her sins could be satisfied only with his execution. It had taken courage indeed for John to point out Herod's wickedness. Like Nathan (2 Samuel 12:7), John drove home the king's guilt, but in so doing John forfeited his life, for Herod, unlike David, refused to repent of his iniquity.

This vile and licentious ruler would not have hesitated to destroy John immediately, but Herod was afraid that he might incur the hatred of the people who looked at John as the successor to the prophets of old. Instead of immediately executing John, therefore, Herod shut him up in prison.

When Herod's birthday was celebrated, the shameless daughter of the infamous Herodias came before the king and his attendants and pleased them by what was evidently a lascivious dance. The old tyrant was so delighted that in his enthusiasm he promised with an oath to give the dancer whatever she might ask. After conferring with her wicked mother the girl came boldly into the presence of the king with the request that he give her John the Baptist's head in a charger. Corrupt as he was, Herod was sorry, for he realized that John had done nothing worthy of death, and doubtless his initial anger had cooled to some extent by this time. But having declared on oath before all his courtiers that he would grant the girl's request, he did not have the courage to acknowledge his folly. He commanded, therefore, that John should be beheaded. The gruesome evidence that the execution had been carried out was brought in on a great platter and given to the damsel, who presented it to her mother. One can imagine how Herodias gloated as she looked at the severed head of the man whom she considered her enemy because he had been bold enough to tell her the truth. He had charged her with the infamy for which she would yet have to give an account unto God.

The incestuous relationship of these two godless rulers had become a public scandal. The country needed a man with the boldness of John the Baptist to say, "It is not lawful for thee to have her." He was martyred because of his faithfulness, but his reward is sure. Herod went from bad to worse until he died in his sins, a wretched victim of his own vices. Vain, willfull, and unclean, Herodias died as she had lived, unrepentant and wicked to the last. Herod and Herodias stand out as warnings to all who would tamper with impurity. After John's death, Jesus did not travel about in Herod's tetrarchy, but remained in that of Philip.

This martyrdom was indeed a terrible tragedy to the brokenhearted disciples of John. They took the body of their master and reverently buried it. And then they "went and told Jesus." There is something very precious about these last words. They went to Jesus in their trouble and distress, assured of His deep understanding and loving sympathy.

Upon hearing of the death of His predecessor, the Lord took a ship and went apart to a desert place. A great multitude out of the various cities near the northern end of the lake followed Him. The Lord Jesus, seeing them, was moved with compassion toward them and expressed His kingly power by healing those who were sick.

Jesus Feeds the Multitude (Matthew 14:15-21)

After the pathetic account of John the Baptist's death, the balance of Matthew 14 tells us of two miracles, both of which demonstrate the power of the Lord Jesus over nature. The first one is the only miracle performed by the Lord before His crucifixion that is given in all four Gospels. It is very evident that there is some special lesson in it that God would have us learn. The hungry multitude, the perplexed disciples, and the grace of Christ are vividly portrayed. In Psalm 132:15 we hear Messiah speaking by the Spirit, saying, "I will satisfy her poor with bread." So God's anointed One took the five loaves and two fishes and multiplied them so that abundant provision was made for five thousand men, besides women and children.

We can understand the concern of the disciples who came to Jesus as the evening drew on, beseeching Him to send the multitude away before the darkness fell in order that they might go into the villages and buy food for themselves. This was not what the Lord had in mind, however. He said, "They need not depart; give ye them to eat." To the twelve this was a most amazing commission. With what were they to feed so many? After looking about they explained that they had found but five loaves and two fishes. These, we are told elsewhere, were provided by a lad who had brought them with him, doubtless as his lunch. Jesus said, "Bring them hither to me." When the small provision was placed in His hands He commanded the multitude to sit down on the grass, and looking up to Heaven He blessed the food and broke it. He then distributed it to His disciples, and they passed it on to the multitude. All were fed and satisfied. After the repast twelve baskets of fragments remained. We might say there was one basket for each apostle after all the rest had received what they desired.

This miracle was but a picture, however, of what the Lord Jesus is doing constantly, for it is He who multiplies the seeds sown in all the cornfields on earth. As a result of the small amount placed in the ground, abundance is provided to satisfy the throngs who are dependent on bread for their food.

Jesus Walks on the Sea (Matthew 14:22-36)

This miracle demonstrates the Lord's power over the elements in a somewhat different way from that in which He stilled the storm mentioned in a previous chapter. This passage is a beautiful dispensational picture. In verse 22 we read how Jesus constrained His disciples to get into a ship and to go before Him back to the other side of the lake, while He dismissed the multitudes. The disciples set out in the ship without the personal presence of Jesus, picturing the circumstances in which the church of God was to be found after the death and resurrection of our Lord Jesus. He who had been with His disciples during the days of His flesh would no longer be visibly present among them. They would be left to make their way alone, as it were, across the troubled sea of earthly circumstances, looking forward to the time when they would again see their Savior.

Christ Himself went up into a mountain apart to pray. This suggests His present ministry on behalf of His people—He has gone up on high where He ever lives to make intercession for us.

While He prayed on the mountaintop, those in the ship were in trouble, for their little vessel was passing through a severe storm and was tossed with the waves. As far as its occupants could see it was likely to be lost. The people of God have been frequently placed in such circumstances during the time that the Lord has been ministering on high in the presence of the Father. God's dear people have often thought themselves forsaken and forgotten, but His eye has always been upon them.

In the fourth watch of the night when the darkness was still great and the wind contrary, He looked down from the heights and saw them in their distress. To their amazement, He came walking on the sea to give them the assistance they needed. As they beheld Him they were distressed rather than comforted, and they cried out in fear, "It is a spirit"—that is, a ghost. But in response to their startled cry came the voice they knew so well, the voice of Jesus Himself saying, "Be of good cheer; it is I; be not afraid."

Ever impetuous but devoted to his Lord, Peter cried out, "Lord, if it be thou, bid me come unto thee on the water." In response Jesus said, "Come." Without a moment's hesitation Peter went down over the side of the ship, and doubtless to his own amazement he found himself actually walking on the water as though on firm ground. All was well as long as he kept his eyes fixed on Jesus, but when he turned and saw the boisterous waves, fear filled his heart, and he began to sink at once. As the waters were rising above him he cried out, "Lord, save me." "And immediately Jesus stretched forth his hand, and caught him, and said unto him, O thou of little faith, wherefore didst thou doubt?" What Peter should have remembered was that he could not walk any better on smooth water than on rough waves, except as sustained by the power of the Lord Himself. That power is just as great in the storm as in the calm.

Jesus and Peter entered the little boat, and immediately the wind ceased. They had witnessed such a display of omnipotent power that all the disciples fell down before the Lord and worshiped Him, saying, "Of a truth thou art the Son of God."

Returning to the land of Gennesaret, which was east of Capernaum and north of the lake, word that Jesus was again in that country quickly spread abroad. A great multitude came to Him, bringing with them many that were diseased that He might heal them. It is very evident that the people of Gennesaret were impressed with Jesus' grace and ability to deliver them from their distressing ailments. They came from all the country round about, in order to lay their sick ones at His feet. They felt that if these troubled ones could only touch the hem of His garment like the poor woman of whom we have read, they would be healed. And we are told that as many as touched His garment were made perfectly whole. The blue border spoke of Him as the holy One of God, the heavenly One who had come down to earth for man's redemption. To contact Him meant life and health.

Jesus continued His wondrous ministry and everywhere His messiahship was attested by marvelous signs, which must have convinced any honest seeker after the truth that He was all He professed to be. But the religious leaders stood coldly aloof or came out in positive opposition because of their unwillingness to humble themselves before God. The "poor of the flock" (Zechariah 11:11) heard Jesus with gladness and were blessed by His gracious ministrations. These glorified the God of Israel for sending His anointed One to them.

CHAPTER FIFTEEN
THE KING DENOUNCES HYPOCRISY

Jesus Condemns the Laws of the Pharisees (Matthew 15:1-11)

Here we read of the King's rebuke of many who were opposed to His claims as Lord and the kingdom He announced. There was a remnant whose hearts were opened to the truth and who gladly received our Lord as the promised Messiah. But it was difficult for many to see in this quiet, lowly man of Nazareth that which answered to their expectations of a great world ruler who would deliver the Jewish nation from the Roman yoke and make them again a great people, such as they were in the days of David and Solomon. Their conceptions of the kingdom were utterly carnal, because they were merely natural men who knew nothing of spiritual realities. Consequently they failed to realize that before the prophecies of a restored Israel would be fulfilled there must be repentance on the part of the nation and a definite return to God individually and collectively.

The question of washing raised by Jesus' critics had to do with a certain ceremonial baptizing of the hands, which all orthodox Jews were supposed to go through before partaking of food. This was something far more than simply cleansing the hands in order that they might be free of impurity as one was about to sit down to a meal. This washing involved quite a lengthy ceremony, and so the Pharisees put the question, "Why do thy disciples transgress the tradition of the elders?" That is, the disciples ignored the regulations of the Pharisees.

As was so often His custom, the Lord answered by putting a direct question to them, "Why do ye also transgress the commandment of

God by your tradition?" He then cited that commandment of the law which begins, "Honour thy father and mother," and also the judgment of the law concerning those who cursed father or mother, as found in Exodus 21:17. While professing to honor the Word of God they really made God's Word ineffectual by one of their own traditions. They allowed a man to ignore the needs of his parents and refuse to be responsible in any way for their support if he dedicated his goods to Jehovah by saying to his parents, "It is Corban, that is to say, a gift" (Mark 7:11). Then the parents were supposed to have no claims on the goods. Thus they were dishonored rather than otherwise, and so the commandment of God was made ineffective. In condemning the actions of the Pharisees, Jesus quoted Isaiah 29:13: "This people draw near me with their mouth [they made a great profession of faith in Jehovah], and with their lips do honour me, but have removed their heart far from me, and their fear toward me is taught by the precept of men." They did not yield heart-allegiance to Him. The Pharisees gave God empty and formal worship, for instead of obeying the Word of God they substituted the commandments of men.

Turning from the Pharisees to the multitudes who were gathered nearby, Jesus addressed the larger throng, drawing their attention to the fact that one is not defiled by what he eats. It is not food going into the mouth that makes one unclean, but that which comes out of the mouth, "for out of the abundance of the heart the mouth speaketh" (Matthew 12:34). Unclean and unholy words defile the speaker, not mere neglect of the regulations for preparing to partake of food. It is evident that the Pharisees were very indignant at the way in which the Lord had dealt with them, but instead of toning down the truth in any way the Lord Jesus only affirmed more definitely that which He desired to impress upon them.

Jesus Defines the True Source of Defilement (Matthew 15:12-20)

The disciples were undoubtedly disappointed to have the religious leaders scandalized by the teaching of their Master. They probably hoped that these men had come as honest inquirers who might be led to receive and enter into the kingdom. They were people of importance in the community, and it must have seemed a pity to some of the apostolic band that these leaders should be stumbled and turned away. But the Lord answered, "Every plant, which my heavenly Father hath not planted, shall be rooted up." In other words, only those who were subject in heart to God and His Word would abide as disciples of the Lord; the rest, no matter how encouraging their attitude might be at first, would eventually turn away. As to these Pharisees, one could only let them alone; they were determined upon their evil course and could be considered only as blind leaders of the blind. Those who followed them, accepting their teaching, would be destroyed with the teachers themselves in the day when God dealt with them.

Peter raised a question regarding what the Lord had already said about defilement. With his natural Jewish prejudices he had doubt- less thought more of physical defilement than of that which was spiritual, and so he asked the Lord to explain the teaching. He considered the words of Christ to be parabolic rather than literal. Jesus explained very definitely the meaning more fully, while gently reproving Peter for his lack of understanding. He pointed out that no man's soul is defiled by what he eats. Food passes through the process of digestion in the body, but does not affect the spirit or the soul of the man. On the other hand, those things that come from the heart and are expressed often in speech do indeed defile the man, for they have to do with his whole course of thinking and therefore make his very mind and spirit unclean. "Out of the heart proceed evil thoughts." It is these unholy things that defile a man; merely eating with unwashed or unbaptized hands could not defile anyone. The Lord thus traced everything back to its source. We read in Proverbs 4:23, "Keep thy heart with all diligence; for out of it are the issues of life," and in Proverbs 23:7, "As he thinketh in his heart, so is he."

Following the conversations, first with the Pharisees and then with Peter, Jesus left that particular scene, and went up into the northern part of the land to the very border of Gentile territory. Here a notable miracle was performed on the daughter of a Gentile woman.

Jesus Rewards the Faith of a Gentile Woman (Matthew 15:21-28)

Tyre and Sidon were cities on which God's judgment had already been poured out because of their wickedness and uncleanness, but they had been somewhat rebuilt and reinhabited—not exactly the original cities but contiguous territory. From this region came a Canaanite woman who had heard of the fame of Jesus, and felt sure He would relieve her daughter's terrible condition. She came to Jesus crying for mercy. Doubtless to her surprise, and perhaps to that of others, Jesus made no reply whatever. It was not rudeness on His part, for He was the holy One of God, but it was in order to teach her a much-needed lesson. As Son of David He had come to minister to Israel and to reign eventually as King on the throne of David. As such, for the present, a Gentile woman had no claim upon Him; and so He answered her not a word. She continued to plead until the disciples became annoyed and begged Him to send her away. He simply replied, "I am not sent but unto the lost sheep of the house of Israel." This must have seemed for the moment a rebuke to the poor, anxious mother. But instead of turning away in despair she bowed down before Him as a worshiper pleading, "Lord, help me." He replied, "It is not meet to take the children's bread, and to cast it to dogs." It was a hard saying, but it was meant to reveal the true attitude of her soul. She responded in humility and faith, exclaiming, "Truth, Lord: yet the dogs eat of the crumbs which fall from their masters' table." Here she used a diminutive—the little dogs, the puppies. She only asked for a few crumbs of blessing that could well be spared since He had dealt so bountifully with Israel.

The heart of Jesus rejoiced to see such an evidence of confidence linked with lowliness of spirit. He granted her request immediately, saying, "O woman, great is thy faith: be it unto thee even as thou wilt." And we are told that her daughter was healed instantly.

Jesus Feeds the Multitude Again (Matthew 15:29-39)

Having completed a circuit from Capernaum through the northern part of Galilee and Iturea (which was the tetrarchy of Philip, the husband of Herodias), Jesus returned to the region of the sea of Galilee, and ascended a mountain with His disciples. As soon as the people knew He was once more in their vicinity, they thronged the roads and ascended the mount on which He sat, bringing with them their sick and maimed friends. He met them all in grace, and healed every one, thus demonstrating again His Messianic authority (Isaiah 35:4-6).

As these country folk saw their friends and relatives delivered from dumbness, lameness, blindness, and various diseases, they were convinced in their own hearts that God had visited His people. They glorified Him as they recognized in these mighty works the credentials of Him who was to be the deliverer of Israel. The people who felt their need and longed for deliverance from sin and its effects received with joy the gospel of the kingdom as proclaimed by Jesus.

In the next miracle Jesus performed we see once more the heart of the blessed Lord going out in compassion to a hungry multitude; this time it was four thousand men, whereas before there were five thousand, besides women and children. On this occasion they had been listening to His ministry for three days and had evidently used up all their own provisions. He was disinclined to "send them away fasting, lest they faint in the way." It seems strange, after the former experience, that the disciples should have ever raised the question, "Whence should we have so much bread in the wilderness, as to fill so great a multitude?" The Lord had already proved His power to multiply loaves and fishes, and one might think that they would have counted on His demonstrating the same ability at this time. But strangely enough, they seemed to have forgotten what He had done in the past.

In answer to His question, "How many loaves have ye?" they replied, "Seven, and a few little fishes." As before, He commanded the multitude to sit on the ground. Then taking into His hands the small amount of food which the disciples had, He gave thanks, broke both the loaves and the fishes, and distributed to the disciples, in order that they might give to the multitude.

We read that "they did all eat, and were filled: and they took up of the broken meat that was left seven baskets full." Two different words for baskets are used in the accounts of the feeding of the two groups. In the first instance, where the Lord fed the five thousand (Matthew 14:13-21), the word translated "baskets" means a wicker traveling basket for small articles, such as people carried with them on a journey. The word used in Matthew 15 means a hamper, a large market basket commonly used by those who went out to buy provisions for the household. This time there were seven of these large baskets filled with the broken bread and fish, enough to provide food for the entire apostolic company for perhaps another whole day.

Just how many people partook of the Lord's bounty that day we have no means of knowing. The records tell us there were four thousand men, besides women and children. There might not have been a great many of the latter classes; yet undoubtedly there would have been a number of women who had come with their husbands and children who had accompanied their parents.

Sending the multitude away the Lord sailed to the coasts of Magdala, the region in which Mary Magdalene had lived, and from which she took her name.

CHAPTER SIXTEEN
THE CHURCH AND THE KINGDOM

The Pharisees Ask for a Sign (Matthew 16:1-4)

The Pharisees and Sadducees were violently opposed to one another in regard to almost every doctrine of the Scriptures, but they were united in their deliberate rejection of the Lord Jesus, God's promised King. Being familiar with prophecy, these religious leaders knew that certain signs were to take place before the appearance of the Messiah. They came to Jesus without any desire to know the truth, simply tempting or testing Him, asking that He show them a sign from Heaven. They meant a sign indicating that the Messianic age was close at hand. Jesus rebuked them for their unbelief. They were quite able to read the signs of the heavens in regard to the weather, but they were absolutely unable to discern the signs of the times. Had their eyes been opened they would have realized that all the miraculous works of Jesus were in themselves the signs of the age to come and told of the presence of the King. Messiah was in their midst. No other sign would be given to them but the sign of the prophet Jonah. Jesus did not explain here what was meant by that sign, but He told us in Matthew 12:40, "As Jonas was three days and three nights in the whale's belly; so shall the Son of man be three days and three nights in the heart of the earth." The deliverance of Jonah pointed to the resurrection of the Lord Jesus. Alas, when the day of His resurrection came, even that miracle failed to convince these legalistic, hypocritical gainsayers; they were shut up to unbelief and hardness of heart.

Jesus Warns His Disciples (Matthew 16:5-12)

After the Lord's colloquy with these religious leaders, the disciples came to Jesus, indicating that they had forgotten to bring bread. In His answer to them He brought in a warning that is not only important in itself, but also helps to serve as a key to the meaning of leaven in Scripture, as we have seen in our study of Matthew 13.

When the disciples acknowledged that they had forgotten to bring bread with them, Jesus said to them, "Beware of the leaven of the Pharisees and of the Sadducees." His followers did not understand what He meant by this, and thought He was warning them against accepting bread from these false teachers. They said among themselves, "It is because we have taken no bread." When Jesus perceived how they were reasoning, He rebuked them. Then He reminded them how readily He had provided bread for the five thousand and also for the four thousand, and how much had been left over in each instance. In view of this, they should have realized that He was not speaking of material bread, which He could supply so abundantly, but He was warning them to beware of the doctrine of the Pharisees and of the Sadducees. The leaven of the Pharisees is explained in Luke 12:1 as hypocrisy. With this was coupled self-righteousness. The leaven of the Sadducees was false doctrine: they denied the authority of all the Old Testament except the books of Moses, and they did not believe in spiritual realities. Such evil teachings work like leaven, spreading throughout any group beginning to tolerate them; hence the warning of the Lord to beware of them.

Peter Declares His Faith (Matthew 16:13-20)

Speculation was rife as to the actual identity of Jesus, and whether He was only what He seemed to be or possibly a reincarnation of another. The Lord wished to put His disciples on record as to their apprehension of the mystery of His person (1 Timothy 3:16). Jesus questioned His disciples not for His own enlightenment, but because He desired to elicit a clear, definite confession from His followers, as He was soon to go with them to Jerusalem, where He was to be crucified. It was all-important that they should know Him in the reality of His divine-human personality.

"Some say that thou art..." They at once began to tell how various ones supposed Him to be John the Baptist risen from the dead, as Herod had thought; or Elijah, who was to herald "the coming of the great and dreadful day of the Lord" (Malachi 4:5-6); or Jeremiah, who many supposed was to reappear and was to fulfill the great prophecy of Isaiah 53 (they assumed Jeremiah 11:19 explained Isaiah 53:7); or one of the prophets, possibly that prophet whose coming Moses had predicted in Deuteronomy 18:18.

"But whom say ye that I am?" Had they learned, through observation and the Spirit's illumination, who He really was? This definite question called for a clear, positive confession, and it was this He desired to obtain from them.

"Thou art the Christ, the Son of the living God." Peter spoke for them all, though no one of the rest seems to have had the boldness to declare his faith openly. *Christ* and *Messiah* are synonymous. Both mean "the anointed." It was the title given prophetically to the coming deliverer (Isaiah 61:1). Of old, prophets, priests, and kings were all anointed. Jesus holds the three offices; He was anointed by the Spirit of God for all three (Acts 10:38). In His human nature He is the Son of David, the Messiah, the Christ. As to His divine nature He is the Son of the living God.

It is all-important that men have a right understanding of the nature and person of our Lord Jesus Christ. Only as He is recognized by faith as the Son of the living God, coequal with the eternal Father, do we dare trust our souls to Him as our Savior. There is an unbridgeable gulf between the highest of all created beings and the Creator Himself. The church of Christ is not founded on any mere man, no matter how holy, enlightened, or devoted he may be. It rests securely upon the revelation of the truth so clearly declared by Simon Peter. And just as the church is built upon this blessed reality, so does the salvation of each individual soul depend upon the fact that God became man in order to give Himself a ransom for our sins.

"Flesh and blood hath not revealed it." Simon Peter had not come to this conclusion by mere intuition or logical reasoning. It was God the Father who had enlightened his understanding and revealed to him the truth as to the person of the Lord and His divine sonship (Matthew 11:27).

"Thou art Peter, and upon this rock I will build my church." "This rock" is Christ (1 Corinthians 10:4). In Peter's great confession we have the sure foundation on which the church was to be built. Peter means a stone, or a piece of a rock. He was to be built into the church. The church was not to be built on him. The heavenly kingdom to be built on earth, is to be founded upon the truth that Christ is the Son of David (2 Samuel 7:12-13). The nations of the world are to share in the blessings of that kingdom because Christ is the Son of Abraham, the seed in whom all nations will be blessed (Genesis 22:18). But the church of our Lord Jesus Christ is built on the precious truth that He is the Son of the living God.

To say that Peter is in any sense the rock on which this divine edifice built of living stones rests, is to deny what he himself taught in 1 Peter 2:4-8. Paul, too, added his testimony that there can be no other foundation but Jesus Christ Himself (1 Corinthians 3:11). This is that foundation of the apostles and prophets to which he refers in Ephesians 2:20.

"The gates of hell [hades] shall not prevail" against the true church, built upon Christ as the Son of the living God. No effort of Satan and his hosts can avail to destroy the church or to stay the progress of its testimony. The only real hindrance comes from within the church itself as other Scriptures show.

Note, Christ did not say, "I have been building," or "I am building," but "I *will* build." The assembly that He called "my church" was still in the future. Hitherto the Lord had been dealing with matters relating to the kingdom of Heaven. Now for the first time He spoke of the church not entirely as dissociated from the kingdom, but rather as connected with it in the new phase it would assume after His rejection and His ascension to Heaven. The building of this spiritual temple did not begin until after He had ascended to Heaven and the Spirit of God came as the promised Comforter. In this house Peter was to be a living stone, but Christ was to be the foundation rock.

"The keys of the kingdom of heaven." Having spoken of the church, Jesus reverted to the kingdom, whose course He had previously outlined in the parables of Matthew 13. The keys of this kingdom were entrusted to Peter. Note, He did not give Peter the keys to Heaven. Such a notion is the grossest superstition. A key is designed to open a door. On Pentecost Peter opened the door of the kingdom to the Jews; in Cornelius' house he opened the door to the Gentiles.

"Tell no man." This may seem strange. But as it was now evident that Israel had rejected Him, it was not the time to proclaim His messiahship and declare that He was the Christ. When He was raised from the dead Peter declared this truth with power (Acts 2:36).

Jesus Teaches of His Death and Resurrection (Matthew 16:21-27)

A new period of our Lord's ministry had begun. From this time on the Lord began to speak more and more concerning His ultimate rejection by the Jews, His sufferings and death, and His subsequent resurrection. But His disciples were very slow to comprehend what He meant. Their minds were still set upon the coming kingdom, and they could not imagine the King being put to death.

In these verses we have a solemn example of how easily one who has been divinely illuminated may fall into serious error if acting on merely human principles. What a poor rock Peter would have been on which to build the church! He became unwittingly the mouthpiece of Satan when he advised Jesus against going to the cross. It is strange that anyone could teach in one breath that Peter was the first pope, and in the next that the pope is infallible. While he was a most devoted and earnest man, Peter blundered perhaps as badly as any of his brother apostles, not only during the days of our Lord's humiliation, but also after His resurrection and ascension to Heaven. Paul told us how he had to oppose Peter because he was to be blamed for dissimulation and the fear of man, thereby compromising the liberty of grace (Galatians 2:11-16).

Jesus told His disciples that the path of discipleship is one of constant self-abnegation. The Lord was preparing His followers for the responsibilities that would be theirs when His prophetic words concerning Himself were fulfilled. They would be called on to ignore fleshly claims and to take up the cross, which meant accepting the place of rejection with Him, and thus they were to follow in His steps.

He who would think to better his condition by avoiding persecution for Christ's sake, thereby saving his life, would really lose it. But he who was ready even to lay down his life for Christ's sake would keep it unto life eternal. Death in this world would only be the introduction to everlasting glory. It would be worth nothing if óne were able to gain even the whole world and yet in so doing lose his soul. The soul is really the life, the self. To lose the soul, therefore, is to miss the purpose for which one has been created. Man was made, as *The Shorter Catechism* declares, to glorify God and enjoy Him forever. He who makes it his object to accumulate wealth, or the favor of a Christless world will lose out and find himself at last bereft of everything that is of any worth whatever.

Note the question, "What shall a man give in exchange for his soul?" It does not say, as one might imagine it would, "What shall a man *take* in exchange for his soul?" Man's soul is forfeited. What can a man give in order to redeem it? He has nothing to give. If l continues in his sin his soul will be lost forever, but if he turns t Christ he will find redemption in Him. When He comes the secon time as the Son of man in the glory of His Father with His angels then He will reward each one according to his works.

Jesus Foresees His Transfiguration (Matthew 16:28)

The closing verse should really be the first verse of Matthew 17. Whoever edited the book of Matthew and divided it into chapters and verses made the break in the wrong place. In this verse Jesus was referring to the great event that followed "after six days"—the transfiguration, which presented the kingdom of God in embryo.

CHAPTER SEVENTEEN

THE GLORY OF THE KINGDOM

The Transfiguration (Matthew 17:1-8)

It seems a great pity, as indicated in our closing remarks in the previous chapter, that its final verse was not made the opening one of this seventeenth chapter. The Lord Jesus Christ had intimated a week before that some would not die until they had seen the kingdom of God come with power. In the corresponding accounts in both Mark and Luke this announcement is linked directly with the transfiguration scene. The announcement is, in fact, the key to a right understanding of this glorious vision that was intended to be a representation of "the kingdom of God come with power" (Mark 9:1). This is confirmed for us by the apostle Peter, who in his second Epistle said, "We have not followed cunningly devised fables, when we made known unto you the power and coming of our Lord Jesus Christ, but were eyewit-nesses of his majesty...when we were with him in the holy mount" (2 Peter 1:16,18). There the Savior appeared in that glory in which He will be manifested when He returns to take His great power and reign (Revelation 11:17).

Jesus took Peter and James and John up into a high mountain (mount Hermon) where He was to give them a vision of the kingdom as it shall yet be displayed. The three favored apostles, who beheld His glory and heard the Father's voice, represent Israel restored to the Lord in the latter day and so entering into the blessings of the kingdom.

The transfiguration was a metamorphosis, a change from within; the glory of Christ's eternal sonship shone out through the veil of His flesh so that the disciples might have ocular proof of His true character as Immanuel—God and man in one person.

"There appeared unto them Moses and Elias talking with him." These two men of a past dispensation represent two groups of believers: Moses represents those who die before the coming in of the kingdom and will be raised in glorified bodies; Elijah depicts those who will be changed at the rapture and caught up without passing through death (1 Thessalonians 4:13-18), preparatory to the bringing in of the millennial glory (John 11:25-26). Elijah and Moses also speak of the law and the prophets, both of which bear witness to Christ's atoning death, whereby God is able to provide a righteousness for men who have none of their own (Romans 3:21,24-25). The subject of their discourse was our Lord's redemptive work, soon to be accomplished (Luke 9:30-31).

"Let us make here three tabernacles." Peter's suggestion came without real consideration. He was so overwhelmed with the glory of the vision that he would have gladly remained on the mount in such wonderful company. But he erred in putting Moses and Elias, eminent servants of God though they were, on a par with Jesus, the Son of God become flesh.

"This is my beloved Son, in whom I am well pleased; hear ye him." A cloud shut out the Old Testament worthies, and Jesus was left alone. The Father's voice spoke from Heaven the second time, attesting the perfection of His Son and His delight in Him, whose voice they were commanded to heed.

Awed by what they had seen and heard, the three apostles fell prostrate as worshipers in the presence of God as seen in the Lord Jesus Christ. Reaching forth His loving hand, our Lord touched each disciple reassuringly, and bade them stand up, fearing nothing. He would have His own feel at ease in His presence, for though He is Lord of all, He is our kinsman-redeemer, who assumed our humanity, apart from sin, in order to bring us to God.

"They saw no man, save Jesus only." There could be no thought of three tabernacles now, for Moses, the law-giver, and Elijah, the restorer, had vanished away. The Lord Jesus alone remained—He who is the same yesterday, today, and forever (Hebrews 13:8).

Jesus is not a mere man who, by dint of spiritual enlightenment and surrender to the Father's will, became more divine than any other man. He is God the Son, one person of the eternal trinity, manifested in the flesh and thus the one mediator between God and man. Peter's confession and the Father's voice after the transfiguration tell the same blessed story. Jesus had to be who He was in order to do what He did. No one less than the Son of God could make propitiation for our sins (1 John 4:10).

The vision passed, but Jesus remained. When the morning came He led His disciples down from that mount of special privilege to face the appalling effects of sin in the valley below, for the time had not yet come for the kingdom to be displayed in universal power and glory.

Explanation of the Coming of Elijah (Matthew 17:9-13)

Foreseeing His rejection Jesus commanded the chosen three to say nothing to anyone of what they had seen in that never-to-be-forgotten time, until after He rose from the dead. The cross must come before the kingdom.

The perplexed disciples asked their Master, "Why then say the scribes that Elias must first come?" These teachers of the law had good authority for this, for in Malachi 4:5-6 it was plainly declared, "Behold, I will send you Elijah the prophet before the coming of the great and dreadful day of the Lord: And he shall turn the heart of the fathers to the children, and the heart of the children to their fathers, lest I come and smite the earth with a curse." The kingdom follows the great and dreadful day of the Lord. It is in fact a continuation of that day, after its preliminary judgments shall have ended. What then of Elijah? Was he to be looked for first?

Jesus replied, "Elias truly shall first come, and restore all things." But He explained that he had come already and his testimony had been rejected and he, himself, put out of the way. And even as they had treated the forerunner, so would they treat the Son of man.

"Then," we are told, "the disciples understood that he spake unto them of John the Baptist." He had come in the spirit and power of Elijah to prepare Messiah's way (Luke 1:17).

It seems clear from the prophetic Scriptures that a similar Elijah-testimony will be given in the dark days of the great tribulation before the manifestation of the Lord in judgment. The vision of the two witnesses in Revelation 11 would appear to confirm this.

As Jesus and the three disciples talked together they came upon a great multitude of troubled people, as depicted in the next few verses.

The Healing of the Demon-possessed (Matthew 17:14-21)

This scene at the foot of the mountain illustrates the effect of the second advent, binding Satan and giving to the troubled nations deliverance from his power. Having descended to the plain after the night of vision, they found a distracted father, who had brought his demon-possessed son to the other nine disciples, pleading with them to help. But they were out of touch and, although commissioned to cast out demons (Matthew 10:8), found themselves powerless in this particular case. Disappointed in the servants, the distressed father recognized the Master as He came toward them, and began at once to implore Him to free his son from the demon. Kneeling, he begged the Lord to have mercy on him and heal his boy, explaining that he had brought him to the disciples, and they could not cure him. One can understand how poignant was the father's grief and how distressed he was when the disciples could not help. In expectancy of heart he turned to the Lord Jesus, pleading as many other fathers since have pleaded for the deliverance of sons who have come under the power of the evil one in various ways.

After rebuking the nine for their lack of faith, Jesus called for the boy to be brought to Him. His heart was moved by the father's plea. Turning then to the demon-possessed youth Jesus rebuked the foul spirit who departed from the boy, and he was cured from that hour.

On the mount the disciples had been taken into God's confidence and given a foreview of the kingdom to be ushered in with power and majesty at our Lord's second advent. In the plain, they beheld anew something of the ravages of sin and Satan, under which this poor world suffers and groans still, and from which it will be freed completely only when Christ returns. But all down through the present age of evil the Lord Jesus is the One who hears the prayer of faith and gives deliverance to those who put their trust in His Word. No case is too difficult for Him. His disciples are often powerless because of unbelief and failure to recognize their own inability to work apart from Him who commissions them to represent Him in this world.

When alone with the Lord, away from the multitude, the perplexed disciples inquired why they had been unable to expel the demon in this case. The answer was, "Because of your unbelief." Again the Lord declared that if they had faith even as a grain of mustard seed, mountains of difficulty could be removed and absolutely nothing would be impossible to them.

But true faith and self-indulgence are never found together; therefore, He added, "Howbeit this kind goeth not out but by prayer and fasting." The flesh and its appetites must be kept in subjection in order that faith may flourish. Occupation with the glorified Christ is preliminary to service for Him in a world where Satan expresses his antagonism to all that God is doing. Satan is overcome only by dependence on Christ as indicated by prayer and fasting. No man is competent to meet Satan in his own strength. Prayer is the expression of dependence upon God, which alone gives victory. Fasting is the evidence of such concern for spiritual blessing that desire to satisfy carnal appetite is held in abeyance. May we not see in these words of the Lord the reason for many of our unanswered prayers?

The Temple Tax (Matthew 17:22-27)

Again Jesus forewarned the disciples of what He was soon to experience, but although their hearts were grieved they did not grasp the full significance of His words. The Galilean ministry of the unrecognized King was soon to come to a close. He foresaw all that would befall Him at the hands of man, but He looked beyond with prophetic eye to His resurrection when God was to bring Him back from the dead. So often had Jesus spoken of this and so plainly that it seems incredible that the disciples should have failed to comprehend His words. Yet it was so. Not until all had been fulfilled did they recall and understand that of which He had spoken so definitely (see Mark 9:30-32 and Luke 9:43-45).

The incident with which this chapter closes reveals another aspect of Peter's impulsiveness, and yet of the Lord's wondrous grace. The tribute money referred to here was the half-shekel of silver that was commanded to be paid as the redemption money at any numbering of the people (Exodus 30:11-16). In the course of time it had come to be considered and levied as a poll-tax for the support of the temple services. The collectors of this tax came to Peter and inquired as to whether Jesus paid it. Without consulting his Master, Peter answered in the affirmative.

When Peter entered the house in Capernaum a little later (probably his own home) Jesus anticipated him and put the question, "What thinkest thou, Simon? Of whom do the kings of the earth take custom or tribute? of their own children, or of strangers?" Peter answered unhesitatingly that it was of strangers. Only a little time before Peter had confessed Jesus to be the Christ, the Son of the living God. Therefore, Jesus was under no obligation to pay this particular tax; so He declared, "Then are the children free." But in His concern for others, that none might be stumbled who did not understand who He really was, He commanded Peter to go to the sea of Galilee and cast a hook and take up the first fish that he caught, and He added, "When thou hast opened his mouth, thou shalt find a piece of money: that take, and give unto them for me and thee." It is not necessary to suppose that the coin was miraculously created at the moment, but rather that it had fallen into the water, and the fish attracted by the glittering object had attempted to swallow it, but the shekel had stuck in its gullet. When Peter drew the fish to land, the money was there as Jesus had said, and could be used to silence all criticism. Was Jesus at this time so poor that He had no other money to pay this tax? Possibly so, or perhaps He chose this method to impress upon Peter the fact that He was Lord of all creation.

CHAPTER EIGHTEEN
CITIZENS OF THE KINGDOM

The Greatest in the Kingdom (Matthew 18:1-14)

Not yet delivered from the desire for prominence in the coming kingdom, the disciples came to Jesus with the question, "Who is the greatest in the kingdom of heaven?" It is a question that would not concern the truly noble soul. But devoted as these disciples were, they could not seem to get away from the thought that the kingdom was to be a place and a time for flesh to assert itself, although the Lord had rebuked them for this on former occasions.

This time He answered both in word and by an object lesson. He called a little child. The wee one responded and came to Him without hesitation, we may be sure. Setting the child in their midst Jesus explained that the true subjects of the kingdom are the meek and lowly who hear the voice of Jesus and come at His call, content with the place of His appointment. The greatest in the kingdom will be the one who is willing to take the lowest place, thus proving himself a follower of Him who came from the glory of God to be a servant in this world of suffering and sorrow.

To receive a little child in His name is to receive Him, because He identifies Himself with all who trust Him. He is the Savior of those who, because of wasted years in sin and debauchery, realize their need of forgiveness and cleansing. He is also the Savior of the little ones who, in their comparative innocence, are attracted to Him because of His tender interest in them.

Whether absolutely true in detail or not, there is much truth in general in the story of the stern-visaged minister who was preaching a sermon on "The Tears of Jesus." He is said to have exclaimed, "Three times we read that Jesus wept, but we never read that He smiled." A little girl below the pulpit cried out, forgetful of where she was, "Oh, but I know He did!" Shocked at the interruption the minister asked, "Why do you say that, my child?" Thoroughly frightened as she realized all eyes were upon her she replied, "Because the Bible says He called a little child and he came to Him. And if Jesus had looked like you, I know the child would have been afraid to come." She did not intend to be rude. It was a child's frankness, but it told a wonderful truth. Children were never afraid of Jesus, and He was always ready to bless and acknowledge them.

Nor did He ever speak more sternly to anyone than to the person who would cause a child who believed in Him to stumble. It would be better for that person if he were cast into the depths of the sea with a millstone tied to his neck. Jesus foresaw such stumbling-blocks but warned His hearers not to be among them. Better to mutilate oneself by cutting off a hand or a foot than to be guilty of using either physical member to point or lead one of these children astray. To do so was to be exposed to the fire of Gehenna—eternal judgment. In the same way He speaks concerning the eyes that, alas, have often led vicious and lascivious men to look wickedly upon childish innocence.

We are warned never to despise these little ones because the Father has a special interest in the children, and in Heaven their guardian angels always appear before His face. Possibly by "angels" here, however, we are to understand the spirits of departed children. Both views have been held by godly men, and it may be best not to be too dogmatic regarding it, for whichever may be intended here, unquestionably both are true.

When speaking of adults in Luke 19:10 Jesus said, "The Son of man is come to seek and to save that which was lost." Here as He speaks of children He simply says He came to save them. While members of a lost race, they have not wandered willfully into paths of sin; so they do not need to be sought.

The parable of the lost sheep gone astray on the mountain of sin follows, for it is not only to save the children that He came. There is rejoicing in Heaven, where myriads of saints are safely gathered, over one wanderer recovered and saved. But if this be so—and it is—how much more the joy when one is saved in early childhood, and so never wastes long years in rebellion against God.

Matthew 18:14 gives the assurance that all children dying before coming to years of accountability are forever saved through the work of Christ. It is not the Father's will that any of them perish; and inasmuch as their wills are not set against the will of God we may be certain they are with Christ in the Father's house.

Discipline in the Church (Matthew 18:15-20)

Two things are brought into juxtaposition in this chapter: the kingdom in its spiritual aspect (verses 1-14), and the church that was to be brought into existence by the Lord after His death and resurrection (verses 15-20). The Lord spoke for the first time of the church which He was to build on the occasion when Peter made his great confession. In Matthew 18 Jesus gave instruction concerning discipline and godly order in that church, which, while one throughout the world, was to be expressed locally as distinct assemblies in various places. The church is seen here in its local aspect as an assembly of believers responsible to maintain principles of righteousness, and therefore to deal in discipline with refractory or trespassing members who refuse to repent.

In some of the best manuscripts the words "against thee" in Matthew 18:15 are omitted after "trespass," so that there may be more involved than trespass against one individual. He who recognizes the trespass and is concerned about it is instructed not to blazon it abroad thereby defiling others who might not otherwise know anything of it. Rather he is told to go to the offender privately and speak to him about the matter, endeavoring to bring him to repentance. This was in accordance with the law of Moses which commanded, "Thou shalt not hate thy brother in thine heart: thou shalt in any wise rebuke thy neighbour, and not suffer sin upon him" (Leviticus 19:17). In Galatians 6:1 we are told, "Brethren, if a man be overtaken in a fault, ye which are spiritual, restore such an one in the spirit of meekness; considering thyself, lest thou also be tempted."

To so act toward an erring one is to fulfill the Lord's admonition, "Ye also ought to wash one another's feet" (John 13:14). It is the duty of the one who is cognizant of the offense to apply the water of the Word to an offending brother's feet. This principle is applied in both the old and the new dispensations.

But if the wrongdoer is stubborn and willful and shows no disposition to put things aright, the one dealing with the offense is to take one or two more brethren and see him again. These witnesses are to hear and give their judgment according to the facts presented. If they agree that wrong has been done, they are to join with the first in seeking to bring the recalcitrant brother to acknowledge his sin and seek forgiveness. If this does not avail, and the trespasser is adamant and refuses to accept their admonition, the matter is for the first time to be put before the local assembly, which will hear the case. If convinced of the righteousness of the plaintiff, the accused one is again to be admonished to acknowledge his wrong and endeavor to put things right. If he refuses to hear the church, he is to be put under discipline and treated as an outsider—as a heathen, or worldling, and a publican.

It is only in this place that we get these words of which Rome makes so much: "Hear the church." This teaching does not call on us to bow to the teaching of the church as such, but in this type of incident the man under discipline is responsible to accept the judgment of the assembly. Nowhere is the church said to be the authoritative teacher. On the contrary, the church is commanded to hear what the Spirit says through the Word.

The binding and loosing of Matthew 18:18 is illustrated in the Corinthian Epistles. It deals with church, or assembly, discipline. When Paul commanded the Corinthian assembly to put away from themselves the wicked person—the incestuous man—Paul was binding that man's sin upon him until he should repent (1 Corinthians 5). When he instructed the assembly to forgive that man upon evidence of his repentance, he was loosing him (2 Corinthians 2:5-11). Such actions, when in full accordance with the Word of God, are bound in Heaven.

Matthew 18:19 suggests something even higher than this. Suppose a case where human judgment is at fault, and the saints are in utter perplexity. They may appeal to the Lord Himself for light and help. Wherever two agree, or symphonize, as the word really is— that is, where even two come to God in prayer in harmony with His Spirit and with one another—He will act for them, doing according to His will in the church on earth as that will is done in Heaven. For every local assembly of believers gathered together in the name of the Lord Jesus may be assured of His presence. This does not refer to some one special group claiming more intimate association with Christ than others, but the Lord's presence is predicated for every company gathered in His name, no matter how small that company is. What comfort this is in a day of ecclesiastical ruin and yet of great religious pretension!

Lesson in Forgiveness (Matthew 18:21-35)

The rest of the chapter deals particularly with forgiveness in several different phases. The whole problem is easily solved for the Christian. We are to forgive as God in Christ has forgiven us (Ephesians 4:32; Colossians 3:13). From the kingdom standpoint, however, forgiveness is based upon the repentance of the offender. Christ's disciples are to maintain an attitude of forgiveness at all times and toward all men. But they are to bestow that forgiveness upon the one who says, "I repent" (Luke 17:3-4). To fail to do this will bring the unforgiving one himself under the chastening hand of God in government, as seen in the parable of the obdurate servant who refused the plea of his fellow-debtor for mercy. This principle abides even in the dispensation of the grace of God, for grace and government go on together. No one is more responsible to show grace to others than he who is himself the object of grace. Much of the chastening that we as Christians have to undergo can be traced to our hard and oftentimes relentless attitude toward those who have offended us. We would save ourselves much sorrow brought by the disciplinary dealing of our Father (Hebrews 12:6-11) if we were more careful and considerate of others.

"How oft shall...I forgive him?" Peter had not risen to the true conception of grace that God had shown toward him, and that he was to demonstrate toward a brother.

Seven is the perfect number. Our Lord raises this, as it were, to its highest power. Our forgiveness is to be like that which God has given to us. Seventy times seven may seem like an impossible number of offenses to forgive, but have we not all exceeded that number many times in our relations with God?

In this parable the disciple is viewed as a subject of the kingdom under the government of God, who though He is our Father, exercises corrective discipline over His people (1 Peter 1:17). Ten thousand talents was an immense sum, whether the talents were of gold or only of silver. It suggests one who has been guilty of great offenses against the divine government.

The offender, having no resources, is morally bankrupt. No man can ever make up to God for the wrong he has done. According to the law then prevailing, the insolvent debtor could be sold into slavery.

"Have patience with me, and I will pay thee all." While no man can meet the full demands of God's holy law, the attitude of this debtor was one of penitence and repentance.

"The lord of that servant...loosed him, and forgave him the debt." Even so does God deal with His erring servants when they face their sins in His presence and bow before the claims of His righteous government. Observe, it is not the case of the forgiveness of an unsaved man that is here before us, but a servant of God who has grievously failed.

"One of his fellowservants...owed him an hundred pence." It was a very trivial sum, as compared with the other great debt. No man can possibly offend any of us to the extent that our sins have offended a holy God. To demand full satisfaction of a brother who has wronged me, when God has dealt so graciously with my greater offense, is to act inconsistently with the principle of grace.

The fellow servant took the same attitude before his creditor as the first servant had taken before the king. The fellow servant should have been given the same consideration. However the creditor was obdurate and not only refused forgiveness, but also cast his fellow servant into the debtors' prison, doubtless hoping his friends would come to his aid and pay the debt.

"His fellowservants...told unto their lord all that was done." Shocked by such conduct, other servants reported the unworthy creditor's evil action to his lord. The indignation of the king was stirred by the perfidious conduct of the one toward whom he had extended such clemency.

"Delivered him to the tormentors, till he should pay all that was due." Governmental forgiveness may be revoked, as in this instance, when the recipient of it forfeits all right to consideration because of his inconsistency afterward. Observe that it is not that eternal forgiveness which God bestows upon the believing sinner that is here in view, but the forgiveness of one already in the kingdom who has grievously failed. The Father deals with the members of His own family, and will not overlook harshness or lack of compassion on the part of His children toward their erring brethren. There are many of God's children who are under disciplinary correction all their days simply because there is someone whom they will not forgive. Let us search and try our own ways as to this matter.

Those who have entered into the kingdom by new birth (John 3:5) are all forgiven sinners who stand before God on the ground of pure grace. Nevertheless, as children in the family of God, they are subject to the Father's discipline and are under His government. The moment our responsibility as sinners having to do with the God of judgment ended, our responsibility as children having to do with our Father began. In this new relationship we are to display the activities of the divine nature, and therefore are called upon to act in grace toward any who may offend us. If we fail to do this, we will be sternly disciplined in order that God may maintain government in His own family.

Different Aspects of Forgiveness. If we do not distinguish the various aspects of forgiveness as set forth in the Word of God, we are likely to be confused because of God's disciplinary dealings with us after our conversion to Christ. When He saves us He forgives us fully and eternally and will never, as Judge, remember our sins again (Hebrews 10:17). But as His children, we are to confess our sins whenever we fail, and He gives restorative forgiveness (1 John 1:9). Certain governmental results, however, may follow these failures, which are not to be construed as indicating that God has not pardoned, but that He would teach us by discipline the heinousness of sin in His sight (2 Samuel 13–14). Since we are forgiven, we are to forgive our brethren who sin against us (Colossians 3:13). Members of the church who offend against God's righteous principles are to be disciplined, but forgiven when they give evidence of repentance (Matthew 18:17; 2 Corinthians 2:7).

Degrees of Guilt. Our Lord's teaching shows us clearly that there are varying degrees of guilt in regard to sin. All sin is wickedness in the sight of God. But the greater one's light and privileges, the greater is his responsibility. Consequently, the sin of one who knows God's Word and has enjoyed years of fellowship with the Lord is far worse than that of one who is comparatively ignorant and immature. Degrees of punishment vary accordingly. See Luke 12:47-48; John 13:17; Romans 2:12; James 4:17; 1 John 5:17.

We see the government of God exemplified in many instances in Scripture. For example, Jacob deceived his father (Genesis 27:18-24); his sons deceived him (Genesis 37:31-35). Moses failed to glorify God at Meribah (Numbers 20:11); God refused to let him go into the promised land (Numbers 20:12). David sinned in the matter of the wife of Uriah (2 Samuel 11:1-26); the sword never departed from his house (2 Samuel 12:9-10). The Corinthians dishonored God at the Lord's table (1 Corinthians 11:20-22); sickness and death of many resulted (1 Corinthians 11:30).

CHAPTER NINETEEN
THE NEW LAW OF THE KINGDOM

Jesus Answers Questions on Divorce (Matthew 19:1-12)

Leaving Galilee Jesus proceeded toward Jerusalem, going down through Perea on the east of the Jordan. By the expression "the coasts of Judea" we are to understand the land bordering on Judea. As He moved majestically on toward His death He continued to exercise His grace and power toward all who came to Him for physical healing. Through His miracles He demonstrated that He was the anointed of Jehovah (Acts 10:38), although unrecognized by the religious leaders and the rulers of the nation.

Some of these proud, haughty Pharisees came to Him and raised a question in regard to divorce, which gave Him opportunity to make clear the new order that was to prevail among those who would be subject to His authority in the days to come. The kingdom predicted by the prophets was in abeyance since Christ had broken with Israel after the flesh for the time being. But His followers needed guidance during the intervening years while the mysteries of the kingdom were being unfolded. Jesus spoke with authority as He provided definite information for the guidance of His followers.

The question asked by the Pharisees was evidently designed to put Jesus in opposition to the law of Moses. In answering them He went back to the original institution of marriage rather than to the Sinaitic or Levitical enactments. The guideline established at creation was to be the rule for His disciples in the future.

So lax were the teachings of some of the more liberal rabbis as to divorce, that a man could disown and divorce his wife upon the slightest pretext. Jesus referred them to what was written in Genesis 2:24: "He...made them at the beginning...male and female." This is the divine ideal: one man for one woman in the sacred relationship of marriage. The entire human race sprang from the first pair thus created by God. Their union typifies, as the marriage ceremony so aptly puts it, the mystical union that exists between Christ and His church (Ephesians 5:31-32).

"They twain shall be one flesh." Observe, it is not "they three," or five, or any other number, but simply "they twain." Anything other than this is a perversion opposed to the original intent of the Creator.

"What therefore God hath joined together, let not man put asunder." Thus, at the very dawn of human (and family) history, we have the inviolability of the marriage contract revealed, as according to the will of God. He who breaks this union disobeys the Word of the Lord.

Naturally His opponents asked, "Why did Moses then command to give a writing of divorcement, and to put her away?" Jesus explained that this was a temporary provision that Moses was authorized to allow because of the callousness of men's hearts. This arrangement was to protect the woman from the hardship of endeavoring to carry on in a home where she was unloved and unwanted and might be subjected to cruel treatment. Far better to send her back to the home of her parents than to make of her a slave to the capriciousness of an unkind husband.

But now that Israel's destined King and Redeemer had come, He reaffirmed the sacredness of the marriage relationship. It is intended by God to be a union for life. The subject believer will never break it. If one violates the tie by unchaste behavior—that is, by illicit relations with a third party—the innocent one is free to divorce the unfaithful one and to marry someone else.

Many have questioned this interpretation of our Lord's words, but His words allow no other meaning. To say, as some have done, that the Lord was referring to fornication committed before wedlock (as in Deuteronomy 22:13-14,20-21), and not to such sin committed after marriage, would be to insinuate that marital unfaithfulness is less evil than the same kind of iniquity committed by those not yet married. To support this theory it has been stated that the word *fornication* refers only to sexual impurity on the part of single people. But

1 Corinthians 5 contradicts this definition. The incestuous man there was living with his stepmother, and he is charged with fornication.

While affirming the high and holy character of marriage according to God's Word, Jesus does not put on the innocent divorced party the burden of going through life alone because of the unfaithfulness of a wicked partner.

Another theory has been put forth in order to nullify the very clear teaching given by Jesus as to divorce: namely, that He spoke as under the law, and that therefore the exception He mentioned does not apply in this dispensation of grace. Those who hold to this view forget that while Jesus came under the law, "the law and the prophets were until John." The preliminary teaching of the new dispensation was given by Jesus, for "grace and truth came by [Him]" (John 1:17). He was laying down the principles in regard to marriage and divorce that were to prevail from that day on.

Christ's teaching perplexed and troubled the disciples, who said that if these things were so it would perhaps be best not to marry at all, as He seemed to put such heavy restrictions on the natural propensities of human nature. The Lord acknowledged that all men cannot receive this teaching; it is for those who are ready to be submissive to the will of God, recognizing the sacredness of the marriage relationship, or for others who, as Paul said in a later day, had such self-control that they could keep themselves pure though unmarried. Such were as eunuchs for the kingdom of Heaven's sake. But Jesus would put no one under bondage as to this. It was for him who was able to accept it.

It is well to remember that the real object of marriage is to bring forth children and so to establish a godly home, which is a marvelous testimony for Christ in the midst of a corrupt world. *Home* to millions is one of the sweetest words in the English language. What memories it evokes! What stirring of the hearts and what thanksgiving to God are aroused as we recall the joyous home circle and think about the impressions made there on our young minds. For though we may have wandered far since, home is still the most sacred place we have known on earth. Yet vast numbers of people have never known its mystic spell. And in many languages of earth there is no word which is the exact equivalent of our word *home*. Few pagan tribes have any synonym for it. They speak of a house, a dwelling-place, or a shelter; but to them home, as we understand it, is something of which they know nothing. Yet "God setteth the solitary in families" (Psalm 68:6), and established homes for mankind long before the rise of governments and before the church was brought into existence.

It takes more than four walls and comfortable furniture to make a home. Home, in the truest sense, is where love rules. The ideal home of Scripture is an abode, whether it be a pilgrim's tent or a grand mansion, where the family live together in love and harmony, each delighting in the company of the others, and all seeking the good of the whole. Such homes were found in Israel when all the rest of the world was steeped in idolatry, and where fear ruled instead of love. Christ lifted home life onto an even higher plane, making it a place of deep spiritual fellowship as well as tender love. The Christian home is a scene where father, mother, and children enjoy together a sense of the divine favor and protection, and where the whole family honors Christ as Savior and Lord. From such a home the voice of prayer and praise will rise up as a continual sacrifice day by day.

The loosening of the marriage tie and the lowering of the home ideals are perhaps the two greatest evils of our times. Divorces are increasing at an alarming rate as people more and more disregard the teaching of Scripture as to the sacred character of marriage, and give free rein to inordinate affections and selfish desires. The children are the greatest sufferers in the breaking up of the home. We are sowing the wind as a nation, and we are destined to reap the whirlwind unless we turn to God in repentance and seek to walk in humble obedience to His Word.

At the rate in which divorces are increasing in this and other lands, family life will soon be a thing of the past in the majority of cases, as far as the unsaved are concerned. The children of God should avoid any complicity in this evil thing by implicit obedience to the teaching of our Lord in regard to the intended permanence of the marriage relationship.

After this somewhat lengthy digression we must pass on to consider the next incident, which follows in beautiful moral order.

Jesus Blesses the Children (Matthew 19:13-15)

Parents brought their little ones to Jesus, beseeching Him to lay His holy hands on them and to bestow a blessing upon them. The bringing of the children was a token of real faith in the grace and power of the Lord. To the disciples this seemed an unnecessary intrusion upon the time and consideration of their Master, and they attempted to restrain those who came desiring Him to take such kindly notice of their offspring.

Jesus interfered immediately, however, and encouraged the parents by saying, "Suffer [or permit] little children, and forbid them not, to come unto me: for of such is the kingdom of heaven." He had shown and declared earlier that, because of their simple faith, children are the ideal subjects of the kingdom. Here He reaffirmed this, and by these words gives encouragement to all parents everywhere who believe in Him and endeavor to bring their children up in the nurture and admonition of the Lord. They can bring their little ones to Him, confident that His blessing will be upon them.

After laying His hands on the children, Jesus left that place to go on toward Jerusalem where He was to lay down His life as a sacrifice for sin.

Jesus Defines the Cost of Discipleship (Matthew 19:16-26)

In order to understand this incident correctly we need to distinguish carefully between salvation and discipleship. God's salvation is absolutely free. It is offered to men on the principle of pure, unmerited grace. But discipleship literally costs all that one has—the loss of all things (Philippians 3:7-8; Luke 14:33). No one can be a true follower of Christ who does not take up his cross—that which speaks of death to the flesh—and follow the Lord Jesus in His path of rejection by the world and devotion to the Father's will.

"Good Master, what good thing shall I do, that I may have eternal life?" The question involves one's ability to earn eternal life by doing. This young man had not yet learned his own utter sinfulness and absolute helplessness.

In addressing Jesus Christ as "Good Master," the young man

evidently meant to do Him honor, but Jesus declared that only God is good. All men are sinners (Romans 3:12). Therefore, if Jesus were only a man, He would not be good, in this absolute sense. If truly good, then He is God. After His solemn declaration, the Lord Jesus took the inquirer up on his own ground. The law promised life to those who kept it (Leviticus 18:5; Galatians 3:12). So the Lord answered, "If thou wilt enter into life, keep the commandments." This declaration was designed to show the man his inability to obtain life by obedience to the law, for if his conscience were active, he would realize he had already violated the law.

"He saith unto him, Which?" This was clearly an attempt to evade the full force of the Lord's words. In reply, Jesus quoted five of the principal commandments and concluded by summing up all of those that refer to our duties to our fellow men by quoting from Leviticus 19:18, "Thou shalt love thy neighbour as thyself." It would indicate an unawakened condition of soul if one could face all these and plead not guilty.

If men would seek to gain eternal life by doing good, the law challenges them to perfect obedience. Because all have sinned, it is not possible for anyone to be justified by the deeds of the law. The law speaks with awful force to an awakened conscience, leading one to realize the hopelessness of ever obtaining eternal life by human merit.

"All these have I kept from my youth up." No doubt these words came from a sincere heart, but they give evidence of lack of real exercise of conscience. Who, knowing himself, could so speak? Outwardly, the life may have been blameless, but if conscience had been active there would have been confession of sin. The words of the young man revealed the smug self-righteousness of one who prided himself on his own morality and did not realize the corruption of his heart. The question, "What lack I yet?" in itself indicates how complacent he was—how self-satisfied.

"If thou wilt be perfect, sell...and give...and follow me." Jesus so spoke in order to jar him from his ill-founded confidence. How could anyone who was wealthy profess to love his neighbor as himself while needy, poverty-stricken people were suffering on every hand. To become a disciple of Christ—to live for others—and thus to lay up treasure in Heaven, had no attraction for this one who talked so glibly of complete obedience to God's commandments from his youth up.

In calling upon the rich inquirer to sell all he had and give to the poor in order that he might have treasure in Heaven, our Lord was seeking to reveal both the deceitfulness and selfishness of the human heart. The challenge to forsake all and follow Christ was a call to yield wholly to His authority, thus to become a disciple in deed and in truth.

It is a poor thing when Christ has merely the first place in one's life. He is intensely exclusive and asks that we give Him full control of our entire being. No one, however closely related, is to be permitted to turn us aside from the path of devotion and allegiance to Him (Luke 14:26-27). So fervent should be our love for Christ that our affection for our dearest friends or relatives will seem as hatred in comparison.

To the flesh, this may seem to be a hard and almost unkind demand. But the truly surrendered soul finds a deeper joy in yielding all to Him who has bought us with His blood, than in living to please one's self. Many have resisted for years the call to such a life of wholehearted allegiance, only to learn at last that they have lost out immeasurably by refusing to own the claims of the Lord Jesus to the exclusion of all else.

"He went away sorrowful: for he had great possessions." It has been well called "the great refusal." Whatever admiration this man had for the Lord Jesus Christ, whatever inward yearning there was for the spiritual life, all were weaker than his love for his wealth and the place it gave him in the social circles of his day. His great possessions stood between him and the salvation of his soul. They meant more to him than the knowledge of life eternal.

To take up the cross and follow Christ in His path of rejection by the world may appear to involve sacrifices too great for flesh and blood to endure. But when the surrender is made and the cross accepted, we find, as the saintly Rutherford expressed it, that "that cross is a burden such as fins are to a fish, or wings to a bird."

"A rich man shall hardly enter into the kingdom of heaven." As we have seen already the kingdom of Heaven is not Heaven itself.

Rather it implies the recognition of and subjection to Heaven's authority while here on earth. It is hard for those to whom God has entrusted great wealth to hold everything they possess as a stewardship, which they are responsible to use for His glory. It was not merely the salvation of this young man's soul that was at stake: Christ was pointing the way to true discipleship.

"His disciples...were exceedingly amazed, saying, Who then can be saved?" They naturally thought it would be easier for those in comfortable circumstances to follow Jesus than for the poor and needy, but throughout the history of Christianity the poor of this world have often been richest in faith.

"With God all things are possible." It is only the omnipotent power of God that leads any man, be he rich or poor, to trust in Christ as Savior and yield obedience to Him as Lord. Every conversion, and every consecrated life is a miracle of grace. Whether men be wealthy or poverty-stricken, or among the fairly comfortable middle classes, it is only when they have been convicted of their lost condition by the Holy Spirit that they ever turn to Christ for deliverance. In Him all class distinctions vanish, and all stand on one common ground before God.

Just what it was that led the rich young man to talk with the Lord Jesus we are not told. He may have felt within his soul that Jesus spoke with all authority and had therefore the right to claim submission to His words. But the young man evidently had no sense of his own need as a sinner. He thought of Jesus as a teacher, not as a Savior. So he was not ready to put Christ first in his life, and like many thousands since who were somewhat attracted to the Lord Jesus, he went pensively away when he learned the conditions of discipleship.

The Right Use of Wealth. It is not sinful to be rich. It is sinful to make riches the ground of overconfidence, and to enjoy the comforts that wealth can give while forgetting the sufferings of the poor and needy. When God commits wealth to any man, it is as a stewardship entrusted to him to be administered for the glory of Him who gave it. It is the love of money, not money itself, that is evil (1 Timothy 6:10). Money may become the means of untold blessing if used in subjection to Christ (1 Timothy 6:17-19).

Jesus Promises Rewards for His Followers *(Matthew 19:27-30)*

The disciples had been silent on-lookers and listeners during the colloquy between their Lord and the rich young ruler. But now that the young man had turned away to go on in his selfish course, Peter spoke up on behalf of them all and expressed the concern in their hearts as to what the final result would be of their own renunciations for Christ's name's sake.

"We have forsaken all, and followed thee; what shall we have therefore?" It seemed to be a natural question, and in one sense it was. In the eyes of the world they had forfeited all hope of riches or advancement. They had risked everything on the belief that Jesus was the promised Messiah. Yet He had spoken darkly of rejection, suffering, and death. For what were they to look in the days to come?

In reply Jesus assured them that when the kingdom was fully displayed, in the days of earth's regeneration, or new birth, they who had been identified with Him in His rejection would be honored and recognized in a very signal manner. They would sit upon twelve thrones, judging the twelve tribes of Israel. In saying this He did not overlook the predicted apostasy of Judas, but it had been arranged in the counsels of God that Matthias was to take his place. Paul's apostleship later on was of an altogether different order. He was not numbered with the twelve, but was the chosen instrument to make known the mystery of the body of Christ in which no distinction is made between Jew and Gentile, as he told us in Ephesians 3.

Not only were the twelve sure of reward. Jesus declared that "every one that hath forsaken houses, or brethren, or...lands, for my name's sake, shall receive an hundredfold, and shall inherit everlasting life." No one ever lost out by excessive devotion to Christ. Whatever has to be renounced for His name's sake will be repaid abundantly, both in this life and in the next. Many who profess such renunciation of worldly profit for His sake will, like Demas, fail of reward because of unfaithfulness (2 Timothy 4:10). Others who might not seem to have endured much for Him but were true at heart in the time of His rejection will be recognized in that day. Thus, the first should be last and the last first.

When Christ fills the soul's vision, it is easy to forsake all else for

His sake. But until He is known, first as Savior, then as Lord, things of earth still seem to be of far greater worth and importance than the things of eternity. Not until one has learned the lesson of his own sinfulness and good-for-nothingness, will he turn to the Lord Jesus alone for deliverance and be prepared to acknowledge His authority in every sphere of this earthly life. Love for Christ makes self-surrender easy. Love of self makes it impossible.

The contrast comes out clearly as we consider the great refusal of the rich young ruler and the devoted allegiance of the apostolic band, who had left all to follow their Lord, in spite of much misunderstanding and failure.

CHAPTER TWENTY
KINGDOM STANDARDS

The Parable of the Workers *(Matthew 20:1-16)*

Matthew 20 opens with a parable of the kingdom designed to show that service for the Lord is to be rewarded according to opportunities embraced, not simply for the amount of work accomplished. As this parable is a likeness of the kingdom of Heaven in its mystery form, the householder necessarily represents the Lord Himself. The laborers are those who hear His call for service in the great harvest field.

With those first engaged the master agrees for a penny—that is, a denarius—a day. While this seems a very small amount—a silver coin a little less than a quarter in size—it was the regular wage for day-laborers at that time, and had much greater purchasing power than any similar piece of money today. Therefore the agreed payment was eminently fair and all that these men would have any expectation of receiving.

As the day wore on, the husbandman went to the market place on four other occasions: the third, sixth, ninth, and even the eleventh hours, answering to our 9:00 a.m., 12:00 noon, 3:00 p.m., and 5:00 p.m., the last being just an hour before the close of the day. Each time he hired any available laborers, telling them he would do what was right by them as to payment for work accomplished. Notice the reason the eleventh-hour workmen gave for unemployment: no man had hired them. They were ready to work but opportunity had not come their way. When it did come, they complied at once with the request to go and work in the vineyard.

After the toil of the day all were called to receive what was considered their due. To the surprise of the entire company those who had worked only one hour received a full day's wage, and those in each group were paid the same. Those who had worked all day took it for granted they would receive a larger sum. When only a denarius was forthcoming, they registered a complaint on the ground that they had borne the burden and heat of the day, yet those who came later were made equal to them. They overlooked the fact that they had accepted the agreement to labor for a denarius a day. The lord of the vineyard made this clear, insisting that no wrong was being done to them inasmuch as he had kept his part of the bargain. It was his liberty to reward the others as he chose to do. He paid according to their needs and according to their readiness to embrace the first opportunity that came to them.

The principle is clear and is emphasized by the words, "So the last shall be first, and the first last: for many be called, but few chosen." All are chosen who heed the call, so none can blame the employer if they are not given the opportunity to serve.

The lesson for us is evident. Every disciple of Christ is expected to obey His call to service. At the day of manifestation every man will be rewarded for his own work according to its character and not merely for the amount of time put in. Jesus Himself did not live long, but He lived deep; and in His three and a half years of service He accomplished far more than anyone else in a long life. In this, many of His followers have imitated Him.

It is sad to observe that, even after hearing this parable, the disciples were still concerned as to who should have prominence in the kingdom.

Dealing with Worldly Ambition (Matthew 20:17-28)

The teaching and healing ministry of Jesus was rapidly coming to an end. He had now steadfastly set His face to go to Jerusalem, where He was to make the supreme sacrifice on our behalf. The religious leaders, blinded by their selfishness and self-righteousness, were to add to all their other sins that of delivering Jesus up to the death of the cross. So far could mere religiousness, apart from spiritual life, carry its devotees.

Again and again our Lord definitely foretold His resurrection on the third day, yet it seemed to make little impression on the minds of His disciples (see Luke 18:31-34).

The mother of James and John evidently expected Jesus to proclaim Himself as the promised Messianic King in Jerusalem, and she was ambitious for her children to have two of the best positions in the new government. Mark told us that James and John themselves concurred in her request (Mark 10:35). She felt her sons were deserving of special recognition and, like many a mother since, she endeavored to push them forward, lest others should gain the choicest offices and they be overlooked.

"Ye know not what ye ask." Jesus was to be rejected and crucified. To share with Him would mean to take the same path—to be spurned and hated rather than to be honored and praised. They were to participate in His cup of sorrow and to have part in His baptism unto death. As to recognition later on, when He would reign in righteousness, it was the Father who appointed His associates.

Christ's Cup and Baptism. He referred to the cup of rejection and hatred He was to drink, and the baptism of death He was to endure. To a certain extent all His disciples share in both of these. There is another sense in which none but He could go through them. The cup of judgment that He drained to the dregs for us, and the baptism of the divine wrath against sin that He endured on the cross were His alone.

Those for Whom It Is Prepared. The displayed kingdom of God on earth will be the sphere in which His saints will reign with Him. In that kingdom each one will be rewarded according to the measure of his devotedness during the time of association with our Lord in His rejection. The Father has decreed that precedence will be given in that day of glory to those for whom it is prepared.

Angered at the temerity of James and John, the rest of the disciples nevertheless all cherished similar ambitions. They felt that an attempt had been made to get possession of places ahead of themselves. In earthly kingdoms men grasp for power and are honored by those beneath them because of their ability to rule and to subject others to their will. It is the very opposite in the kingdom of God. In the world the great man is the one of determined will and effective initiative who can triumph over his fellows. But in the kingdom of Christ true greatness is characterized by intense lowliness and a readiness to serve rather than rule.

In the heavenly kingdom it is meekness and unselfish service that have the pre-eminence. To prefer others before oneself, to minister in grace rather than to rule in power, is to exemplify the spirit of our royal leader. There is no room for earthly pomp or worldly glory in the circle of Christ's followers. To seek for personal advancement and to endeavor to lord it over one's brethren is thoroughly contrary to the spirit of Him who became servant of all, though He created the universe. The spirit of a Diotrephes (3 John 9) is far removed from the spirit of Christ and should be avoided by all His servants; but that of an Epaphroditus (Philippians 2:25-30) should be emulated. The spirit of Christ is demonstrated by a rivalry, not to be great but to be little, not to be highest but to be lowest. The principles of His kingdom are exemplified where service is at a premium and worldly ambition is frowned upon.

"To give his life a ransom for many." Here our Lord tells us exactly why He came into the world. He did not leave the glory that He had with the Father before the world began (John 17:5) in order to seek for greater glory in this world. He came to serve mankind, not only in ministering to temporal or even spiritual needs day by day, but also in redeeming us from sin and its penalty by giving His life for us, dying a sacrificial death, to make propitiation for sins (1 John 4:10).

Our Lord Jesus Christ has given to mankind a new ideal. He has shown us that the truly great man is the one who seeks not his own good, but the blessing of others. Even here on earth the unselfish life is the most satisfactory one. To Baruch of old the message came, "Seekest thou great things for thyself? seek them not" (Jeremiah 45:5). This runs contrary to the pride and self-assertion of the natural man: "Men will praise thee, when thou doest well to thyself" (Psalm 49:18). But after all is said and done, the truth abides that "for men to search their own glory is not glory" (Proverbs 25:27). Our Lord, because of His very nature, had every right to assert Himself and seek recognition and honor from the men whom He created. Yet He chose to take the place of servant of all. He humbled Himself to become man, but that was not enough. As man, He took the servant's place, and at last gave Himself up to death for us in the sacrifice of the cross, that He might redeem us to God. He has glorified and exemplified the dignity of service and self-abnegation in such a way as to give an altogether new standard of greatness. He has stained the pride of all earthly glory (Isaiah 23:9) and shown it to be mere selfishness, and thus opposed to that which has the approval of God. The laudable ambition of all who know Him as Savior and Lord should be to serve, not for present gain, but to bless and help others. Thereby we express our gratitude to God for His grace and love so freely bestowed on us in Christ Jesus.

The things that are highly prized among men are often thoroughly opposed to the mind of God (Luke 16:15). It is the ambitious, energetic man, pressing to the front and striving to excel above his fellows, who has the admiration of men of the world. They suppose that present gain is the great thing to be desired, but Jesus taught us that it is the meek who inherit the earth (Matthew 5:5). The meek are content to be passed over and to be unnoticed by men. The approval of the Lord means more to them than all else; these are they who overcome the world by faith (1 John 5:4). They can afford to relinquish present advantage, for they know they shall find a sure reward at the judgment seat of Christ.

The Healing of the Blind (Matthew 20:29-34)

The Lord and His disciples were now well on their way toward Jerusalem. They had entered the city of Jericho. It was there Luke told us that Jesus met Zacchaeus, whose whole life was changed by coming to know Christ; and there two blind men received their sight.

To the casual reader there seems to be a discrepancy between the accounts given here and in Mark, and that given by Luke. The latter told us that "it came to pass, that as he was come nigh unto Jericho, a certain blind man sat by the way side begging" (Luke 18:35), whereas both Matthew and Mark told us that this incident occurred as they departed from Jericho. There is no confusion, however, if we understand that Bartimaeus sat by the wayside begging as Jesus drew near to Jericho, but the actual healing took place as He was departing from that city.

These seeming discrepancies in the Gospel records make it more certain that there was no collaboration on the part of the different writers, but that each related the incident according to information that he had and as guided by the Holy Spirit. It is a well-recognized principle in taking testimony in court that where several witnesses use exactly the same language, it is evident that they have been in consultation together or instructed by a lawyer as to what they should say. The same story may be related with minor differences that upon full investigation do not conflict with each other at all, but emphasize the viewpoint of the one giving the testimony.

Matthew told us here that there were two blind men sitting by the wayside, whereas Mark and Luke spoke of only one, and that one named Bartimaeus. There were two. The Holy Spirit guided Matthew from any error in regard to this, but it is very clear that Bartimaeus was the stronger character of the two, and the one on whom attention is focused in the accounts of Mark and Luke.

Learning that Jesus was passing by, these blind men cried out, "Have mercy on us, O Lord, thou son of David." This was a recognition of His messiahship on their part. They believed Him to be in very truth the promised Son of David who would give sight to the blind and perform other marvelous works.

The multitude rebuked them, calling on them to be quiet, as though Jesus was not to be troubled by poor wretches such as they. But they refused to be silenced and cried out the more, pleading with Jesus for the help they needed so badly. He stood still and called them to Himself and tenderly inquired, "What will ye that I shall do unto you?" He knew well what they wanted, but He always likes to have people tell Him what is on their hearts. Without a moment's hesitation they replied, "Lord, that our eyes may be opened." In His infinite compassion Jesus granted their request. He touched their eyes and immediately they received their sight, and followed Him in the way. While the great and the mighty in Israel refused Him, these two, who for years had been blind mendicants, recognized Him as the rightful King of Israel and gladly owned Him as such.

CHAPTER TWENTY-ONE

THE KING IN JERUSALEM

The Triumphal Entry (Matthew 21:1-11)

The so-called triumphant entry of our Lord into Jerusalem took place at the beginning of the last week of His earthly ministry, which culminated in His death and burial, followed by a glorious resurrection. This triumphal procession was in partial fulfillment of Psalm 118, where He is presented as the rejected stone, eventually to be made the head of the corner. He is first accepted by a few who cry, "Hosanna" ("save now") and "Blessed be he that cometh in the name of the Lord" (Psalm 118:25-26). But instead of the kingdom being set up then, the next thing was His crucifixion, when He was bound, as it were, like the sacrificial animals to the horns of the altar (Psalm 118:27).

How His heart must have been stirred as He drew near to the city. Once called holy, it was now polluted by sin and characterized by a form of godliness without power. The hour had come when He was to present Himself as King, and in preparation for it He sent two of His disciples into a nearby village to procure a donkey and her colt. Evidently the owners of these beasts were among those who knew Jesus and recognized His claims, for they acknowledged immediately His right to take the animals for His use at this time.

Zechariah had prophesied that the King would come into His royal city "riding upon an ass, and upon a colt the foal of an ass" (Zechariah 9:9). All this was fulfilled literally as Jesus came down the slope of Olivet and into Jerusalem riding on the unbroken colt. The disciples spread some of their garments on it as a saddle and seated the Lord

Jesus Christ upon them. It is significant that this humble creature was more subject to Him—its Creator—than men whom He had come to save.

Doubtless those who welcomed Him into Jerusalem as He rode on the donkey into the holy city thought the hour of His triumph had come. They believed that He was about to assert His royal authority and begin His beneficent reign over Israel and the subjected nations, making Jerusalem the capital of a regenerated world. All this will indeed be in God's appointed time, but He had other work to accomplish first. So the entrance into the city amid the plaudits of the populace was but preliminary to His death on a Roman cross, where He was to make propitiation (rather than reconciliation) for the sins of the people (Hebrews 2:17, RV). For Him there could be no kingdom without the cross.

We need not question that the welcome He received was sincere. His own words in answer to the criticism of the chief priests and scribes make that clear (Matthew 21:16). But those who thus rejoiced in His coming to them little realized the true state of affairs, nor did they understand the predictions of the prophets: how Christ must first be rejected and suffer many things before He could enter His glory (Luke 24:25-27).

Every move that the Lord Jesus Christ made as He went through this world was in exact accord with the prophetic Word and therefore in obedience to the Father's will. As He entered Jerusalem, He knew that crucifixion, not the kingdom, was to be His portion in the immediate future. But nothing turned Him aside from His path of perfect submission to the One who had sent Him. He adorned every position that He took. His matchless perfections were revealed in everything He did. He accepted the praise of the children and of the older ones, who hailed Him as David's Son, with the same grace that enabled Him to endure the cold, cutting criticism of His enemies. The one paramount object of His life was to glorify the Father.

"A very great multitude spread their garments in the way." It was a truly oriental setting. Part of the throng carpeted the road before Him with their robes, and others cut down palm branches and strewed them on the path He was to take, thus acclaiming Him as their rightful King.

"Hosanna to the son of David." This and the words following, as we have noted already, were quotations from the Psalm of triumph (Psalm 118) in which His royal subjects acclaim their King, "Great David's greater Son." The complete fulfillment of the Psalm awaits His second advent, as He Himself predicted later (Matthew 23:39).

The singing and rejoicing were heard throughout all Jerusalem, and the populace, stirred with wonder, inquired as to who it was whose entrance to their city had caused such an ovation. It was a repetition of what had taken place centuries before when Solomon was welcomed as king (1 Kings 1:38-40). He of whom Solomon was but a type was now among them; yet many knew Him not. With fervent faith, the rejoicing multitude declared Jesus to be a prophet. They were doubtless, for the most part, Galileans themselves who had become convinced that He was all that He claimed to be.

The children and others who welcomed Jesus so vociferously were acting according to the Word of God when they acclaimed Him as the true Son of David, who is yet to reign in Zion. As on so many other occasions, the chief priests and scribes, though familiar with the letter of the Word, proved themselves altogether out of touch with this momentous occasion.

Zechariah's Prophecy. It is interesting to note how the two advents of our Lord are linked together in Zechariah 9:9-10. In verse 9 we see the King riding into His earthly capital, presenting Himself to the people as their rightful ruler. But although verse 10 follows this so closely, the events depicted in it will not be completely fulfilled until He comes again. It is then that He will speak peace to the nations, and His dominion will be set up over all the earth.

Psalm 118. This Psalm deals largely with the time when the Lord will arise for the deliverance of Israel. At that time all their trials will be ended and they will enter into the blessedness of that rejoicing and salvation that will then be found in the tabernacles of the righteous (118:15). But all this blessing depends on the One who was first to be bound as a sacrifice to the horns of the altar. It was settled in the purpose of God from eternity that there could be no kingdom till after the work of the cross was accomplished. While the welcome that Jesus received was quite in keeping with the divine plans, those who would have crowned Him as king at that time had to learn that He must first suffer many things, be crucified, and rise from the dead. In God's due time the remainder of the prophecy will have a glorious fulfillment.

The Cleansing of the Temple (Matthew 21:12-16)

Upon entering the city Jesus proceeded to visit the center of all Jewish worship and to exercise His authority there as He had done on an earlier occasion, as related in John 2:13-17.

The cleansing of the temple was Christ's assertion of His authority as the Son of the Father, whose house had been so grossly defiled. That temple was the place where, of old, Jehovah had set His name, but it had become defiled and polluted. It had been turned into a place of merchandise under the guise of assisting the many pilgrims who came from all parts of the world to keep the annual feasts, or set times, of Jehovah (see Leviticus 23).

"My house shall be called the house of prayer." This was the divine purpose, as declared by Isaiah the prophet (Isaiah 56:7). In the coming day of the kingdom, when Jerusalem becomes in truth the worship center of the world, a new temple will arise, to which all nations shall resort. The one which then stood on mount Moriah had become "a den of thieves," dishonoring to God and a stumbling block to men.

He who was the Lord of the temple was there to reveal His delivering power. Those who were suffering from various physical infirmities sought Him out, "and he healed them" in His grace and compassion.

"The chief priests and scribes...were sore displeased." These proud, haughty legalists were scandalized by the very goodness and lovingkindness of Jesus. The plaudits of the grateful populace were as gall and bitterness to these religious leaders. When they heard the people crying, "Hosanna to the son of David," they were indignant that such honor should be paid Him. They had no thought of joining in this glad recognition of Him whose words of power bore witness to the divinity and authority of His message (John 5:30).

They blamed Jesus for permitting the people to address Him as the Son of David, which was equivalent to acknowledging Him as their

Messiah, and called on Him to rebuke the multitude. But Jesus refused to heed their angry criticisms and referred them to a passage in the Psalms that exactly fitted the case: "Out of the mouth of babes and sucklings thou hast perfected praise" (Psalm 8:2). In their honesty and simplicity, the children and the common people, whom the self-righteous leaders despised, proved they had been taught of God. They honored Jesus Christ as the sent One of the Father, who had come into the world to be the Redeemer of Israel.

The Fig Tree Cursed (Matthew 21:17-22)

As the evening drew on, Jesus left the city and went out to Bethany. So far as the record goes He did not spend a night in Jerusalem until He was arrested and taken to the house of Caiaphas. He may have found lodging with His friends, Lazarus, Martha, and Mary, or in some other convenient place. The home of Lazarus in Bethany was very dear to the heart of Jesus. We may well imagine that He was in close touch with the little family there during these closing nights of His stay upon earth.

Each morning He wended His way with His disciples to the city. As they went in on the second morning Jesus saw the fruitless fig tree and pronounced a solemn judgment on it. The fig tree is the well-known symbol of Israel (or rather Judah) nationally: a fig tree planted in a vineyard. When Jesus came to Israel there were the leaves of religious ceremony but no fruit for God. So the Israelites were given up to judicial barrenness for all the present age.

The fact that this tree was covered with leaves would naturally imply fruit, for the figs appear before the leaves in most varieties of fig trees. Jesus knew well the facts of the case, but He chose to go to the tree to search for fruit in order to make of it an acted parable. There are three fig tree passages that are definitely linked together and give us a dispensational picture of God's dealings with the Jews: Luke 13:6-9; Matthew 21:17-20; Matthew 24:32-33.

"And presently the fig tree withered away." The disciples noted with wonder that this fruitless tree, which had been so verdant and fair to look upon, was dried up and withered. Noticing their amazement, Jesus took occasion once more to impress on them a lesson as to the importance of faith. He used the same illustration as before (Matthew 17:20) of the mountain being cast into the sea in response to faith as a grain of mustard seed. This time He added the definite and soul-heartening declaration that "all things, whatsoever ye shall ask in prayer, believing, ye shall receive."

This is not to be understood as an assurance that God will grant every request we make, or give us whatever we ask. To pray believingly implies that we pray in accordance with the revealed will of God, and that we do not regard iniquity in our hearts (Psalm 66:18). But where one is right with God and his prayer is in faith because it is in harmony with the known will of God, the divine response is sure.

The Authority of Jesus (Matthew 21:23-27)

While teaching in the temple Jesus was challenged by the religious leaders regarding His authority to act as He did. These priests and elders acted often on very dubious authority, but they questioned the right of Jesus to cleanse the temple of those who had made it a "den of thieves" and to teach the people as He did.

Following the custom He had so often used in dealing with cavilers such as these priests, Jesus replied by putting a leading question to them. What about John's baptism? Was it of divine origin or was John acting from a purely human standpoint?

Realizing they were trapped in their own crookedness and dishonesty, they replied by saying, "We cannot tell." They knew that if they admitted John was sent by God, they would be unable to explain why they had not believed him. Believing John would have involved receiving Jesus, whom John had declared was the promised Messiah. On the other hand, if they dared to deny John's heavenly commission, it would stir the ire of the populace against them, and they would lose their influence over the people, who generally believed John was a prophet of the Lord.

When they admitted their ignorance or inability to answer, Jesus calmly replied, "Neither tell I you by what authority I do these things." To attempt to convince them would be but wasted time, for as we often say, "There are none so blind as those who will not see."

The Parable of the Two Sons (Matthew 21:28-32)

Matthew 21 closes with two parables, both designed to show the seriousness of refusing immediate compliance with the testimony and the demands of the Lord.

The first of the two closing parables concerns a man and his two sons. The two sons portray two types of men: those who give lip-service, and those who are genuine in their interest in spiritual realities. In the first lad we see the willful son, persisting in disobedience until subdued and brought to repentance by divine grace. In the second son we see the legalists in Israel. At the base of Sinai they said, "All that the Lord hath said will we do, and be obedient" (Exodus 24:7), but their history was one of insubjection to God (Romans 2:24).

"The publicans and the harlots go into the kingdom of God before you." It is the self-confessed sinners who feel their need of grace, turn to God in repentance, and enter through new birth into the kingdom (John 3:3,5).

John came proclaiming the righteous demands of God upon His creatures and calling to repentance those who had failed to attain this standard. The legalists turned indifferently away, but needy sinners obeyed.

It is a terribly dangerous thing to trifle with the mercy of God. Little did the Jewish leaders realize that they were sealing their own doom in rejecting Jesus, the One sent of God to bring them into fullness of blessing if they received Him. They lost their opportunity because they were blinded by self-interest. They failed to recognize their Messiah when He came in exact accord with the Scriptures of the prophets whom they professed to reverence. Mere knowledge of the letter of the Word saves no one. It is those who believe in the Christ of whom the Book of God speaks who are made wise unto salvation (2 Timothy 3:15). To reject Him is fatal.

This is a solemn theme. Who can portray adequately the perils of rejecting Christ? God has used some of the most striking figures imaginable to warn us of the dire fate that awaits the one who spurns His grace and refuses the Savior.

The fruitless fig tree, cursed by Jesus, represents the religious nation that bore no fruit for God and so was rejected and has ever since been dried up, as it were, from the roots. The parable of the two sons contrasts the legalistic self-righteous leaders of the Jews, who pretended to an obedience they did not execute, with poor sinners, both Jews and Gentiles, who have heard and obeyed the truth of the gospel. The parable of the vineyard (Matthew 21:33-46) tells of God's care for and patience with His earthly people until they fulfilled their own Scriptures in rejecting His Son. The story of the marriage feast (Matthew 22:1-14) emphasizes the same truth; the parable shows how the door of faith was to be opened to the Gentiles and warns against mere profession, which can mean only judgment at last, as in the case of the man who refused the wedding garment.

The Parable of the Vineyard (Matthew 21:33-46)

The second of the two closing parables in Matthew 21—the parable of the vineyard—had both a backward and a forward application. It traced God's ways with Israel in the past and their rejection of His messengers. It also looked on prophetically to what was to be accomplished in the next few days when Jesus Himself was to be repudiated by His own people and delivered up to death.

The householder was God Himself. The vineyard was Israel (Isaiah 5:1-7). The husbandmen were the leaders in Judah who were responsible to guide the people aright. The servants were the prophets who came from time to time as Jehovah's representatives to press His claims upon the people.

"Beat one, and killed another, and stoned another." Thus had Israel and Judah treated those who came to them in the name of the Lord (Acts 7:52).

"He sent unto them his son." How vividly does this portray the grace of God in sending the Lord Jesus! He was in Palestine as the representative of the Father (John 6:38; 7:28-29). Christ was the heir sent by the Father in grace to call the leaders in Israel to a path of obedience and responsibility. But He knew they would spurn Him as they had persecuted the prophets that went before. The rejection of Christ by His own people was the fullest possible expression of the hatred of the natural heart, moved by Satanic malignancy, toward the God of all grace (Acts 2:23).

It is useless to try to absolve the leaders in Jewry of the crime of delivering our Lord up to death (1 Thessalonians 2:14-15). Actually it was the Gentiles who crucified Him, but potentially it was the Jews who killed Him. Both are implicated in the greatest crime in all history, the murder of the Christ of God (Acts 4:26-27).

"What will he do unto those husbandmen?" Foreseeing their treatment of Himself, Jesus put the question directly to those who had followed the parable thus far. He would have them pronounce their own condemnation.

"He will miserably destroy those wicked men." Without realizing it, they declared what God was about to do. Their words were fulfilled in the destruction of Jerusalem and the setting aside of the Jew in favor of the nations of the Gentiles.

"The stone which the builders rejected." Jesus called their attention to the definite prophecy of Psalm 118:22. He Himself was the rejected stone. But in His resurrection God was to make Him the head of the corner in the new temple of living stones He was about to erect.

A Jewish legend explained this verse by declaring that at the building of Solomon's temple a stone was sent up from the quarries at the very beginning for which the workmen could find no place, so it was thrown down into the valley below mount Moriah. Later they sent word that they were ready for the cornerstone, but the masons declared it had been sent up already. Finally someone recalled the disallowed stone, and a search in the valley brought it to light, and it was hoisted up to the mount again, and made the head of the corner.

"The kingdom of God shall be taken from you, and given to a nation bringing forth the fruits thereof." Israel after the flesh was to be put aside. The kingdom for which they had waited so long was to be lost to them forever. A new and elect nation, a regenerated Israel, will possess the kingdom eventually. Meantime the grace of God is going out to the Gentiles.

Christ is the stone of salvation; He is also the stone of judgment. The Jews stumbled over Him and were broken (Isaiah 8:14). Some day He will come again, as the stone falling on the image of Gentile power to grind it to powder (Daniel 2:34-35).

There could be no doubt in the minds of our Lord's hearers as to the application of the parable. Recognizing a picture of themselves in the unfaithful husbandmen, the Pharisees gave no evidence of repentance, nor of a desire to obey the Word of God. Instead, they seemed to become even more determined in their opposition to Jesus, God's anointed One. Had they dared they would have laid hands on Him and endeavored at once to put Him out of the way, but again they were deterred by their fear of the multitude who believed Him to be a prophet. Such is the incorrigible evil of the natural heart unless subdued by divine grace!

CHAPTER TWENTY-TWO
THE KING AND HIS OPPONENTS

Parable of the Wedding Feast *(Matthew 22:1-14)*

In this striking parable, which our Lord spoke to the people of Jerusalem toward the end of His ministry, He gave a remarkable dispensational outline of the way God is dealing with men in this world. Jesus presented this parable shortly before going out to the garden of Gethsemane and from there to the judgment hall and to the cross. It is another parable of the kingdom of Heaven. It has to do with the sphere of profession, and tells us of what was to go on during the time of the absence of the Lord.

The "certain king" is God; the son is Christ Himself; the marriage is the union of believers with Christ. Those who put their trust in Him are united to Him as in marriage. The marriage supper is really the gospel feast—the feast of good things that God has provided for all who will accept His gracious invitation. But observe, the feast is prepared by God for the joy and glory of His own beloved Son. The thought was in the heart of God, and He expressed it by sending the Lord Jesus Christ into the world to save us from our sins.

The king "sent forth his servants to call them that were bidden to the wedding: and they would not come." This first invitation was to the lost sheep of the house of Israel, bidding them come to the marriage feast that the King had prepared. They refused the gracious invitation. "He came unto his own, and his own received him not" (John 1:11). The question has been asked often by Jewish people, "If Jesus is really the Messiah, as you say He is, why is it that Israel has been suffering all these years instead of being blessed?" The answer is: He came to save Israel, but when they refused Him, the invitation was extended to the Gentiles. The King sent His servants to call the people of Israel; they had an invitation to the marriage, but they would not come. Jesus said, "Ye will not come to me, that ye might have life" (John 5:40). They would not enter in and partake of the feast that had been spread. To accept the invitation one must trust Christ for himself.

Notice that a second invitation, a most urgent one, was extended to the same people, telling them that the feast was ready. Still they would not come. The king said, "Go again and call them!" After the Lord Jesus ascended to Heaven we find Peter and the other apostles, in the early chapters of the book of Acts, pleading with Israel to repent of the rejection of Christ and turn to Him and trust Him, confessing Him as their Savior. A few accepted Him, but the great majority spurned Him and actually persecuted His servants.

"But they made light of it, and went their ways, one to his farm, another to his merchandise." Is there anything wrong in owning a farm? Anything wrong in being a merchant? Not at all; unless it keeps you out of Heaven! If you get so occupied with your farm, or so taken up with your merchandise that you cannot lift your eyes above the earth, then there is something tragically wrong with it. Things that are proper in themselves may become wrong if we put them in place of Christ and the gospel. These men to whom the message came said, "We have too many other things about which we must be concerned: we have our farms to work, merchandise to sell. We cannot consider the king's invitation."

"And the remnant took his servants, and entreated them spitefully, and slew them." There were some who were simply indifferent, and others were positively antagonistic. These actually murdered the servants. Even in those early days hundreds of God's dear people were put to death by those who spurned His message.

Someone reading this may say, "Well, I am not against Christ; I have nothing against the church, nothing against Christianity. The only thing is I am not really interested. I have too many other things to occupy my mind." You are just like the first class—those who "went their ways, one to his farm, another to his merchandise." Others may be antagonistic to Christ. But notice this: both classes failed to get into the marriage feast. Whether one is simply indifferent or actually antagonistic to the gospel of God, the end will be the same. The question found in Hebrews 2:3, "How shall we escape, if we neglect so great salvation?" has never been answered. In order to be lost forever it is not necessary to be opposed to Christ. It is not necessary to say definitely, "I reject Jesus." Just neglect Him and you will never get in to the feast. "The road of by-and-by leads to the house of never." You may say, "Some day when conditions are different I am going to think about my soul." But alas, while you are waiting for a more convenient season the end of life may come, and you will find yourself shut out in the darkness forever.

"But when the king heard thereof, he was wroth: and he sent forth his armies, and destroyed those murderers, and burned up their city." After Christ had been rejected and crucified, God waited for some forty years for Israel to repent, but they would not. Then "he sent forth his armies." He is the God of hosts; He is the God of armies. And when a nation has sinned against Him to such a degree that He must deal with them in judgment, He sends the armies of some other people to visit judgment upon them. God permitted the Roman armies to invade the land of Israel and destroy Jerusalem. The final destruction of that city was the fulfillment of the words of the Lord Jesus, "There shall not be left here one stone upon another, that shall not be thrown down" (Matthew 24:2).

The Father thinks so highly of His Son that when men deliberately reject and spurn Him, God's indignation is stirred. In His dealings with Israel He really caused Jerusalem to be destroyed, and the people have been scattered ever since all over the world. They have shown themselves to be unworthy of eternal life.

Is God then going to have an empty banquet hall? Will there be no one who will accept His invitation and be present for the glory of His Son? Oh, no! God is going to see that His wedding feast is furnished with guests, and He will find them in the most unlikely places. We read, "Go ye therefore into the highways, and as many as ye shall find, bid to the marriage." We see the gospel going out to the Gentiles. Israel had their opportunity; they had an invitation to the feast, but they refused to accept it. So God says to His servants, "Go out into the hedges and the highways; go out among all classes everywhere. No matter what the condition in which men may be, no matter how unclean, no matter how vile and sinful, bid them to the marriage feast; invite them to come in." And so we read that the servants "went out into the highways, and gathered together all as many as they found, both bad and good: and the wedding was furnished with guests." It is a graphic picture of what has gone on for the last nineteen hundred years. God's servants have been going from city to city, from land to land, and out into the uttermost parts of the earth. They have been going everywhere inviting poor lost men to come to the marriage feast that God has prepared for His Son. Many have accepted the invitation. But oh, how many there are among the Gentiles who have rejected Christ and refused to come! Are you one of those? You may have been born in a Christian home and heard the message all your life. Perhaps the first name you learned to pronounce, after learning to say "father" and "mother," was the name of Jesus; and yet you are still unsaved, still in sin and without Christ. Oh, the unspeakable danger in which you stand, for it is written in the Word of God, "He, that being often reproved hardeneth his neck, shall suddenly be destroyed, and that without remedy" (Proverbs 29:1)! Now God is waiting in grace to save you. The invitation is extended. Will you come? Will you take Christ for yourself? Tomorrow the door may be closed.

Some people profess to accept the gospel invitation and yet never really trust Christ as their own Savior. We read, "And when the king came in to see the guests, he saw there a man which had not on a wedding garment." According to eastern custom, when a great personage made a marriage feast for someone in his family, he himself provided suitable garments to be worn by the guests when they sat down to the banquet. Everyone had an opportunity to wear a wedding garment. So today God provides a robe of righteousness that all are obligated to accept and wear. You may say, "I am not fit for Him and for Heaven; I am not fit to be numbered among the redeemed." My dear friend, it is because you are not fit; it is because you are a sinner that you are invited to come, and it is He who makes you fit. Will you trust Christ as your Savior? "All the fitness He requireth is to feel your need of Him." Lack of fitness is therefore no excuse. When sinners come in repentance, trusting in Christ, then He

clothes them with the garment of salvation, with the robe of righteousness. This is the wedding garment that makes one presentable at
the marriage supper.

There was one man at this feast who professed to accept the invitation, but he did not avail himself of the wedding garment. This man
was like many who say today, "I do not think I am so bad. I do not need
a Savior; I am good enough as I am." They are trusting in their own righteousness. We read in Romans 10:3, "For they being ignorant of God's
righteousness, and going about to establish their own righteousness,
have not submitted themselves unto the righteousness of God."

I can visualize this man coming in. The king's servants were
handing out robes to the guests as they entered the door. But when
this particular man came he said, "I do not think I need to bother with
that robe. I just bought a new outfit, and I do not think I need anything
else; I am quite presentable just as I am."

"But the king himself has provided this robe. He wants all to wear
one," the servant replied.

The man insisted, "Oh, I do not think it will make any difference
in my case; the king will be satisfied with me just as I am." And the
servant allowed him to pass in.

The time came when the guests were gathered at the table. The
king came in and looked over the guests. He saw the man without a
wedding garment, and asked, "Friend, how camest thou in hither not
having a wedding garment?" The man was speechless. He had
accepted the invitation to the feast, but had refused the wedding
garment so graciously provided.

He is like many who join the church but do not receive Christ as
their personal Savior. This parable shows what will take place some
day. When the King looks over the guests He will inquire, "Friend,
how camest thou in hither not having a wedding garment? How did
you dare take your place among those who profess faith in My Son
when you are not really born again? How did you dare associate
yourself with a Christian company when you were never saved?"
And in that day no one will dare offer a word of excuse. Oh, I imagine
a little while before, this man was quite ready to explain to the king's
servants. He made a good case for himself, but when it came to facing
the king, "he was speechless."

You may be relying upon your good works for your soul's salvation. You may be resting on the fact that you have joined some particular church, perhaps in childhood, and you think that will get you into Heaven. You may be relying on the fact that you were baptized and take the sacrament of the Lord's supper, or the fact that you have reformed your life and are no longer living the way you used to live; but "there is none other name under heaven given among men, whereby we must be saved" (Acts 4:12), except the name of Jesus.

Saul of Tarsus at one time refused the wedding garment. He thought he was fit for God without it, and thought that he did not need Christ; he had a righteousness of his own. But on the Damascus road he found out that all his righteousnesses were as filthy rags. He caught sight of Christ in glory sitting at God's right hand in Heaven, and he exclaimed:

> What things were gain to me, those I counted loss for Christ. Yea doubtless, and I count all things but loss for the excellency of the knowledge of Christ Jesus my Lord: for whom I have suffered the loss of all things, and do count them but dung, that I may win Christ, And be found in him, not having mine own righteousness, which is of the law, but that which is through the faith of Christ, the righteousness which is of God by faith (Philippians 3:7-9).

That is the wedding garment—the righteousness of God received by faith. This garment is offered to all but is only worn by those who believe in Christ. Are you wearing the wedding garment? If the King came in to see His guests tonight, would He say to you, "Friend, how camest thou in hither not having a wedding garment?" You would have nothing to say; you would be speechless. Oh, would it not be best to take your true place in repentance before God and receive Christ as your Savior? Confess to Him now, "I have not been born again; I am still in my sins with all my religious profession. I am a lost sinner needing a Savior." If you will make this confession and turn to Him, He is ready to save you.

"Many are called, but few are chosen." Do you say, "I may not be among the chosen"? You never will be unless you heed the call. The invitation is the call. How many are chosen? Those who respond to the call, those who accept the gift of righteousness, those who trust Christ. Millions are called, but thousands are chosen because the great majority refuse to take God at His Word.

Will you take Christ as your Savior now? You are called; will you be among the chosen? Will you yield your heart to Him? He waits for your answer. If you refuse, you have only the misery and wretchedness of the outer darkness to look forward to. This means banishment from the King's presence in eternal woe.

That this parable made no impression on the sin-hardened hearts of many of our Lord's hearers is evident from what followed immediately.

Lesson on Paying Taxes *(Matthew 22:15-22)*

As we read these verses we marvel at the manner in which the Lord exposed the hypocrisy and deceitfulness of the leaders in Judea. They were very punctilious about the niceties of will-worship, but knew nothing of divine love welling up in their souls. He who is truth incarnate was in their midst. Yet they sought only to make Him appear to be an offender against the law of God and their own customs, in order that He might be discredited before the people, and that their own wickedness in rejecting Him might be excused. But He turned the light upon them, revealing the evil that they tried to cover by a cloak of religiousness.

They sought "how they might entangle him in his talk." There was no reality with these religious leaders. They endeavored to set a trap for Jesus, hoping He would incriminate Himself in some way so they could hold Him up to the scorn of the people or report Him to the governor as a rebel against Roman authority.

The Herodians constituted a pro-Roman party in Jewry, who were venal and corrupt and thoroughly worldly-minded. These joined with the professedly pious Pharisees, and came tempting Jesus. "Master, we know that thou art true." It was a subtle effort to flatter the Lord Jesus and to inveigle Him into saying something that could be used against Him.

"Is it lawful to give tribute...or not?" This was a vexatious question in Judea. The Pharisees generally answered in the negative, the Herodians in the positive, though both obeyed the law.

"Jesus perceived their wickedness." He "knew what was in man" (John 2:25; 16:30), and so discerned at once the hypocrisy of these crafty questioners.

"Shew me the tribute money." Jewish Palestinian coins were not used for paying taxes, but special Roman currency, which was of far greater value. These coins bore the emperor's likeness and a Latin inscription of his name and rank.

"Render therefore unto Caesar the things which are Caesar's; and unto God the things that are God's." With these words Jesus answered their question by showing that the people of God are responsible to Him in spiritual things, but must be obedient to the powers that be in civil and national matters.

"They marvelled, and left him, and went their way." They perceived the rightfulness and the wisdom of His reply, but they evinced no desire to become His disciples. Willfully they turned away from Him to follow their own devices.

To stress the first part of the words of Jesus, "Render...unto Caesar the things which are Caesar's," while forgetting the last part, "unto God the things that are God's," is to miss altogether the truth He was insisting upon. Are we as much concerned about loyalty to God as we are about loyalty to the country to which we belong and the government under which we live?

Lesson on the Resurrection (Matthew 22:23-33)

It was the materialistic Sadducees who attempted to put Jesus in opposition to the law of Moses, and to entangle Him in a discussion as to the possibility of the physical resurrection of the dead. It is questionable whether such an incident as the Sadducees described ever actually occurred. The whole story may have been an imaginary one, designed to cast ridicule on the doctrine of the resurrection. According to the Sadducees one woman had been the wife in turn of seven brothers, each one taking her after the brother next older than he had died. Finally, the woman was said to have died, after she had outlived them all. The question raised was, Of whom would she be the wife in the resurrection? Doubtless this seemed an unanswerable question to these cunning deniers of the reality of life after death and a final resurrection. It was designed to show the absurdity of the doctrine of the resurrection that the Pharisees taught and Jesus proclaimed to be true.

But the Lord met them in such a way as to silence their objections, using the only part of the Scriptures that they recognized as inspired: the Torah, or the five books of Moses. He declared their question was based on ignorance of the sacred writings and the power of the omnipotent Creator. Then He cited Jehovah's words to Moses when He revealed Himself at the bush that burned with fire but was not consumed. There God had said, "I am the God of thy father, the God of Abraham, the God of Isaac, and the God of Jacob" (Exodus 3:6). He did not say, "I *was* the God of these patriarchs while they lived on earth." He was their God at the very time He spoke to Moses, centuries later. He is not the God of the dead (that is, of men completely obliterated by death) but of the living, for all (even though dead as far as their bodies are concerned) live unto Him. And this necessarily involves a future resurrection, for God had made promises to Abraham, Isaac, and Jacob that were never fulfilled during their lives on earth, but will be fulfilled when they rise again from the dead.

For this appeal to the Torah, the Sadducees had no answer, and the listening multitude were astonished at the manner in which these supposedly astute theologians had been silenced.

Lesson on the Greatest Commandment *(Matthew 22:34-40)*

It was now the Pharisees' turn to interrogate Jesus. The question put by their chief spokesman was really antagonistic in character. It was designed to draw out the Lord in order to see whether His teaching coincided with the law of Moses, or was in opposition to it.

Jesus had silenced the Sadducees by teaching the resurrection of the dead, a doctrine which they denied but the Pharisees believed. Now a Pharisee, evidently an expert in the law of Moses, sought to confuse and bewilder Jesus by a question that many of the Jewish

authorities had debated for centuries. His question concerned the
relative importance of each of the ten commandments.

"Thou shalt love the Lord thy God." Jesus replied by quoting from
Deuteronomy 6:5. If God is loved supremely no one will violate
anything He has commanded. This covers particularly the first table of
the law, which sets forth man's duty to God. To violate this law of love
was therefore, in the legal dispensation, the greatest of all sins.

"Thou shalt love thy neighbour as thyself." This was a quotation
from Leviticus 19:18, and covers all of the second table, for "love
worketh no ill to his neighbour" (Romans 13:10). He who loves
mankind in this way will not violate any of the laws that have to do
with the rights of others (Romans 13:8-9).

Where love reigns all else will be as it should be, for no one who
truly loves God and his neighbor will intentionally wrong either
(Matthew 7:12). All the law and the prophets hang therefore on these
two commandments cited by Jesus, for every sin that we might
possibly commit is either a wrong done to God Himself or to our
fellowmen. The salvation provided for us is first of all an atonement,
or propitiation, to meet all our sins, and then a regeneration to enable
us to love God and our neighbor so as to cease from sin.

When the heart is right with God, and He is loved supremely, man
too will be loved unselfishly, and so the whole life will be ordered in
obedience to the divine Word. Love delights to serve the one loved,
and thus it preserves one from committing acts that would grieve
God or injure his neighbor. But no natural man has ever thus fulfilled
the law. The selfishness that is inherent in our very natures renders
this impossible. When renewed by divine grace, the love of God is
shed abroad in the heart by the Holy Spirit (Romans 5:5). Our Lord's
teaching was designed to convict of sin and to reveal the need of
regeneration. Man has become alienated from God through the fall.
When born again by the Word and the Holy Spirit, he receives eternal life. It is the very nature of this new life to love, because it is
divine (2 Peter 1:4). Therefore love becomes the controlling principle of the life of the man in Christ. The righteousness of the law
comes to fulfillment in the one who walks not after the flesh but after
the Spirit (Romans 8:4). The Christian finds it as easy to love God and
his neighbor as it was easy to live in selfishness and ill will toward

others before regeneration. A new power dominates him. This is the positive evidence of the new birth (1 John 3:14; 5:1-2).

Lesson on Jesus' Identity (Matthew 22:41-46)

Having thus answered all the questions put to Him, Jesus turned the tables upon His adversaries by asking them: "What think ye of Christ? whose son is he?" After nearly twenty centuries since Jesus asked these questions they are as pertinent as ever, and still demand honest answers from every man to whom the message of the gospel comes. For that gospel concerns Him who is both Son of God and Son of David (Romans 1:1-4). According to the Scriptures the Christ—that is, the Messiah, Israel's promised King—is more than man. His "goings forth have been from of old, from everlasting," declared Micah when he foretold the place where Christ was to be born (Micah 5:2). According to Psalm 2 Jehovah owned Him as His Son. Many other Scriptures attest the same thing—Scriptures that were well known to these Pharisees. Ignoring the passages that indicated His divine paternity however, they answered, "The son of David."

This was true, but it was not all the truth. So Jesus directed their attention to Psalm 110 where David spoke of Messiah as his Lord, saying, "The LORD said unto my Lord, Sit thou at my right hand, until I make thine enemies thy footstool." It is well known that *LORD* in small capitals in our English New Testament stands for "Jehovah." The second word translated *Lord* means "Master." So David, looking forward in the Spirit to the exaltation of his Son sees Him seated on Jehovah's right hand, and owns Him as his Lord. How could this be explained? The Pharisees had no answer, nor did anyone after this dare ask Jesus any more questions.

It is a solemn thing to be so determined to take one's own way that the heart refuses to bow even to the plainest words of Holy Scripture.

CHAPTER TWENTY-THREE
THE KING'S INDICTMENTS

Warning against Seeking Earthly Glory (Matthew 23:1-12)

The Lord Jesus came not to condemn the world but to save all who would believe in Him. However, He expressed Himself in terms of great severity against those who professed to be the guardians of the Scriptures, but lived hypocritically and opposed the truth that He proclaimed, thereby misleading their unwary followers. The term "Moses' seat" indicates the place that the Pharisees and the scribes occupied as the recognized teachers of the law given by Moses. When they read and explained its precepts their hearers were responsible to obey, not because of any inherent authority vested in these teachers, but because of the truth they taught. But He drew a marked distinction between their words and their ways. They expounded and preached to others what they did not attempt to practice themselves. It is a terrible thing for those who occupy the place of preachers or teachers of the Word when they simply traffic in truth that has never affected their own lives.

These leaders in Israel formed a kind of clerical caste and were most outspoken in denouncing the sins and frailties of the people in general. But they themselves were simply complacent as they gave punctilious attention to the outward signs of religion. They knew nothing of genuine piety and holiness of heart and life.

They were not concerned about the approval of the God they professed to honor, but were constantly looking for men's applause.

It is always a snare when one feels he has a certain reputation of godliness to maintain before his fellows. It is so easy to succumb to the temptation of trying to appear more devoted than one really is. The only right thing is to live before God and to be utterly indifferent to men's praise or blame.

The Pharisees sought to attract attention to their religiousness even by their garb. Wearing the broad phylacteries that seemed to indicate greater reverence for the Scriptures than others had, and with the fringes on their garments conspicuously enlarged, they delighted in the respect accorded them. They were given the seats of honor at the appointed feasts and in the services of the synagogue. In public places generally they were greeted with their highly prized titles of "Rabbi, Rabbi." Who can fail to see in all this a picture of what is very common today in many ecclesiastical circles?

Against all this outward show of piety Jesus solemnly warned His disciples, "Be not ye called Rabbi." They were not to seek honorable recognition from their fellows but were to realize that Christ was their teacher, or Master, and they were but brothers—all of one great family. As born from above they were to call no man "father" on earth, for God alone was their Father. Is it not strange that this definite command is so flagrantly disregarded by those who call their priests "Father"?

Because of the readiness with which His disciples were inclined to seek honor one over another, Jesus repeated the admonition, "Neither be ye called masters: for one is your Master, even Christ." The word really means "leader," but was generally understood as teacher or master.

Certainly Jesus did not mean that His followers were to despise the gifts He gives—among which are teachers. His gifts are given for edification and are to be appreciated and valued by the saints. But we are not to admire people because of worldly advantage.

Those entrusted with a special ministry should not be self-seeking, but serve in love, following Christ's own example. For he who exalts himself will be abased in due time, even as he who humbles himself will be exalted by the Lord, who values all service that is done with a single eye to His glory.

Woes against the Religious Leaders   (Matthew 23:13-33)

The Lord pronounced judgment on the religious leaders whose spirit and behavior were so opposed to their profession. The first woe (verse 13) was a judgment pronounced against the scribes and Pharisees because of their lack of interest and opposition to the word of the kingdom. They endeavored to hinder others who might become concerned. It is a very serious thing to stand in the way of anyone who might otherwise be prepared to enter into the kingdom of Heaven.

The second woe (verse 14) was against those who used a profession and outward appearance of piety as a cloak. Solomon told us that the prayer of the wicked is an abomination to the Lord (Proverbs 28:9). How much more when such prayer is used to build up a reputation for godliness for one who is actually living in hypocrisy.

The third woe (verse 15) was against hypocritical leaders who proselytized. It is characteristic of sectarians generally that they are far more concerned about obtaining adherents to their special beliefs than winning lost souls for Christ. The new adherents become ardent advocates of the system with which they now identify themselves. As a rule, those thus perverted trust in their new association for ultimate salvation, so entering into a worse state than before they were proselytized. It is harder to reach and awaken the adherent of a false cult than to bring a godless worldling to see his lost condition and his need of salvation.

The fourth woe (verse 16) was against those who used vain and profane oaths. When anyone lays greater stress on secondary things than on matters of major importance, he gives striking evidence of his illogical reasoning. These blind guides, as Jesus called them, put more emphasis on the gold with which the temple building was enriched and adorned than on the sanctuary itself. To take an oath on the gold of the temple meant more to them than to swear by the sacred building which God had inhabited.

In the same spirit they ranked the offering above the altar in holiness; although it was the altar that sanctified the gifts placed on it. That altar typified Christ, and the gifts and offerings represented various aspects of His work. But He had to be who He was—the eternal Son of God become flesh—in order to do what He did. To swear by the altar was therefore to swear by all that was placed on it. To swear by the temple was to swear by Him who dwelt therein, even as to swear by Heaven (a most frequent thing) is to take an oath by the throne of God and by Him who sits on it. All such oaths were forbidden very definitely by the Lord on a former occasion (Matthew 5:33-37).

The fifth woe (verse 23) was pronounced on those who were inclined to overemphasize trifling details of the law while utterly ignoring the weightier matters with which it dealt. To tithe even the cheapest of herbs was quite right in itself. But to lay special stress on this tithe and advertise it as though indicating remarkable scrupulosity, while neglecting matters of far greater importance, indicated a conscience that was unexercised and a spirit insubject to God. He would have those who profess obedience to His law careful to exercise discernment and mercy and faith. The person who practices these greater virtues will not neglect things of less weight and importance.

The sixth woe (verse 25) was against those who set a great value on ceremonial cleansing, while overlooking the importance of a clean heart and a pure life. They were likened to a housekeeper who was very careful to have her cups and other vessels clean outwardly, while inside they were filthy. God desires truth in the inward parts. Where the heart is purified by faith, the outward behavior will be in accordance with that faith.

The seventh woe (verse 27) is somewhat similar, but was an even stronger condemnation of those who tolerated hidden corruption while pretending to godliness and devotion. These hypocrites were like beautifully adorned and whitened tombs that appear pleasant and often majestic in the sight of men, but are full of decaying bodies and of all uncleanness. Such are they who appear to be righteous before men but within are full of dissimulation and lawlessness.

The last woe (verse 29), making a complete octave of denunciation of hypocrisy, was pronounced against those who honored the memory of the former prophets while refusing to obey their words. How characteristic was the glaring error of these pretenders. The Pharisees honored the memory of Isaiah, whom their fathers sawed asunder;

Jeremiah, who was imprisoned in a filthy dungeon by the religious leaders of his times; and Zechariah, who was slain between the porch and the altar by zealous opponents. In the same way the descendants of those who vilified Martin Luther in his day and generation now vie with one another in lauding his genius and intrepidity. And the children of those who detested the stand taken by Abraham Lincoln are now often loudest in his praise. Yet there was no evidence that the scribes and Pharisees accepted and acted upon the admonitions of those prophets whose sepulchers they garnished. They showed by their attitude toward the King in their midst that they were of the same spirit as their ungodly fathers.

While boasting that if they had been alive in the days of old their response would have been different, their present behavior proved the opposite. It was for them to fill up the measure of their fathers in the final rejection of the Lord of glory.

Deserved judgment therefore awaited them. Their words and their behavior proved them to be a generation of vipers, the seed of the serpent—that old serpent which is the devil and Satan. How then could they escape participation in his judgment?

Doom of the Unbelieving Generation (Matthew 23:34-39)

Messenger after messenger had been sent by God to Israel, but they had spurned and rejected them all. They would do the same to those who rebuked their sins and hypocrisy. Morally they were no different from those who had shed the blood of all the righteous from Abel to the last of the prophets. Their hearts remained unchanged and their consciences seared; therefore, the ire of God must be vented on them.

To be consistent with His holy character God could not do otherwise than to deal with them in judgment because of their wickedness. Nevertheless the heart of the Lord grieved over them and longed even yet for their deliverance.

Pathetic indeed is the lament (verse 37) with which He concluded this most solemn discourse. Jerusalem, the city of the great King, knew not the time of her visitation. He who would have saved and brought in the promised kingdom blessings, was in their midst and they knew Him not. Had they only turned to Him in repentance He would have sheltered them from judgment as a hen protects her chickens from the hawk seeking to destroy them. But they would not receive Him. They were responsible, therefore, for their own condemnation.

Because they rejected Him, He rejected them nationally for the present time. They would not see Him henceforth until they were ready to own Him as their King and cry (in the words of Psalm 118 with which "the poor of the flock" had greeted Him as He rode into the city a few days before), "Blessed is he that cometh in the name of the Lord."

Before that day this whole dispensation of grace was to come in— the period of the revelation of the mystery of the church as the one body of Christ. At present God is gathering out of all nations a people to the name of His Son; not till that work is completed will Israel as a nation look on Him whom they pierced and acclaim Him as their Redeemer and King.

CHAPTER TWENTY-FOUR
THE KING REVEALS THE FUTURE
PART ONE

Characteristics of the Present Age (Matthew 24:1-8)

Matthew 24 and 25 are very closely linked together. They give us what Sir Robert Anderson has called the second sermon on the mount. All that we have in these two chapters was uttered by our Lord on the mount of Olives in answer to the questions of His disciples, "When shall these things be? and what shall be the sign of thy coming, and of the end of the world [or age]?" (24:3) His answers deserve a much more careful consideration than we can give them here. In Matthew 24 He shows the conditions that will prevail in the world during the time of His rejection. The prophet Daniel called this period "the time of the end," the great tribulation immediately preceding our Lord's return as Son of man to set up the kingdom of Heaven on this earth in power and glory.

After His most solemn denunciation of the hypocritical scribes and Pharisees and His expression of grief over the blindness and insubjection of the people of Jerusalem in Matthew 23, the Lord left the temple courts where He had been preaching and teaching. With His disciples, Jesus walked across the brook Kedron to the mount of Olives. Before they left the city the disciples attempted to arouse His admiration for the beautiful buildings on the temple site. Jesus' words (Matthew 24:2) must have seemed a prophecy that was unlikely to be fulfilled. In the eyes of His followers those buildings looked substantial enough to stand for many centuries. Yet His words were to be proved true after a probationary period of forty years.

Evidently the disciples linked the prediction of Jesus to what He had said on former occasions concerning His second coming. Therefore after they had reached the mount that overlooked the fair but doomed city, they put three questions to Him. Note the questions in order:

1. "When shall these things be?" That is, when will Jerusalem be destroyed? The answer to this is given more fully in Luke's report of Jesus' discourse (Luke 21:20-24).

2. "What shall be the sign of thy coming?" Both Matthew 24 and Mark 13 give the answer to this.

3. "What shall be the sign of...the end [consummation, or full end] of the world?" They were not asking about the end of the world as such, but about the end of the age. This is answered here and also in Mark 13. Each evangelist wrote as guided by the Holy Spirit.

The conditions depicted in Matthew 24:4-8 have marked all the centuries since the Lord returned to Heaven. They do not in themselves tell us of the nearness of His return, but they show us how badly this poor world needs a competent ruler and how all creation groans as it waits for His advent.

"Take heed that no man deceive you." Satan works by imitation. He seeks to ensnare by counterfeiting everything that is of God. Hence the necessity to be on guard constantly against his deceptions. We need to test everything by the Holy Scriptures.

"Many shall come in my name, saying, I am Christ." The number of impostors or antichrists have been legion. Often such men, and occasionally women, have given every evidence of paranoia; but many have been willful deceivers. No one would ever have been led astray by such pretenders to messiahship if they had remembered that Christ is not coming again to earth as He came before through the gate of birth. He will come as the Lord from Heaven accompanied by the whole celestial train.

"The end is not yet." Ever since He ascended to Heaven wars and rumors of wars have been constant reminders of man's folly in rejecting the Prince of peace; but these are not evidences of the closing up of the age. It is a mistake to look on the conflicts of nations as being in themselves signs that the second advent is close at hand.

Verse 7 depicts a series of great wars in which many nations and kingdoms will be engaged. Such conflicts have been frequent during the past nineteen hundred years and have increased in intensity and frightfulness during the last century; the world wars of 1914-18 and 1939-45 were the worst mankind has ever known. Famines and pestilences invariably succeed widespread warfare. Matthew adds earthquakes in many places to these plagues, which would seem to imply a great increase in natural convulsions as the end draws nigh.

"All these are the beginning of sorrows." These events are to be followed by far worse and more startling conditions before the Son of man appears in person to bring in the kingdom which was rejected when He was here the first time.

The secret of the rapture of the church prior to the endtime is not introduced here in this great prophetic discourse. That was still a hidden mystery when Jesus spoke these words. There is no time set for it, nor are there any signs indicated. The signs here all have to do with His revelation from Heaven as the King who is to return to take His great power and reign. The coming of the Son of man refers always to this event, never to the rapture.

Signs of the Last Days (Matthew 24:9-14)

The conditions depicted in verses 9-14 fit perfectly with the first half of the unfulfilled seventieth week of Daniel; and therefore it is quite possible that the rapture should be fitted in between Matthew 24:8-9. On the other hand, similar conditions have taken place again and again during the so-called Christian centuries, but they will be accentuated in the time of the end.*

"Ye shall be hated of all nations for my name's sake." The martyrdom of the saints, first under pagan rule, then under papal Rome, and later under various other evil systems, is not to be ignored when considering this prophecy. Martyrdom will not cease when the church of God is caught away. Then the Lord will call out a new testimony when He gives Israel another chance. Many of His witnesses in those dark days will be called on to lay down their lives

---

*The perplexed reader might find help in the author's *Lectures on Daniel the Prophet* and *The Great Parenthesis*. In these the prophecy of the seventy weeks is fully explained.

during the reign of the imperial atheistic beast-power of the last days and his satellite, the personal antichrist. So these predictions will have a double fulfillment—during the present age of grace, and in the coming period of judgment.

Then there will be great apostasy when many will be stumbled, and faithful servants of God will be betrayed by their closest relatives. This too has had a partial fulfillment during this dispensation. History repeats itself, both in the professing church and in the world.

The closer we come to the end the more active Satan will be, knowing his time is short. So "many false prophets shall rise, and shall deceive many."

Because of abounding iniquity those professing allegiance to Christ will be grievously tested; and where love was only superficial it will become cold, and so apostasy will prevail.

The test of reality in any age is endurance. So it is now, and so it will be in the day of grief and sorrow that lies ahead of Christendom. "He that shall endure unto the end, the same shall be saved." In order to fit these solemn words into the truth revealed elsewhere of the believer's eternal security, it is not necessary to say that they apply solely to the tribulation period. It is true always that only those who endure will be finally saved. But when one has been born of God and so received eternal life, he will endure. "Whatsoever is born of God overcometh the world: and this is the victory that overcometh the world, even our faith" (1 John 5:4). He who makes a profession of faith in Christ and then in the hour of testing repudiates it and goes back like a dog to his vomit, or a sow that was washed to her wallowing in the mire (2 Peter 2:20-22) gives evidence that he was never born of the Word and Spirit of God. Had such an one been a sheep belonging to the Good Shepherd he would never have been attracted to the hog wallow.

The Great Tribulation (Matthew 24:15-28)

The great tribulation in its full sense will begin in the midst of the seventieth week (the last seven years) of Daniel's great time-prophecy. It will be ushered in by the setting up of the abomination that maketh desolate (Daniel 12:11). In Matthew 24:15-28 we have a graphic portrayal of the outstanding events of the time of trouble, "such as never was since there was a nation even to that same time" (Daniel 12:1).

The abomination of desolation of old (Daniel 11:31) was an image set up by Antiochus Epiphanes, king of Syria, in the temple at Jerusalem, after he had defiled the sanctuary by offering a sow on the altar and sprinkling its blood in the holy places. The abomination of desolation in the future will evidently be some outward acknowledgment of the apostate power and the antichrist. Forewarned by this prophecy, saints in those days will recognize this sign of coming distress and will flee from Jerusalem and from Palestine to "the wilderness of the people" (Ezekiel 20:35), where they will be hidden from the wrath of the beast and his followers "until the indignation be overpast" (Isaiah 26:20). These saints will be "the brethren" of the Lord and will be living on the earth when the Son of man will come in His glory. Christ speaks of these people in Matthew 25:31-46, when He pictures the judgment of the nations.

These faithful Jews, the remnant so often mentioned in the prophets, will flee in haste, not waiting to take their goods and chattels with them, lest the fury of the antichrist burst upon them. They are exhorted to pray that their flight be not in the winter nor on the sabbath day. This warning, in itself, indicates a different condition of things from that prevailing in this present age. While this remnant will be waiting for the manifestation of Messiah, they will be on Jewish ground, under law, not yet having entered into the liberty of grace.

"Then shall be great tribulation"—such distress as had not been known from the world's beginning unto that time. So terrible will be the conditions that unless God in mercy shortens the days no flesh would be saved. But for the sake of the elect—not the elect of the church but of Israel—He will shorten the days. They are numbered as actually 1260 days in the book of Revelation. This would be 3½ years, made up of 30-day months, and so considerably shorter than the full time if the years were counted as having 365 days each.

In the time of trouble all who have turned to God will be looking for the Son of man to return and give deliverance. Satan will attempt to deceive them by offering false christs, and above all, presenting the personal antichrist as the expected one. But those who know God and rely on His Word—"the very elect"—will be prepared to refuse all such deceptions.

If told that Messiah has come already and is manifesting Himself in the desert, they are not to seek Him there. If told He is hidden in some secret place, they are not to believe it. For His coming will be in visible glory when He shines forth from Heaven as lightning flaming across the sky.

As the great tribulation moves on to its culmination, apostate Judaism, centering in Jerusalem, will be as a putrid carcass against which the eagles (or vultures) will be gathered together. This is a vivid picture of the gathering of the armies of "all nations against Jerusalem to battle," as foretold in Zechariah 14 and other Scriptures.

The Coming of the Son of Man (Matthew 24:29-31)

The second advent will take place at the very time when it will seem as though Satan's triumph is complete. "Immediately after the tribulation of those days…then shall appear the sign of the Son of man in heaven." There are many who hold and teach that the great tribulation is past already: that it referred to the great persecution for over two centuries under pagan Rome, or to the worse persecutions under papal Rome in the years preceding and following the Protestant Reformation. But our Lord tells us definitely here that His second advent is immediately after the close of that time of trouble; so that it is evident that this day of trial is yet in the future. When it comes to its complete fulfillment there will be remarkable manifestations among the heavenly bodies and the Son of man will be seen "coming in the clouds of heaven with power and great glory." The tribes of the earth, or more properly, of the land, will then mourn when they look on Him whom they once rejected, and whom they pierced (Zechariah 12:10-12). They will realize at last that He is the King, the anointed One for whose coming they have waited so long.

Then the great trumpet will be blown (Isaiah 27:13). The angels will gather together the elect from all quarters of the earth, those who in that time of testing will have received the kingdom message and so are prepared to welcome the King at His return. This is not at all the same event as the rapture of 1 Thessalonians 4. There the saints living and dead will be changed and raised from the grave, and caught up to meet the Lord in the air. But when the Son of man descends to the earth His elect will be gathered from the four winds to greet Him as their King and deliverer. Thus at long last the throne of David will be set up again in Jerusalem, and the law will go forth from mount Zion, where Christ Himself will reign in righteousness for a thousand glorious years (Revelation 20).

The Sign of Christ's Coming (Matthew 24:32-35)

In these verses the Lord answers the disciples' question, "What shall be the sign of thy coming?"

The pre-eminent sign that the time for the appearing of the Son of man has drawn near is that of the budding fig tree. The fig tree is the well-known symbol of Israel nationally. For many centuries the scattered Israelites, once claimed by God as His own covenant people, have had no national existence. But today they are returning to Palestine in large numbers and once more indulging in the sense of again being a distinct nation. Thus the fig tree is putting forth its green leaves, and thereby proclaiming the near return of Him who is yet to be acknowledged as their Messiah and King. At present they are going back in unbelief, as the Scriptures indicate they would, for it is after many have returned to the land that the nation will be regenerated. If the new life displayed in the fig tree heralds the approach of the day of Israel's blessing, how near must be the hour of the rapture!

How Matthew 24:33 should speak to the people of God today as well as to the remnant of Israel in days to come! "When you see all these things, you know that he is near, at the very gates" (RSV). His return is certain, for His Word can never fail. Though Heaven and earth should pass away His words will never pass away.

The Time of Christ's Return (Matthew 24: 36-41)

The comparison of the antediluvian world with that which will exist at the Lord's return contradicts the idea indulged in and propagated by many that all mankind is to be converted before that day comes. Such an expectation is but an idle dream without any Scriptural teaching to support it. As it was in the days of Noah so will the coming of the Son of man be. In the days preceding the flood men lived carelessly and self-indulgently. Corruption and violence filled the earth. God's message given through Noah was spurned as an idle tale. The flood came and destroyed them all while they were insensible to their danger. So will it be at the Lord's coming.

Then two will be working in the field, one a believer and the other an unbeliever. The latter will be taken away by judgment; the other will be left to enter the kingdom and enjoy its blessings. It will be likewise with two women grinding corn for the morning meal. This passage is often applied to the separation at the rapture, and it is quite possible so to use it. But in that case we would understand the righteous would be caught away to meet the Lord in the air, and the other left to endure the judgment of the tribulation era.

No one can know beforehand just when the Son of man will return. It will behoove all, therefore, who live in that day of trial to be ever watching lest He come as a thief in the night.

Our Duty to Watch   (Matthew 24:42-51)

Responsibility to live for God and witness for Christ while waiting and watching for His appearing is stressed in the closing verses of Matthew 24. It is a great responsibility to be put in trust with any measure of divine truth. What is given is not for our own information alone but to be passed on to others. "It is required in stewards, that a man be found faithful" (1 Corinthians 4:2). Those to whom the Lord has made known His purpose and counsels are therefore called on to act as good stewards of the manifold grace of God, sharing with the household of faith the spiritual food for their encouragement and edification.

The servant who fulfills his responsibilities along this line will be duly rewarded in the day of manifestation. But if anyone attempts to trifle with the truth, putting far off the coming of the Master, and lives selfishly, displaying a haughty overbearing spirit, he will have to face the Judge at an unexpected hour and will be given his portion with the hypocrites. Such a false servant is of course not a true child of God at all, but he will be judged nevertheless according to the profession he has made. It is a very serious thing to use one's knowledge of the truth of God for selfish enrichment, with no real concern for those to whose needs one is called to minister. All service is to be in view of the coming again of the King when His faithful servants will have their places appointed in the kingdom according to the measure of their devotedness during the day of testimony.

CHAPTER TWENTY-FIVE

THE KING REVEALS THE FUTURE

PART TWO

The Parable of the Ten Virgins (Matthew 25:1-13)

We have in Matthew 25 a continuation of the same discourse as that reported in the previous chapter. There are three parables, each designed to present special aspects of truth in connection with the second coming of Christ.

The first parable, that of the ten virgins, has been the subject of considerable controversy. Confusing and contradictory questions have been raised as to its exact application. It would seem to apply to the entire period during which the professed people of God are waiting for the fulfillment of the promised return of the bridegroom. The parable depicts the responsibilities resting on His people during His absence and the importance of being ready to greet Him when He returns. It is definitely a parable of the kingdom of Heaven in its mystical form, as are all the kingdom parables in the Gospel of Matthew from chapter 13 on. Therefore, it would be a mistake to shift the application solely to the tribulation period and say the virgins represent only the Jewish remnant rather than the church in accountability or responsibility.

It is well to remember that the word virgin means also "maiden." Too much should not be made of the former usage here. The ten virgins do not necessarily represent born again people, but those who by profession are in the place of testimony on earth. The lamps speak of the testimony of these people. Five maidens are wise and five foolish. The wise have the oil of grace to replenish their lamps; the

foolish have lamps but no oil. All professedly go out to meet the
bridegroom, and while he tarries they all slumber and sleep. This
answers perfectly to what took place in Christendom when in the
dark ages the hope of the Lord's return was forgotten. The whole
professing church slept until awakened when the darkness was
deepest by the clarion call: "Behold, the bridegroom cometh; go ye
out to meet him"! Ever since the Reformation this midnight cry has
been sounding but becoming ever clearer as the end nears. With it
there came a great awakening.

The wise unto salvation trimmed their lamps: their testimony
became brighter. But those who were unreal found that they were
without oil to replenish their lamps. The wise could not give them oil
but directed them to the source of supply; and we are told that the
bridegroom came while they went to buy. Those who were ready
went in to the marriage, but the rest were left outside. Later they
knocked for admittance but found they were too late. From within
came the voice of the bridegroom saying, "I know you not." They
were shut out forever.

The admonition that follows is simply, "Watch therefore, for ye
know neither the day nor the hour." The words "wherein the Son of
man cometh" are not found in the best manuscripts. In view here is
not the coming of the Lord as the Son of man to set up His millennial
kingdom, but the return of the Lord as the bridegroom to rapture His
church.

The Parable of the Talents (Matthew 25:14-30)

As we consider this parable we should be careful to distinguish
between reward for service and salvation by grace. All who trust in
the Lord Jesus are saved, and this altogether apart from human merit.
But all who profess to believe in Him are responsible to serve Him,
to use whatever gift or ability or means they have for His glory, and
to further His interests in this world. There are those who profess to
be servants who are not even born of the Spirit. But God holds men
accountable for what they know and profess. It is incumbent on all
who believe His Word to serve wholeheartedly in view of the day
when every one of us will give an account. In that solemn hour no

one will regret having been too much concerned about living for Him, but many will rue the hours spent in selfishness and folly that might have been used for His glory. Many will regret wasting or hiding talents that if properly invested in the light of eternity would have earned Christ's "Well done." He will reward all work that is in accordance with His Word (1 Corinthians 3:13-14).

If we use whatever gifts we have, no matter how small and insignificant they may seem, in dependence on God, we will find our capacity for service increasing constantly. We are told to covet earnestly the best gifts (1 Corinthians 12:31) and to use them in love.

Nothing is gained by quibbling as to the exact dispensational place of this lesson. The principle is the same whether applied to the church now or to the remnant of Israel after the rapture. The important thing is to see that we use aright what we have received of the Lord.

"A man travelling into a far country." Note that the italicized words in the KJV ("the kingdom of heaven is") should be eliminated. This parable has a very broad application. It refers to all of Christ's servants during His absence from earth. He has "delivered unto them his goods." They are to act for Him as His representatives in the world until He returns.

"Every man according to his several ability." All have talents that we are responsible to use to further the work of the Lord in this world. "It is required in stewards, that a man be found faithful" (1 Corinthians 4:2). Both the five-talent man and the two-talent one were faithful with what they had. Each doubled his lord's money by using wisely and carefully what was entrusted to him. This was all that could be expected of them.

The third servant thought he had so little, as compared with the others, it was not worth endeavoring to do anything with it. He hid it in the earth, thinking that the best he could do would be not to squander it. He was an unworthy servant, without vision or a true sense of responsibility.

"The lord of those servants cometh, and reckoneth with them." On his return he called each one to account for the use of that which had been committed to him. So it will be at the judgment seat of Christ when our Savior returns and every servant will be called to give account for whatever ability has been entrusted to him (2 Corinthians 5:9-10).

He will summon His servants to stand before His judgment seat, not to be condemned for their sins, for that judgment is past (John 5:24), but to render an account of their service. Both for Israel and the church rewards are to be given out at His coming. See Isaiah 62:11; Revelation 22:12.

"I have gained…five talents more." This servant was able to give an account with joy (Hebrews 13:17). He had used his talents faithfully, and he could be certain of his lord's commendation.

"Thou hast been faithful over a few things, I will make thee ruler over many things." Because of his integrity and wisdom during his lord's absence, the servant was rewarded by a special place of trust and confidence when his lord returned. It will be so at Christ's return for those who have been faithful to Him in this time of testing.

"He also that had received two talents came." This man had less to do with, but he was as truly faithful as his fellow servant who had so much more. We are held accountable for what we have, not what we do not have (2 Corinthians 8:12).

"Well done, good and faithful servant." This man receives the same commendation as the other, for he too had doubled what was entrusted to him; so he also is accorded a place of authority in the kingdom.

"I knew thee that thou art an hard man." The one-talent man seeks to put the blame of his failure to produce upon his master. He was like those who blame the Lord because of their limited gifts and shirk their responsibility to use faithfully what they have. They do not realize that to whom little is given, of him shall little be required. On the other hand, he who has received much is the more accountable (Luke 12:48).

"There thou hast that is thine." He had failed utterly in regard to the very purpose for which the talent was entrusted to him, yet he sought to justify his negligence and supposed his lord would be satisfied.

"Thou wicked and slothful servant." It is wicked to be disobedient. It is slothfulness to fail to act energetically. This servant had to suffer because he failed to carry out the purpose of the master, as made known to him. The wicked and slothful servant does not represent a child of God, because he is cast into the outer darkness.

He represents those who, while professing to be Christ's servants, do not really know Him at all and so do not seek to obey His Word. It is otherwise with those who are regenerated. Of them it is written that in that day, "shall every man have praise of God" (1 Corinthians 4:5). This refers, of course, not to every man as such, but to every one of those who appear at the judgment seat of Christ, where only believers will stand. Eternal issues hang on the right use of what we receive from the Lord.

"Then at my coming I should have received mine own with usury." If nothing else, the servant should have put out the money at interest and thus have added something to what he had received. He has nothing for which he can be rewarded. The slothful servant lost everything; even his profession was taken from him. The Lord's words may sound strange, but they are readily understood if we realize that what is in view is profit as a result of using his talent aright. That which he had misused was taken from him and added to the ten talents held by the first servant; while the unprofitable one was cast into outer darkness—an Oriental expression for the disfavor of the master. There he wept over his loss even while he gnashed his teeth in anger because of the judgment inflicted on him.

The Sheep and the Goats (Matthew 25:31-46)

"When the Son of man shall come in his glory." The coming of the Son of man refers always to our Lord's second advent, when He will come back to the earth, in manifested glory, to set up the kingdom which the prophets foretold. This expression is never used in connection with the rapture of His church—a mystery still unrevealed when this discourse was given (1 Corinthians 15:51).

"Before him shall be gathered all nations." This sessional judgment is to be distinguished from the judgment of the great white throne of Revelation 20:11-15, that will not take place on the earth at all, but will be the judgment of the wicked dead. Matthew 25:32 refers to a judgment of living nations prior to the millennium when the Son of man will come in the clouds of Heaven with his holy angels and sit on the throne of His glory. The other judgment—that of the great white throne—is after the millennium (the kingdom age) ends and the heavens and earth of the present order have vanished away. These two judgments are separated by a thousand years. There is a noticeable contrast between the events of Revelation 20:11-15 and Matthew 25:31-46, but both judgments are according to works.

In the premillennial judgment the sheep are those in whom divine life is revealed by their loving care for those who belong to Christ. The goats are bereft of divine life, and represent the unrepentant who did not respond to Christ's messengers. The right hand is the place of acceptance; the left hand, the place of rejection.

"Inherit the kingdom prepared for you from the foundation of the world." The kingdom mentioned here is that spoken of in Daniel and other prophetic Books (Daniel 7:13-14). It is not to be confused with the heavenly inheritance, but will be set up on this earth at our Lord's second advent, when He shall be revealed as King of kings and Lord of lords (1 Timothy 6:15), and His world-kingdom will supersede all human dominions (Daniel 2:44).

"I was an hungred, and ye gave me meat." We are not to suppose that the salvation of these Gentiles will be on the ground of works, but their works will prove the reality of their faith. The same principle comes out in John 5:28-29, where our Lord speaks of the two resurrections—the first for those who have done good, and the second for those who have done evil. In each case, works demonstrate the state of the heart.

"Then shall the righteous answer him, saying, Lord, when saw we thee an hungred...?" Notice these "sheep" are designated "the righteous." This in itself speaks of new birth, for apart from that there are none righteous (Romans 3:10). These disavow any recognition of merit in themselves. They will not even be conscious of having ministered to Christ in any worthy manner. Hence their question as to when such services had been rendered.

"Inasmuch as ye have done it unto one of the least of these my brethren, ye have done it unto me." The Lord Jesus ever recognizes anything done for one of His own as done unto Himself (Matthew 10:42; Mark 9:41), and He also considers any harm done to His own as though it were done against Him (Acts 9:4). In its strictest sense, the "brethren" here will be part of a Jewish remnant in the last days who will be witnesses for God in the dark days of the time of Jacob's trouble, the great tribulation (Daniel 12:1-3; Jeremiah 30:7). This will be after the rapture of the church and prior to the establishment of the kingdom, for that time of trouble ends with the coming of the Son of man, as we have seen in Matthew 24:21,23,29-30. As the King's messengers go through the world there will be some who receive them and believe their message: these are the sheep. Others will refuse the messengers and spurn their testimony: these are the goats.

Christ's Brethren. While there is a sense in which all believers are brethren of Christ, it is evident that here the term is used in a special sense, for there are three classes of people in view: the sheep, the goats, and those called by the Son of man "my brethren." These brethren are those of Israel who are related to Christ, both physically and spiritually, and will be His authoritative witnesses in the coming time of tribulation, when the present church age is ended.

"Depart from me, ye cursed, into everlasting fire, prepared for the devil and his angels." This sentence of eternal doom will be pronounced on those who have shown by their cold, indifferent behavior to His servants that they did not believe the message the servants carried through the world. It would seem that this is the final judgment for those on the left hand, as their sentence coincides with that of the unrighteous dead who stand before the great white throne after the thousand years are finished (Revelation 20:7-15).

"I was an hungred, and ye gave me no meat." The charge against these lost ones is not concerning any flagrant violation of the moral code, but it is their indifferent attitude toward Christ that seals their doom. They showed they had no faith in Him or His message by their unconcern about the sufferings of His representatives. This principle is as true now as it will be in the coming tribulation era.

"Lord, when saw we thee an hungred...and did not minister unto thee?" They spoke as men utterly unconscious of having given offense. But they failed to recognize and honor the Son of man in the persons of His brethren who were sent to call them to repentance in view of His coming kingdom.

"Inasmuch as ye did it not to one of the least of these, ye did it not to me." Failure to have compassion on the poorest and weakest suffering one is failure to minister to Christ Himself, for He makes their cause His own. While in strictest interpretation this has to do with the Jewish remnant mentioned before, it may be applied to all who belong to Him.

"These shall go away into everlasting punishment: but the righteous into life eternal." The issues of this judgment are for eternity—either endless punishment or endless life, which is far more than mere prolonged existence. The wicked will be destroyed and go into their awful destiny at once. The righteous will enter into eternal life in the millennial kingdom and then have their portion with Christ through the unending ages that follow the destruction of the present creation. These are the saints of Daniel 7:18 who will enjoy the blessings of Messiah's glorious reign on the earth.

Two Elections. It will help to get the dispensational setting of this parable clear if we notice that there are two different elections in the New Testament. In Ephesians 1:4 we see the church of this age, consisting of those chosen in Christ before the foundation of the world. In this present passage the saved are given a place in the kingdom "prepared...from the foundation of the world" (Matthew 25:34). This agrees with Revelation 13:8, where we have the same people in view. In Ephesians we have a heavenly election; in Matthew an earthly election. To confuse these in our thinking is to fail to rightly divide the word of truth (2 Timothy 2:15).

In Matthew 22–25 we read of our Lord's controversy with the Pharisees, Sadducees, and other leaders in Israel, and His great prophecies as to His second advent and the judgment of the nations. Throughout this section one thing stands out crystal clear: that which counts with God is not slavish adherence to legalistic forms, rites, or ceremonies, but a life controlled by divine love. This is the paramount evidence of the new birth (1 John 3:14), and in the present dispensation is the specific proof that one is indwelt by the Holy Spirit (Romans 5:5).

It is important that we have a proper understanding of Matthew 22–25, viewing this section in connection with God's dealings with the Jewish nation, and in connection with the Gentiles' attitude toward Israel. On the other hand, we will lose a great deal for our own souls if we limit the implications of this section to this dispensational aspect. We need to remember that moral and spiritual realities are the same in all ages, and the love that is here declared to be the fulfillment of all the law and the prophets will be displayed in the lives of all "who walk not after the flesh, but after the Spirit" (Romans 8:4).

Love is, therefore, in the truest sense, the law or controlling principle of the new life. It is that perfect law of liberty of which the Epistle of James speaks (1:25). Love is so designated because the renewed soul delights to do that which glorifies God and blesses his fellowmen, whether brethren in the faith or belonging to the wicked world (1 John 5:19). The Christian will love the sinner even while he hates his sin. And in this he but manifests the divine nature, for this is God's attitude toward the world.

We show our love for Christ by our concern for His own. This is true in all dispensations, for in every age the new nature that believers receive is the same. Its very first characteristic is love. After the church has been caught up to meet the Lord in the air, a new witness will be raised up on earth. The wise in Israel, enlightened by the Word and sealed as the servants of God, will go to the nations, proclaiming the everlasting gospel. The attitude of the nations toward them will determine their destiny when the King returns and sets up His throne of judgment.

CHAPTER TWENTY-SIX

THE KING FACES THE CROSS

Mary's Devotion (Matthew 26:1-13)

The time was drawing near when Jesus was to die. All events had been foreseen from eternity, and He had come to earth for this express purpose—to give His life a ransom for many. Yet as the hour drew near, His holy soul was deeply moved.

Jesus had completed His last public discourse and the dark shadow of the cross was falling across His spirit as He spoke of the coming feast of the Passover, after which He was to be betrayed and crucified. He alone knew the real meaning of that Passover, for He was the antitypical paschal lamb, whose blood was to provide a shelter from the judgment of God for all who put their trust in Him.

Meanwhile the chief priests, scribes, and elders were meeting clandestinely in the house of the wily Caiaphas, who was the high priest that year through the favor of the Romans. There they plotted how best and with greatest safety to themselves they might get Jesus into their power in order to put Him to death. In their zeal for the Jewish religion, which they felt was threatened by His teaching, they were ready to go to any lengths to get Him out of the way, provided the course of action did not embroil them in a conflict with the people. The leaders considered it best not to attempt to take Him on the approaching feast day as that would most certainly provoke an uprising against them.

It is refreshing indeed to turn from consideration of these nefarious, scheming murderers to the beautiful account of Mary's devotion. We know nothing of Simon the leper. His name is recorded here, with the added word telling of the disease to which he was still subject or, more likely, from which he had been healed by the Lord. There is also the possibility that he had passed away. Although the house was designated as his, John's account would seem to make it the home of the two sisters, Martha and Mary, and their brother Lazarus. If this be true, Simon may have been the father of the three devoted friends of Jesus, none of whom are mentioned by name in Matthew's account.

We know that the woman who brought the alabaster box of ointment and anointed Jesus was Mary (John 12:3). John told us she anointed His feet. Matthew and Mark mentioned the anointing of His head. All three statements were true. The anointing was an act of loving devotion. To Mary, Jesus was the King. As He sat or reclined at the table, her spikenard filled the room with its fragrance (Song of Solomon 1:3,12). To Mary there was nothing too precious for Jesus. She lavished her best upon Him.

The disciples, led in this instance by Judas (John 12:4), objected, complaining of what seemed to them to be a waste. They reasoned that the ointment might have been sold for a great sum and the proceeds given to the poor. Judas could not understand a love like that of Mary's, which would lead her to pour her choicest treasure on the head and feet of Jesus. To him it was a great waste.

Jesus rebuked the complainers and vindicated the woman, declaring she had done a good (literally, a beautiful) work. They would always have the poor to whom they could minister. As the law had said, they would never cease out of the land; but He was about to leave. Mary, who perhaps understood more clearly than any of the rest what was about to take place, had anointed His body for His burial. Her devotion was appreciated so deeply that Jesus added, "Wheresoever this gospel shall be preached in the whole world, there shall also this, that this woman hath done, be told for a memorial of her."

Is Christ Himself so real and precious to us that we are ready to make any sacrifice in order to show our devotion to Him?

The Last Passover (Matthew 26:14-25)

In vivid contrast to Mary's love and faithfulness the treachery of Judas now comes into view. The wretched traitor sought out the cabal of priests with whom he had evidently been familiar. He demanded a definite amount to be paid over to him on condition that he would betray Jesus into their hands. Without seeming to recall the prophecy of Zechariah in regard to the betrayal of the Shepherd of Israel, they covenanted with him for thirty pieces of silver (Zecharaiah 11:12). With all their boasted knowledge of the Scriptures, they were unwittingly fulfilling them in the bargain to which they agreed.

Judas continued to consort with Christ and His apostles as he waited for a convenient opportunity to carry out his part of the agreement—a covenant with Hell. This must at times have caused his guilty conscience to protest sternly against the awful course he had chosen.

Matthew 26:17-25 tells us of the last Passover. The feast of unleavened bread lasted seven days. On the first day the Passover lamb was slain and the prescribed meal took place. During all the seven days no leaven was permitted in the homes of the Israelites. The Jewish day began at sunset; so the Passover was "between the two evenings" (literal translation of Exodus 12:6). Jesus kept the feast after the first sunset of Passover day and died as the true Passover lamb before the next sunset.

"I will keep the passover at thy house with my disciples." It was considered a pious thing by the inhabitants of Jerusalem to reserve a guest chamber where visitors in the city might observe the feast. Jesus availed Himself of this privilege. Tradition says that it was in the home of John Mark that the last Passover was held by the Savior and His disciples. They spread the table with the roasted lamb, the bitter herbs, and unleavened bread, as God had directed. What must all this have meant to Jesus, who knew He was the One prefigured by this typical feast! (1 Corinthians 5:7-8).

"He sat down with the twelve." Judas had not yet gone out into the night. He who had already agreed to betray his Lord sat with the rest.

"One of you shall betray me." He who knew all things was aware of the wicked plot into which Judas had entered, but He gave him space even yet to repent, had his conscience been active.

"Lord, is it I?" We are told that every one of them asked this question: eleven in real sorrow and bewilderment, and one with the guilty knowledge that he had entered deliberately into a covenant to do this wicked thing. How sin does harden the heart and sear the conscience!

"He that dippeth his hand with me in the dish." Up to the last Judas was permitted to enjoy the tenderest expressions of the love of Jesus, even sharing with Him in the dish of bitter herbs.

"It had been good for that man if he had not been born." The vain hope of the universalist is destroyed by these words, for they tell us of one man at least for whom it would have been better not to have lived. This could not be true if Judas were ever to be saved.

Evidently feeling he was the object of the suspicion of the rest, Judas asked again with ill-concealed fear and yet visible effrontery, "Master, is it I?" Jesus answered in the affirmative in such a way that the rest either did not hear or did not understand. According to John's Gospel, it would seem that at this juncture Judas hastily arose and left the room (John 13:30). If this be correct, he was not actually present when the next event took place, but went out after the Passover. This has long been a disputed point, however.

The Lord's Supper (Matthew 25:26-30)

These verses record the institution of the Lord's supper, the sacred ordinance that in the Christian church takes the place of the Passover among the Jews. The two are intimately linked together, for it was after the celebration of the paschal feast that Jesus offered His disciples the bread and the fruit of the vine. He tenderly requested them to partake of the bread and the cup representing His body about to be offered on the cross, and His blood soon to be shed for the remission of sins. Since that solemn night, nearly two millennia have elapsed during which untold millions of grateful believers have participated in this memorial in remembrance of Him who loved them even unto death.

"Take, eat; this is my body." Jesus took one of the unleavened loaves into His hand, blessed and broke it, and gave it to the disciples, bidding them eat it as His body. Clearly there was no transubstantiation there, for He sat before them in His actual body and they ate of the bread. It was as when one shows a portrait and says, "This is my mother." The one represents the other.

"He took the cup." We are not told exactly what was in the cup. We know from verse 29 that it was the "fruit of the vine," but whether fermented wine or the juice of boiled raisins (it was too early for fresh grapes), the record does not say, nor should we quibble about it. It is what is signified that is important.

"This is my blood of the new testament." That precious blood had not yet been shed for the remission of sins, but Jesus was speaking of it as though the work of the cross were accomplished already. The cup did not contain His blood, but that which would call it to mind in after-years.

"When I drink it new with you in my Father's kingdom." Jesus did not participate in that which was to be a memorial of His own death. He looked forward to the time when, as a result of that sacrifice, He would have all His own gathered about Him in the Father's kingdom, to celebrate together the full glorious fruitage of redemption. Then He will see of the travail of His soul and be satisfied (Isaiah 53:11).

"When they had sung an hymn." Tradition says this was Psalm 135, known to the Jews as the "little hallel" celebrating Israel's deliverance from Egypt, or, as others think, Psalms 115–118.

The memorial feast of love, the central ordinance committed to the church, is designed to bring Jesus Himself before the soul. It is an appeal to the affections. He was going away. He did not want to be forgotten by those He loved so tenderly. So He instituted this holy supper that wherever and whenever it was observed, it might vividly recall Him to mind. His was a love that was even stronger than death, which the many waters of judgment could not quench (Song of Solomon 8:6-7). He needs no symbols in order that He may remember us. But our love is very inconstant. We forget so soon. Therefore we need that which may quicken our affections and revive our thoughts of Him. Then, like Mary, we shall bring our alabaster boxes and break them in His presence, pouring the perfume of our worship and adoration on Him till the house is filled with the fragrance that is thus set free. It is fitting that the story of her devotion to Christ should precede that of the supper He instituted.

It is only unconfessed sin that should hinder a Christian from partaking of the holy supper, and the sooner that sin is judged in the light of the cross, the sooner one will be restored to communion. David said, "My meditation of him shall be sweet" (Psalm 104:34). Do we delight to sit at His table and think of His love?

The Romish doctrine of the mass and the real presence of Jesus in the sacrament is the very opposite of the truth. To teach that under the form of bread and wine the very body and blood of Jesus are offered in continual sacrifice for the sins of the living and the dead, is to deny Christ's personal absence because of which we remember Him. This doctrine also impugns the perfection of His one offering on the cross, never to be repeated.

The communion (1 Corinthians 10:16) is not in any sense a sacrifice. It commemorates the one perfect sacrifice offered by our Lord once for all when He gave Himself for us on Calvary. Neither should it be celebrated with any thought of its having saving value or inherent merit. It is the reminder that when we were utterly lost and helpless, Christ died for us to redeem us to God. The sacrifice of praise (Hebrews 13:15) should ever accompany the communion as we contemplate the great cost at which we were saved, and rejoice that He who endured such grief and shame for us is now alive forevermore, never again to have to submit to the pain of death. We call Him to mind as the "author and finisher of our faith; who for the joy that was set before him endured the cross, despising the shame, and is set down at the right hand of the throne of God" (Hebrews 12:2), from whence He shall soon return to claim the purchase of His blood. Till then we keep this feast with worshipful hearts, while we look back to the cross and on to the coming glory (1 Corinthians 11:26).

When we rightly observe the communion, we approach the Lord's table as those redeemed to God by His blood. We come with a desire to call anew to mind His glorious person and His all-prevailing love in giving Himself as a sacrifice on the cross for our sins. It is the blood of Christ that makes us worthy to partake of the Lord's supper. But we need to beware lest we participate unworthily: that is, in a light or careless manner.

Observe how the two comings of the Lord Jesus are linked together by the feast of remembrance. We show His death until He comes.

Jesus' Warning (Matthew 26:31-35)

As they passed slowly along the way from the place where these things had transpired to the mount of Olives where Jesus resorted so often with His disciples, He began to warn them of what was to take place soon, and to impress on them the untrustworthiness of their own hearts. Jesus referred to another of Zechariah's prophecies when He told the disciples that all should be stumbled, or scandalized, because of Him that night. Long ago this prophet, speaking by the Spirit of God, had said: I will "smite the shepherd, and the sheep shall be scattered" (Zechariah 13:7). These words were about to have a literal fulfillment, though at the moment the disciples all felt it could not be that any of them would forsake Him whom they loved so dearly. But no man can ever measure the depths of evil in his own heart. Grace alone can overcome that evil.

Jesus added the reassuring promise that when He rose again, He would go before them into Galilee. There He would keep a sacred tryst with them. However at that moment the promise was meaningless to them.

Peter, not realizing the weakness of his flesh, protested that although all the others should be stumbled, it would not be so with him. But Jesus declared that before cockcrow—that is, before early dawn, he would deny his Master three times. Self-confident Peter insisted this would never be. Even though called to die for Jesus, he would never deny Him. In this they all shared. Alas! How little they knew themselves! Their self-confidence led them to make protestations they found themselves unable to carry out when the hour of trial came. The flesh is prone to declare its own goodness (Proverbs 20:6).

The Garden of Gethsemane (Matthew 26:36-46)

Reaching the mount of Olives they came to the garden on the western slope where Jesus often had prayed and communed with His Father. "A place called Gethsemane." The name means "the oil press." It was a garden of olives, just across the brook Kedron. It was easily reached from the city of Jerusalem.

Gethsemane! What depths of woe, what bitter grief does the word suggest! It seems to express, as nothing else could, the inner meaning of our Lord's words, "I have a baptism to be baptized with; and how am I straitened till it be accomplished!" (Luke 12:50). Jesus had often resorted to Gethsemane with His disciples (John 18:2), and frequently He had enjoyed uninterrupted communion with His Father there. In that garden He was to enter into His soul's agony as He contemplated the reality of being made sin on our behalf, "that we might become the righteousness of God in Him" (2 Corinthians 5:21, RV). As He looked forward to it, He exclaimed, "Now is my soul troubled; and what shall I say? Father, save me from this hour: but for this cause came I unto this hour" (John 12:27).

Psalm 102 has often been designated the Gethsemane Psalm. As we read it, we hear the breathings of our Savior's heart as He entered into a sense of the loneliness of One forsaken of God and despised by the very men whom He came to save. This was the cup from which His holy, human nature shrank. It was unspeakably horrible and appalling that He, the perfect One in whom the Father had ever found His delight (Luke 3:22; 9:35), should be treated as an outcast because of taking the sinner's place. True, He had come from Heaven for that very purpose. He had assumed humanity that He might die in our stead. But as the hour drew near when He was actually to undergo the baptism of divine judgment against sin, He would not have been the holy One He was if He had not shrunk from so terrible an ordeal.

Yet we need to remember that the suffering endured in Gethsemane was not in itself atoning for sin. It was at Golgotha, on the cross of shame, that our sins were laid on Him, and He endured the full penalty that should have been ours if God had not intervened in grace and "sent his Son to be the propitiation for our sins." Gethsemane was anticipatory to Calvary, where He drained to the dregs the cup of wormwood and gall that our iniquities had filled.

Jesus left eight of His disciples near the entrance, while He went deeper into the grove to pray. It is evident that all the disciples did not have an equal sense of love and sympathy.

"He took with him Peter and the two sons of Zebedee." There was a closer tie with these than with the rest, because they seemed to understand and appreciate Him more. He expressed to them the perturbation of spirit under which He was laboring. These three shared the more intimate experiences of Jesus on other occasions (see Matthew 17:1; Luke 8:51). They saw that Jesus was in great sorrow though they could not really understand the cause.

"Tarry ye here, and watch with me." The time came when they too had to be left behind, but they were commanded to watch and pray lest the coming trial be too great for their faith (Luke 22:40).

"My soul is exceeding sorrowful, even unto death." His words must have perplexed them greatly, for they still did not realize what was involved in that of which He had spoken to them earlier—His betrayal, death, and resurrection.

"He went a little farther." They could not follow as He poured out His heart to His Father, saying, "O my Father, if it be possible, let this cup pass from me." His resignation to the Father's will was perfect, but He pleaded that if by any other means salvation might be procured for sinners, it would be revealed.

"What, could ye not watch with me one hour?" Returning to the three, He found them asleep, their very grief for Him having overpowered them. He gently reproved Peter for lack of watchfulness, inasmuch as he had spoken so strongly of his love and loyalty (John 13:37).

"The spirit indeed is willing, but the flesh is weak." Jesus recognized the devotion of His followers, but He also realized the untrustworthiness of the human heart, even in the best of saints; so He bade them "watch and pray" that temptation might not take them unawares. He implored them to be on their guard and to ask help of God lest in the hour of testing they fail to stand. He well knew that in their spirits they desired to be true, but He warned them of their weakness as men still in the body.

"If this cup may not pass...except I drink it, thy will be done." His was a perfect resignation to the Father's will, no matter what sorrow and agony this meant to Him. He had come into the world for this very purpose (Hebrews 10:7; John 4:34). There was no conflict of wills. Jesus acquiesced in whatever pleased the Father. No matter how bitter the cup, He would drink it if salvation for lost sinners could be obtained in no other way.

"He came and found them asleep again." They did not realize what He was going through on their behalf, and so they failed to watch with Him in the hour of His soul's distress. Our Lord was as truly man as He was God, and as man He craved human sympathy and understanding. He looked for some to take pity (Psalm 69:20). His dearest disciples failed Him, thus adding to His grief.

Let us challenge our hearts as to how far we have entered into the fellowship of Christ's suffering (Philipians 3:10). Are we able to watch and pray in this time of His rejection by a godless world? No man will be able to stand in the moment of severe temptation who has been slothful instead of watchful, and indolent instead of prayerful. Would we not be more alert to use the opportunities He gives to draw from Heaven needed grace for testing times if we realized that prayerlessness is positive disobedience to His Word? Prayerlessness is as truly sin against God as cursing or swearing.

"He...found them asleep again." It was a sad commentary on poor, frail, human nature, even at its best, as seen in those who really loved Jesus but could not rise to the seriousness of the occasion.

"Prayed the third time." Again Jesus bowed alone before the Father in perfect submission, though His holy soul shrank from the awful ordeal before Him—an ordeal that our poor hearts are too deadened by sin ever to understand in its fullness.

"Saying the same words." He had condemned vain repetitions in the sense of useless ejaculations (Matthew 6:7). But He had shown importunate prayer to be according to the mind of God (Luke 11:5-10). In this He is an example for us as He repeatedly spread out His concern before the Father.

"Sleep on now, and take your rest." Another translation turns His words into an exclamatory sentence: "Sleeping still, and taking rest!" And this, with the betrayer almost in view! How little they understood the solemnity of that hour of testing! While they were so drowsy that they did not realize their danger, the emissaries of the priests were entering the garden.

"He is at hand that doth betray me." There was no effort to escape. His hour was come, and in perfect calmness Jesus went forth to meet the betrayer and the rabble horde who had come to arrest Him. The agony was over. He was now perfectly composed as He went forth voluntarily, like a lamb to the slaughter, to meet those who were seeking Him in order to destroy Him.

The utter resignation of Jesus to the Father's will shines out in all these closing experiences, but particularly in that of Gethsemane. While the horror of becoming the great sin offering overwhelmed His human soul and spirit, He was perfectly subject to the divine will and had no thought of turning aside. There are depths here that our minds can never fathom, but all is perfection on His part. If He could have contemplated with equanimity all that was involved in the sacrifice of the cross, He would not have been the perfect man that He was. But knowing it all and realizing there was no other way by which He could become the captain of our salvation (Hebrews 2:10), He faced the ordeal unflinchingly in order that God might be glorified and sinful men saved from judgment.

The Meaning of the Cup. The cup represents not simply death or physical sufferings. Jesus did not shrink from these. The fierce indignation of Jehovah against sin filled that cup about to be presented by the Father to His holy Son. The impending wrath caused the bitter agony of soul that so affected His body that bloody sweat was forced through the pores of His skin. Some have intimated that the cup consisted of the fear that Satan might kill Him before He reached the cross, or that He might be driven insane by Satanic power and so be unable to offer Himself voluntarily as a sacrifice for sin. But these unworthy suggestions fail to take into account the fact that Satan could have no power against Christ except as allowed by God, and none could take His life until He laid it down of Himself (John 10:17-18). He had bound already the strong man (Matthew 12:29), and He did not fear him in the garden.

The cup of wrath is mentioned in the Old Testament. It is reserved for the wicked (Psalm 11:6); it is a cup of divine indignation against sin (Psalm 75:8); it is a cup of trembling (Isaiah 51:17, 22); it is the cup of Jehovah's fury (Jeremiah 25:15). All this and more were involved in the cup that our Lord had to drink in order that we might have the cup of salvation (Psalm 116:13).

> Death and the curse were in that cup,
>   O Christ, 'twas full for Thee;
> But Thou hast drained the last dark drop,
>   'Tis empty now for me.

The holiness of Jesus is seen in His shrinking from drinking the cup of judgment, which involved His taking the sinner's place and bearing the weight of our iniquities (Isaiah 53:5-6). Because of His infinite purity He could not contemplate with other than horror all that it would mean to be made sin for us. He became the antitypical sin offering in order that God might receive to Himself in peace all who would avail themselves of the offer of life through His death, and justification through His condemnation. His agony was as much an evidence of the perfection of His humanity as was His utter submission to the will of His Father. Gethsemane made it evident that He was the unblemished, spotless lamb whose blood could avail to cleanse from sin and shield from judgment.

"If it be possible." In Gethsemane was settled once and for all the impossibility of sin being atoned for in any other way than by the infinite sacrifice of the Son of God upon the cross. Had there been any other method that would have satisfied the claims of divine justice, it would have been revealed then, in answer to the impassioned prayer of our blessed Lord. But there was none. No other name is given (Acts 4:12), no other way is known (Acts 13:38-39), whereby guilty sinners can be justified before the throne of God.

Let me repeat: It was not in Gethsemane, but on Calvary, that the sin question was settled and expiation made for iniquity. But the agony in the garden was a fitting prelude to the darkness of the cross. In order to make an adequate propitiation for our sins, it was necessary that the substitute be a man, but more than man; otherwise his sacrifice could not have been of sufficient value to be a ransom for all. He must be a man who had been tested and proved to be absolutely sinless, having never violated God's holy law in thought or word or deed. Christ was a man on whom death and judgment had no claim. But this very sinlessness of Jesus explains the suffering He endured in the contemplation of being made sin on our behalf. There was no conflict of will though. He was prepared to carry out the Father's purpose whatever the awful cost to Himself.

It is noticeable, and an evidence of divine design in Scripture, that while in the three synoptic Gospels our attention is focused on Christ's agony in the garden, there is no mention of this in the Gospel of John. Neither does John mention the transfiguration or the rending of the veil when Jesus died. In the synoptics, emphasis is placed on the humanity of our Lord. In John's Gospel it is His essential deity that is before us; the glory is seen shining out in every act of His life and in every word that He spoke. The design is perfect, for Scripture is given by inspiration of God (2 Timothy 3:16).

Jesus' Arrest (Matthew 26:47-56)

What were the thoughts of Judas as he stealthily led the chief priests, elders, and the rabble with swords and staves (clubs) to the rendezvous where he was certain he would find Jesus in prayer? If deeply perturbed, as he would have been if his conscience were at all active, he gave no outward evidence of it as he brazenly led the multitude to where he saw Jesus standing with the three disciples. He had given them a sign saying, "Whomsoever I shall kiss, that same is he: hold him fast." One feels horror-stricken as he contemplates such infamy; yet every deceitful, natural heart is capable of such an act.

Boldly Judas stepped up to Jesus and exclaiming, "Hail, master," kissed Him repeatedly, as the original has it. Calmly Jesus looked at him and asked, "Friend, wherefore art thou come?" Then He permitted His enemies to lay hold of Him and to arrest Him.

Suddenly, spurred by intense emotion, Peter drew his sword and struck a servant of the high priest and cut off his ear (see John 18:10). Peter was asleep when he should have been alert, watching and praying. Now, when he should have been calm and trustful, he was excited and active. But it was the activity of the flesh. Slashing about with the sword, he cut off the ear of Malchus, one who had very little responsibility as far as the matter of arresting Jesus was concerned. Nothing was really accomplished that would tend to avert the catastrophe Peter evidently dreaded.

Jesus rebuked him for his unwise act, bidding him sheathe his sword. Carnal weapons were not needed to protect or defend the Christ of God. He had only to ask of the Father to have twelve legions of angels sent to deliver Him. But how then would the Scriptures that foretold His death as a substitute for sinful men have been fulfilled?

Turning to the mob surrounding Him, Jesus inquired, "Are ye come out as against a thief with swords and staves?" He reminded them that He might have been found any day in the temple teaching. There was no necessity for this strange midnight foray. But in all these things the Word of God given through the prophets was being fulfilled.

Jesus yielded Himself submissively to the mob. Had He not submitted voluntarily to this indignity, His enemies would have been helpless before Him. But He gave Himself into their hands that the will of God might be carried out. We may see in this submission the expression of His love both to the Father and to those for whom He was about to die.

The disciples became panic-stricken and every one of them fled from the scene. They forgot their promises and left Him alone.

Jesus' Accusers (Matthew 26:57-68)

Those who had arrested Jesus hurried Him to the house of Caiaphas shortly before cockcrowing, corresponding to our three o'clock after midnight. A group of the leaders had been waiting there to pass speedy judgment on Him. This was in defiance or forgetfulness of their own law, which forbade the trial of any person charged with crime between the hours of sunset and sunrise. Christ's teaching had caused many to lose confidence in the authority of the Jewish leaders and they feared He might gain a large following if He was not soon put out of the way.

Peter, who had recovered from his first fright, joined the company, following Jesus at a distance to see what the result might be of all these unlawful proceedings. He entered the corridor of the high priest's palace and sat with the servants in a place where he could see what was transpiring within.

Witnesses were hastily summoned to give testimony against Jesus, but they were all men prepared to perjure themselves in order to curry favor with the leaders in this plot against Jesus. Even so, their testimonies did not agree. Finally two men were brought in who testified that Jesus had said on one occasion, "I am able to destroy the temple of God, and to build it in three days." A half-truth is a whole lie. Jesus had said something similar to this, but they so reported His words as to completely subvert His meaning.

As Isaiah had prophesied, Jesus attempted no defense. Like a lamb led to the slaughter and a sheep before its shearers, He opened not His mouth (Isaiah 53:7). This so annoyed Caiaphas that he exclaimed, "Answerest thou nothing? what is it which these witness against thee?" But Jesus did not deign to reply until the high priest put Him on oath, adjuring Him by the living God that He say whether He was the Christ, the Son of God. Then the Lord solemnly declared: "Thou hast said"—that is, "It is as you have said."

"Hereafter shall ye see the Son of man sitting on the right hand of power, and coming in the clouds of heaven." This was a clear, positive declaration of both His messiahship and His deity as the eternal Son. To Caiaphas it was blasphemy. Forgetting the admonition of the law that forbade a priest to rend his garments (Leviticus 21:10) he tore his robe in two, signifying by this very act, though he did not realize it, that his priesthood was ended. God no longer recognized the priests of the Levitical economy. With a great pretense of reverence for God he charged Jesus with blasphemy and declared no more witnesses were needed. He appealed to the rest of the council saying, "Behold, now ye have heard his blasphemy. What think ye?" And they all replied, "He is guilty of death." In fact, they had already prejudged the case and settled on the verdict.

Then in the most shameless way these men, who should have been guardians of the rights of the poor and defenseless, began to spit in the face of Jesus and to beat and buffet Him with their open hands. Taunting Him, they said, "Prophesy unto us, thou Christ, Who is he that smote thee?" He did not answer, but bore all patiently.

Peter's Denial (Matthew 26: 69-75)

Peter sat in the court of the palace, giving no sign of his interest in the holy sufferer whom the council was contemning. A maidservant who had been eyeing him came boldly up to Peter and charged him with having been in the company of Jesus of Galilee. Taken unawares, he did not have the courage to confess that it was indeed true. On the contrary, he denied the charge before them all, insisting that he knew nothing of what was being said.

Going out into the porch, he was challenged by another maid who exclaimed, "This fellow was also with Jesus of Nazareth." With an oath Peter again denied all knowledge of the man who was enduring such suffering inside the palace. Later a man spoke up and said, "Surely thou also art one of them; for thy speech bewrayeth thee." Peter's Galilean brogue branded him before them all as a man from the north country. Excited and thoroughly frightened, Peter lost all control of himself and began to curse and to swear, again taking an oath that he knew not the man. He did not even call Him by name. To what depths can even a child of God sink when he is out of communion with his Master and is under the domination of the flesh!

Even as the poor backslidden disciple spoke he was startled to hear a cock crow. The words that Jesus had spoken came back to him. Realizing something of his terrible failure, he left the company assembled there and went out into the darkness and wept bitterly. Those were grateful tears, for they told of the work of restoration begun in his soul. "Godly sorrow worketh repentance to salvation not to be repented of" (2 Corinthians 7:10). This was the beginning of true contrition, which was to result in full restoration of soul after Jesus rose from the dead.

There is a difference between apostasy and backsliding. Judas was an apostate. He had never known the reality of the new birth. Though chosen as an apostle, he was a devil (John 6:70-71). For him there was no recovery. But in Peter we see a typical backslider. He was a real child of God, who failed through self-confidence and lack of prayerfulness but was afterwards restored and became a faithful witness for Christ. Apostasy is giving up truth that one formerly professed to believe. Backsliding is spiritual declension from an experience once enjoyed. The difference is immense. To see this distinction clearly will save from much confusion of thought.

CHAPTER TWENTY-SEVEN
THE CONDEMNATION AND DEATH OF THE KING

Judas's Remorse (Matthew 27:1-10)

The Levitical law condemned a blasphemer to death (Leviticus 24:15-16), but the Jews had no authority under the Roman regime to inflict the death penalty on anyone. Therefore they were unable to carry out their desire to execute Jesus unless they took things into their own hands, as they did later on in the case of Stephen who, like his Lord, was charged with blasphemy (Acts 7:54-60).

The chief priests and other leaders were anxious to shift the responsibility for Jesus' death to the Romans, in order that the people who had gladly heard Jesus might not in indignation turn on them. Therefore, having declared Him worthy of death, their next move was to bring Him before Pilate, the procurator of Judea at that time.

As soon as circumstances permitted, Jesus, bound with chains, was brought into Pilate's court. No doubt the governor had known something of Him and possibly thought of Him as a harmless zealot of some Jewish sect. Now he was called upon to pass judgment on Jesus as a seditionist who was endeavoring to arouse the populace to rebel against Rome and accept Him as their King instead of Caesar.

At this juncture Judas the traitor appeared before the chief priests and elders. He was filled with remorse as the full import of the deed he had done began to dawn on him. Many have tried to excuse Judas on the ground that he may have been overanxious to see the kingdom of Messiah established, and that he thought possibly by betraying his

Master to the clique that sought to destroy Him, he would force Him to declare Himself at once as the King of the Jews. But of this there is no hint in Scripture; nothing except that Judas is described as a covetous man, who sold the Lord for thirty pieces of silver.

Now that he began to realize the probable fate awaiting Jesus, he was seized with fear. In his crushing anxiety Judas endeavored too late to undo the fearful wrong of which he had been guilty. The repentance of Judas was not true self-judgment for the sin he had committed. The word used here for *repented* is not the ordinary one, which implies a complete change of mind or attitude. It rather means "to be remorseful," and there may be bitter remorse apart from genuine repentance.

Bringing the thirty pieces of silver back to those from whom he had received them, Judas exclaimed, "I have sinned in that I have betrayed the innocent blood." He knew well the holiness and righteousness of Jesus. Judas had kept company with Him for three or more years, and he realized there had been no flaw in His character, no evil in His behavior.

Coldly the priests replied, "What is that to us? See thou to that." These calloused hypocrites had their prey in their power, as they believed, and they were unconcerned as to the truth or untruth of the charges brought against Him. They were determined upon His condemnation.

In his horror and despair Judas threw down the money in the temple, and rushing out in an insane frenzy he sought a secluded spot where he committed suicide by hanging himself. Peter supplied details omitted here. He told us that "this man purchased a field with the reward of iniquity; and falling headlong, he burst asunder in the midst, and all his bowels gushed out" (Acts 1:18). Putting the two accounts together we gather that the wretched man, who was probably somewhat corpulent, hung himself, possibly from some tree or beam that broke under his weight, so that his body was so ruptured in falling to the earth that the condition depicted by Peter resulted. It was a sad and terrible end indeed to a life that once promised so much!

The priests were too punctilious to put the blood-money into the temple treasury. After some consultation, they decided to buy with the money a potter's field—that is, a piece of ground from which clay had been extracted for the making of pottery. In this way Judas himself really purchased the field with the reward of iniquity. This wasteland was set apart as a cemetery in which to bury strangers for whose interment no other arrangements could be made. Significantly it was called "the field of blood"—a constant reminder of the nefarious transaction in which the priests and Judas had participated.

There have been questions raised as to the proper understanding of Matthew 27:9. In Zechariah 11:13 we read, in reference to the thirty pieces of silver, "Cast it unto the potter: a goodly price that I was prised at of them. And I took the thirty pieces of silver, and cast them to the potter in the house of the Lord." While this verse is very similar to that which is quoted in Matthew 27:9-10, it is not quite the same: "And they took the thirty pieces of silver, the price of him that was valued, whom they of the children of Israel did value: and gave them for the potter's field, as the Lord appointed me." There is the possibility a scribe may have inadvertently written *Jeremy* or *Jeremiah* in place of *Zechariah* because he was thinking of another manuscript telling of Jeremiah's visit to the potter's house. Later copyists, finding this name in the text, may not have felt free to alter it. On the other hand, it may not be Zechariah's prophecy that is definitely referred to at all, but rather something handed down by tradition that was spoken, not written, by Jeremiah.

J. N. Darby suggested that the book of Zechariah formed part of a scroll that began with the prophecy of Jeremiah, and therefore would bear his name. So this particular passage could be spoken of as an utterance found in "Jeremiah." In any case we may be sure that there is nothing here to invalidate the authority of holy Scripture.

Leaving the sordid story of Judas, we turn our attention back to the prisoner.

Pilate's Court (Matthew 27:11-18)

In response to the governor's question, "Art thou the King of the Jews?" Jesus calmly replied, "Thou sayest." That is, "You have said that which I am." Thus, before Pontius Pilate, Christ witnessed a good confession (1 Timothy 6:13). While He made no answer to the false and vindictive charges brought against Him by His enemies,

He unhesitatingly declared the truth when the procurator addressed Him.

Pilate was astonished at the quiet confidence that the Lord displayed. No accusation perturbed Him. He did not attempt to defend Himself. Assured in his own mind that Jesus was innocent of any crime, and yet knowing the implacable character of His accusers, Pilate sought for some way whereby he might release Jesus, and yet not displease these wily and unscrupulous religious leaders. It was Passover time, and for some years—as a favor to the Jews—it had been customary to release some notable prisoner of their own nation. If they were sincere in charging Jesus with sedition, might they not appreciate the dismissal of the charge and the freedom of the prisoner? Another seditionist was awaiting execution at the time—Barabbas, who had led an insurrection against the government. So Pilate put the two names before the crowd and asked, "Whom will ye that I release unto you? Barabbas, or Jesus which is called Christ?" Both were charged with the same offense. Why then might not Jesus be released and so the people be satisfied?

Pilate's Weakness (Matthew 27:19-26)

While the matter of which prisoner was to be released was being debated excitedly by the accusers of Jesus and the rabble who had gathered about them, a message came to the governor from his wife. Church tradition has made a saint of Claudia Procula, the wife of Pilate. Legend says she was a Jewish proselyte who became a believer in Jesus. But Scripture tells us nothing more than what is recorded here. She sent a message to her bewildered and time-serving husband, bidding him have nothing to do with "that just man," because of whom she had suffered much in a dream.

We are not told of Pilate's reaction to this, except that we find him casting about still for some way whereby he might not have to face the issue before him. If he treated the case of Jesus in a thoroughly legal and judicial manner, the result could only be the acquittal of the prisoner. This would arouse the intense indignation of His accusers, who would then, in all probability, go to any length to destroy the governor by misrepresenting him to caesar as an untrustworthy servant of Rome. They would accuse him of failing to do his duty concerning One who should have been condemned as a seditionist.

He waited for the people to make their choice. Who should be released: Jesus or Barabbas? The answer was not long in coming. Moved by the chief priests and elders, the multitude vociferously gave their voices in favor of Barabbas.

"What shall I do then with Jesus which is called Christ?" Pilate asked weakly. It is a question every man has to ask himself sooner or later wherever this story of Jesus is known.

The throng cried as with one voice, "Let him be crucified." Thus the King of Israel, the anointed of Jehovah, was definitely rejected; and so, for the time, the hopes of the Jews were destined to be obliterated. There could be no kingdom for them when their rightful ruler was spurned and slain.

Recognizing his impotence in dealing with this mob of excited religionists, Pilate called for water and dramatically washed his hands before the multitude, as he exclaimed, "I am innocent of the blood of this just person: see ye to it." Yet he was there as the representative of the imperial throne, and he was responsible to condemn the guilty and to acquit the innocent. How little he realized that for all time to come his name was destined to be linked with that of the patient sufferer whom he weakly surrendered to His prejudiced accusers. Untold millions yet unborn were to intone in all the centuries to come, "I believe in God...and in His Son Jesus Christ...crucified under Pontius Pilate." No water could ever wash away the stain of the blood of the Son of God!

In recklessness the Jews invoked a fearful malediction on themselves as they cried, "His blood be on us, and on our children." The awful anguish and suffering the unhappy nation has endured throughout the past two thousand years can be traced back to the choice made that day when they preferred a murderer to the One who came in grace to redeem them. For every individual among them, as for all others who will turn to God in repentance, the curse has been turned aside because of the Savior's intercession, "Father, forgive them; for they know not what they do" (Luke 23:34).

Yielding to their demands Pilate delivered Jesus to their will, and He was turned over to the soldiers, who heaped added indignities upon Him. In accordance with the horrible custom of the times Pilate gave the order to scourge Jesus—a most cruel ordeal that involved the tearing of His flesh into ribbons as He was beaten on the bare back by a whip of several lashes, on which were fastened pieces of metal. His body must have been literally bathed in His own blood. Yet no word of reproach escaped His holy lips.

The Soldiers' Cruelty (Matthew 27:27-32)

Knowing Jesus was condemned because He had claimed to be a King, the soldiers stripped Him of all His outer garments and put a discarded scarlet robe on Him. They crowned Him with thorns, then mockingly bowed before Him. They knew it not, but their action was most significant as they pressed the thorny circlet on His pallid brow. When God cursed the earth for man's sin He caused thorns and thistles to grow (Genesis 3:18). The thorn is the fruit of the curse; and Jesus was made a curse for those who so basely treated Him and for all men, that all who would trust in Him might be redeemed from the curse of the law.

The ribald soldiers made obeisance before Jesus, in whose hand they placed a reed for a scepter, and cried in jeering tones, "Hail, King of the Jews!" To them it was all a huge joke that this meek, defenseless prisoner should ever have imagined Himself a king or permitted His followers to think of Him as a king. In their eyes there was nothing regal about Him. Yet to the eye of faith, He was never more royal than when He endured such contradiction of sinners against Himself with such holy patience and resignation to the will of the Father. The soldiers spat in His face, as the Jews had done in the house of Caiaphas. Jew and Gentile were one in their rejection of Him.

When the soldiers wearied of their coarse and vulgar treatment of Him, they took the robe off Him and put His own garments on Him, and so led Him away to crucify Him. Tradition, not Scripture, tells that He fell beneath the weight of His cross three times, but this rests on no authentic records. However, it seems evident His physical strength was so weakened by loss of blood and excessive suffering that even the callous soldiers saw He needed help in bearing His cross. So they laid hold on Simon, a Cyrenian, who was coming that way, and compelled him to assist. What a privilege was Simon's! We would like to know for certain that he appreciated it. The early Christians said that Alexander and Rufus, mentioned as his sons in Mark 15:21, both became ardent followers of Jesus along with their father. We may hope this is more than an unfounded tradition.

The Crucifixion (Matthew 27:33-44)

At last they reached the little hill outside the walls of Jerusalem, called *Golgotha* by the Jews; and by the Latins, *Calvary,* "the place of a skull." There the tragedy of all ages was to be enacted. There the sacrifice of which all the offerings of the Old Testament were types was to be presented to God on our behalf.

It was customary to give one who was being put to death by crucifixion a stupefying draught to make it easier for him to endure the fearful ordeal. Such a drink, composed of sour wine (or vinegar) mingled with gall, or myrrh, was offered to Jesus, but He refused it. He would not take anything that might benumb His mind or alleviate the sufferings He was undergoing.

Below the cross the soldiers who were responsible for His execution divided His garments among themselves and cast lots, gambling for His seamless tunic, in accordance with David's prophecy uttered a thousand years before (Psalm 22:18). During these six hours one prophecy after another was fulfilled.

Matthew 27:36 might well speak to all our hearts: "And sitting down they watched him there." For *watched* we might better read "were keeping guard," yet the sentence as it stands is most suggestive. These hardhearted, indifferent soldiers looked carelessly at Him as He hung on the tree. You and I, my reader, may well turn aside and see this great sight—the holy Son of God suffering unspeakably at the hands of men whose very lives depended on His mighty power. We may learn much as we sit down and behold Him there, bleeding and dying for sins not His own.

It was customary to indicate with a placard the crime for which one was being punished. So Pilate provided a sign that read: "This is Jesus the King of the Jews," indicating that Christ was being crucified for setting Himself up as King in rebellion against Caesar.

Two thieves were crucified with Him, one on either side. Thus He was numbered with transgressors.

The hearts of those passing by were untouched by the Lord's affliction. They continued to mock Him, raising again the old accusations and saying, "Thou that destroyest the temple, and buildest it in three days, save thyself." They even challenged Him to descend from the cross if in very truth He was the Son of God.

The religious dignitaries also joined with the rest in belittling and ridiculing Him. Yet they uttered a great truth that they did not comprehend when they said, "He saved others; himself he cannot save." Our Christian poet was right when he wrote:

> Himself He could not save;
> He on the cross must die,
> Or mercy could not come
> To ruined sinners nigh.

Oblivious to the real meaning of His death these priests and elders challenged Him, as the rabble had done, bidding Him come down from the cross if He was indeed the King of Israel. They declared they would believe Him in that case. They even quoted from Psalm 22 without seeming to realize it, saying, "He trusted in God; let him deliver him now, if he will have him." He had said He was the Son of God. They called on Him to demonstrate His claim by descending from the cross.

The thieves also reviled Him. Matthew did not tell us of the subsequent repentance of one of these. It is recorded for us in Luke 23:39-43.

Jesus' Death (Matthew 27:45-56)

Up to this point, which takes in a period of three hours, from 9:00 a.m. to 12:00 noon, Jesus had been suffering at the hands of men. It was not these sufferings that paid for sin. Matthew 27:45-49 summarizes the awesome events of the next three hours, when He endured the wrath of God as the great trespass offering—"Then I restored that which I took not away" (Psalm 69:4).

No finite mind can fathom the depths of woe and anguish into which the soul of Jesus sank when that dread darkness spread over all the land. It was a symbol of the spiritual darkness into which He went as the man Christ Jesus was made sin for us that we might become the righteousness of God in Him. It was then that God laid on Him the iniquity of us all and His soul was made an offering for sin.

> The tempest's awful voice was heard;
> O Christ, it broke on Thee.
> Thine open bosom was my ward;
> It bore the storm for me.

We get some faint understanding of·what this meant for Him when, just as the darkness was passing, we hear Him cry, "My God, my God, why hast thou forsaken me?" Each believer can reply, "It was that I might never be forsaken." He took our place and endured the wrath of God our sins deserved. This was the cup from which He shrank in Gethsemane; now it was pressed to His lips, and He drained it to the dregs.

> His the wormwood and the gall:
> His the curse; He bore it all;
> His, the bitter cry of pain,
> When our sins He did sustain.

Some who heard His piercing cry in Aramaic did not know the meaning of the words, "Eli, Eli, lama sabachthani?" and thought He was calling on the prophet Elijah for help. One ran and filled a sponge with vinegar and put it to His parched lips, giving Him a drink. This He received. Others said indifferently, "Let be, let us see whether Elias will come to save him." But there was none who could deliver Him: He must endure the pains of death that we might never die.

When He had accomplished all that was given Him to do, Jesus cried with a loud voice, "It is finished" (John 19:30). Then He dismissed His spirit. He did not die of exhaustion, but He laid down His life voluntarily when His work was done.

The veil in the temple, separating the holy from the most holy place, was immediately torn in two from the top to the bottom. The unseen hand of God tore that curtain apart to signify that the way into the holiest was now revealed. No longer would God dwell in the thick darkness. He could come out to man, in the light; and man, redeemed by atoning blood, could enter with boldness into the very presence of God.

Matthew alone mentioned certain natural phenomena that occurred—a great earthquake, splitting rocks, and opening graves. Saints whose bodies had been sleeping in the tombs were raised and came out of the graves after His resurrection and appeared unto many.

The centurion in charge of the soldiers who were detailed to guard the crucified victims was so impressed by all he had seen and heard that he was filled with awe, and declared, "Truly this was a Son of God." He did not use the definite article, as given in the KJV. Like Nebuchadnezzar of old when he saw the mysterious fourth One in the furnace (Daniel 3:25), the centurion was persuaded that the holy sufferer who had just died on that central cross was more than man.

Many devoted women stood afar off with hearts filled with conflicting emotions. They were true to Jesus to the last, though they could not understand why He was left to suffer and die unaided. Among these were Mary Magdalene, Mary the mother of James and Joses, and also the wife of Zebedee, who was the mother of James and John.

Jesus' Burial (Matthew 27:57-66)

It is worthy of note that as long as our blessed Lord was taking the sinner's place in His vicarious offering of Himself unto God, His enemies were permitted to heap on Him every kind of shameful indignity. But from the moment the blood and water flowed from His wounded side (John 19:33-34), God seemed to say, as it were, "Hands off." In 1 John 5:6,8 we read that the water, the blood and the Holy Spirit are the witnesses to accomplished redemption. From the instant Christ's body was pierced by the sword no unclean hand touched it. Loving friends took it down from the cross, wrapped it in the new fine linen clothes with the spices sent by Nicodemus (John 19:39-40), and laid it in the new tomb of Joseph of Arimathaea. It was the burial of a King (see 2 Chronicles 16:13-14).

"A rich man...named Joseph, who also himself was Jesus' disciple." He was one of the few of those who had riches who waited for the kingdom (Matthew 19:23-24; Mark 15:43), but hitherto he had not openly proclaimed himself a follower of Jesus (John 19:38). He had been a secret disciple, but he proved loyal and brave when the test came. He requested the body of Jesus and Pilate ordered that it be given to him. Thus the body of Jesus was preserved from further indignity, and Isaiah 53:9 was fulfilled. He must be with the rich in His death.

As was customary in Jewish burials, the body was entirely swathed in long linen strips, not simply covered with a shroud. A great stone covered the entire entrance to the tomb and was probably like a great millstone, fitted into a groove cut in the face of the cliff.

Mary of Magdala, out of whom seven demons had been cast (Luke 8:2), and Mary, the mother of Joses (Mark 15:47), were looking on, taking note of everything that was done. They planned to come to the tomb after the sabbath was past and properly embalm the body of the One they had loved and on whom all their hopes were set, but who now was cold in death.

Christ died on the 14th Nisan, the first day of Passover, also called the day of preparation. For the Jews the new day began at sunset, so the words, "the next day," refer to the evening of the day on which Christ died. As the evening that ushered in the 15th of the month began, the Pharisees and others hastened to Pilate to request that Jesus' tomb be secured.

"We remember that that deceiver said...After three days I will rise again." Strange that they, His enemies, should remember what His own disciples had forgotten! It is evident that His prediction had become well known.

"Command therefore that the sepulchre be made sure until the third day." They were taking no chances. They realized that if the least ground were given for starting a rumor that Jesus had fulfilled His promise, their efforts to destroy the effect of His teaching would be in vain. The disappearance of His body from Joseph's new tomb would be, in their estimation, a tragedy and would be accepted by many as a proof of His resurrection. So they were afraid His disciples might arrange to rob the sepulcher and hide the body away; therefore, the importance of effectually thwarting any such attempt.

Pilate was probably not only incensed, but even amused by their fears and anxiety. He gave them a detachment of Roman soldiers and appointed them to guard the tomb. His grim words, "Make it as sure as ye can," seem almost sardonic. They were soon to learn how helpless they were when God's hour struck.

"So they...made the sepulchre sure, sealing the stone, and setting a watch." The Jewish leaders felt that none of the disciples would dare to break the seal, which would be a crime of the first magnitude. The guard of soldiers would ensure that no one would be able to steal the body before the three days had elapsed.

It is evident that Jesus' declaration that He was to rise again the third day (Matthew 20:19) had made a deeper impression on the minds of His enemies than on the hearts of His own disciples. Although He had mentioned it on several occasions, they never seemed to comprehend the meaning of His words. They wondered what the rising from the dead could mean (Mark 9:10,31-32; Luke 18:33-34). So even after He was crucified they had no expectation of His resurrection (John 20:9). But the leaders of the people, who had so definitely opposed Him, remembered His words. While they did not expect His prediction to be fulfilled, they were fearful that by some kind of trickery His disciples might be able to persuade the credulous populace that He had actually triumphed over death; hence their errand to Pilate and their request that every precaution be taken to prevent the disappearance of His body from the tomb. But all their precautions were in vain, for in spite of the sealing of the stone that covered the entrance to the sepulcher and the watchfulness of the Roman guard, the stone was rolled away. The Savior rose from the dead and appeared to many reputable eyewitnesses, who testified to the reality of His resurrection.

CHAPTER TWENTY-EIGHT
THE RISEN KING AND THE ROYAL COMMISSION

The Resurrection (Matthew 28:1-10)

The Jewish sabbath was now ended. A new era was about to begin, to be characterized by a new day. On the morning of the feast of the first fruits, the first day of the week following the first sabbath after the Passover, Jesus was raised from the dead and so became the first fruits of them that slept (Leviticus 23:9-14; 1 Corinthians 15:20,23).

Early in the morning of the day following the sabbath the two Marys went out "to see the sepulchre," preparatory to taking steps for the embalming of the body, which had been so hastily laid away on the day of death. They found the stone at the mouth of the sepulcher rolled away. This stone was not rolled back to let the risen Lord out, for He had left the tomb already. No barriers could restrain Him in His resurrection body. The stone was rolled back to let the women and the disciples in.

"The angel of the Lord descended...His countenance was like lightning." Angels are supernatural beings, pure spirits, who assume the human form at will and can disappear suddenly. "Like lightning" is suggestive of those who are said to be as "a flame of fire" (Hebrews 1:7). In fright at the appearance of the celestial messenger, the hard, sturdy soldiers of the guard fainted, unable to look at his terrifying countenance. Quieting the fears of the women, the angel assured them that he knew their quest exactly. But he had good news for them.

"He is not here: for he is risen." This is the foundation of all our hope. It is not true, as Arnold wrote, that the body of Jesus still sleeps in a Syrian tomb. That tomb is empty. "The place where the Lord lay" bore mute evidence of His resurrection in the presence of the unruffled graveclothes that had enswathed His body (John 20:3-8). The attention of the two Marys was directed to the empty crypt, where that precious body had reposed as it lay cold in death. No earthly hands had removed it. Jesus arose at God's appointed hour and left the sepulcher behind forever.

"Go quickly, and tell his disciples that he is risen from the dead." It was the privilege of these godly women to be the first evangelists of the new dispensation—to carry the glad news of a risen Savior to the sorrowing, because unbelieving, disciples. Before going to the cross, Jesus had told them, "After I am risen again, I will go before you into Galilee" (Matthew 26:32). The women were commanded to tell the disciples to meet their risen Lord as a group at that appointed rendezvous. Love and joy gave wings to the feet of the women as they hastened to carry the glad tidings. There was no doubt in their minds as to the truth of the angel's message.

"As they went...Jesus met them, saying, All hail." He appeared to them Himself, so that now they had not only the word of an angel and the sight of the empty sepulcher to rely on, but they could also testify that they had seen the Lord Himself in the body of His resurrection, and thus their faith had turned to sight. Jesus directed them to convey the good news to the disciples and to bid them go into Galilee to the rendezvous appointed, where He had promised to meet them.

His resurrection is the proof that redemption has been accomplished. Because of His perfect satisfaction in the work of His Son, God raised Him from the dead (Acts 4:2) and seated Him at His own right hand, thus acknowledging Him as Lord and Christ (Acts 2:33, 36). Had the body of the Lord Jesus Christ never come out of the tomb, it would have been silent evidence that He was either a deceiver or deceived when He declared that He was to give His life a ransom for many (Matthew 20:28). He would have been simply another martyr to what He believed to be the truth, or else to His own ambitions. But His resurrection, in accordance with His prediction that the third day He would rise again, confirmed His claims and proved that His death was actual propitiation for sin and that God had accepted it as such.

On Calvary the Lord Jesus Christ took the sinner's place and bore the judgment that we deserved. That judgment involved eternal separation from God for the wicked. The Lord Jesus was made sin and cried to God, "Why hast thou forsaken me?" Because He is infinite and we are but finite, His sacrifice and suffering were a sufficient propitiation for the sins of the world. When expiation had been made, it behooved God the Father to bring Jesus Christ back from the dead, thus fully vindicating Him from any charge of personal failure for which He should be "stricken, smitten of God, and afflicted" (Isaiah 53:4). All His atoning sufferings were for others, not a penalty for any sin of His own. In raising Him from the dead, the Father attested the perfection of the work of His Son.

The empty tomb of Jesus is the silent yet effectual witness to the fact of His resurrection. Had it been possible to find His body, His disciples would have received it and given it careful burial again. And if His enemies could have produced it, they would have displayed it in fiendish glee as a positive proof that His prediction—that He would rise again the third day—had been utterly falsified. But neither friend nor foe could locate it, for God had raised His Son from the dead in token of His perfect satisfaction in the sacrifice of the cross. The tomb was empty on that first Lord's day morning, not because the disciples had come by night and stolen the body while the soldiers slept (an unheard-of proceeding). Nor was the tomb empty because the chief priests and their emissaries had dared to break the Roman seal on the stone that covered the entrance to that rock-hewn grave. The tomb was empty because Jesus had fulfilled His words when He declared that if they destroyed the temple of His body, He would raise it again in three days. The resurrection is attributed to the Father (Hebrews 13:20), to the Son (John 2:19-21; 10:17-18), and to the Holy Spirit (Romans 8:11). The entire trinity had part in that glorious event, the supreme miracle of the ages, when He who died for our sins rose again for our justification. When preparing the new tomb that was to be the dwelling place for a few hours of the dead body of Him who is now alive forevermore, Joseph of Arimathaea little thought of the honor that was to be his.

The Guards' Report (Matthew 28:11-15)

While the women were hastening to carry the news of the Lord's triumph over death to the apostles, the Roman soldiers were in a state of great perturbation over the events of the early morning, and had made their way to the city to tell the chief priests what had occurred. There are no depths of deceit and chicanery too low for religious bigots who are determined to pursue a chosen course to the bitter end, no matter what may be involved. When the soldiers explained what had taken place, these priests and the elders counseled the soldiers to say that the disciples of Jesus had come by night, while the guard slept, and stolen the body away.

Such an acknowledgment, if true, would have exposed them to severe penalties, but the chief priests promised to intercede for them if the matter came to the ears of the governor. They gave large bribes to the soldiers to ensure their collaboration in the matter. So they went away and told the story as they were instructed, and their story was commonly reported, Matthew told us, "until this day"—that is, for some years at least after the resurrection.

Christ's Final Command (Matthew 28:16-20)

During His last days with His disciples, as they were drawing near to Jerusalem, Jesus had told them of His approaching death and His resurrection. He mentioned a definite mountain in Galilee where He would meet them after all had been consummated (Matthew 26:32; 28:7; Mark 16:7). Though He appeared earlier to individuals and to various groups, it was in Galilee that He manifested Himself to "above five hundred brethren at once" (1 Corinthians 15:6). At least most commentators consider this to be the case, though He evidently met first with the eleven apostles on the occasion recorded in Matthew 28:16-17, before appearing to the larger number.

"They worshipped him." When they saw Him and knew it was indeed the risen Christ they were looking upon, they worshiped Him, knowing Him to be the Son of God come forth in triumph from the tomb (Romans 1:4). "But some doubted." What a proof of the incorrigible evil of the human heart! Unbelief can be overcome only by the power of the Holy Spirit. It was some time before all the little group believed (Mark 16:14). This helps us to understand Mark 16:17. It was promised only to the believing apostles that miraculous signs would follow and thus authenticate their testimony.

"All power [authority] is given unto me in heaven and in earth." As the obedient One, who had humbled Himself to the death of the cross, Jesus was exalted by the Father to the place of pre-eminence over all things (Philippians 2:9-11). He is set as Son over His own house (Hebrews 3:6), to whom all God's servants are to be subject. It is He Himself who is the general director of the missionary program of the present age.

"Go ye therefore, and teach all nations ... in the name of the Father, and of the Son, and of the Holy Ghost." This gives the primary commission. The command is to teach, or make disciples, of all nations. The words "baptizing them" are secondary. It was not to baptize that they were sent, important as that is, but to instruct the nations in the way of life. Those receiving the word were to be baptized as the outward expression of their faith.

The baptismal formula was in the name of the trinity, as was their preaching and teaching—not in the names, but the name of the Father, and of the Son, and of the Holy Spirit. Each person of the godhead had and still has a part in the work of salvation; therefore all are recognized and confessed in Christian baptism. The Father sent the Son, who gave His life in the power of the eternal Spirit.

"All things whatsoever I have commanded you." During the forty days between His resurrection and ascension, Jesus unfolded to His disciples the program He would have them carry out, and gave the commandments that they were to teach the people of all nations (Acts 1:2-3).

"Lo, I am with you alway." His presence by the Spirit was promised to all who sought to carry out His commission. "Even unto the end of the world." The last word is really *age*. It refers to a time-world, rather than the material universe. Strictly speaking, the age to which He was referring will not end until He appears in glory to set up His kingdom over all the earth, but the period of the calling of the church from Pentecost to the rapture must be included in that word *unto*. During all that time from the hour in which He spoke these words to the bringing in of the kingdom age, the gospel is to be preached, and His Spirit will be with His faithful messengers, to enable them to proclaim the message in power for the blessing of mankind.

The great commission to evangelize the world is not given as a whole in any of the Gospels, but we need to read all related passages in the three Synoptics and in Acts 1 to get it in its entirety. Different aspects of the commission are emphasized in each place. Then, in addition, we have the Lord's command to the eleven as given in John 20. These all agree in this: that it is our responsibility to carry the message of grace to all men everywhere, while we wait for our Lord to return, according to His promise. In keeping with the character of Matthew's Gospel as revealing the King and the kingdom, the commission as given here has specially in view the bringing of all nations to acknowledge the authority of Christ, and proclaim their allegiance by baptism into the name of the holy trinity. In its fullest sense this commission has never been fulfilled as yet. It will be completed after the church age has ended, and a Jewish remnant will carry out the Lord's instructions preparatory to setting up the kingdom. But this does not relieve us of our responsibility to carry it out as far as possible in the present age. Mark stressed the importance of faith on the part of those who carry the message, which was to be authenticated by "signs following." Luke, both in his Gospel and the Acts, linked the subjective with the objective—repentance on the part of the sinner, forgiveness on the part of God. John dwelled on the authority of the risen Christ who commissions His servants to proclaim remission of sins to all who believe and retention of sins to those who spurn the message.

But all alike declared the urgency and the importance of carrying the witness-testimony, the proclamation of the gospel, to all the nations of the world in the shortest possible time. Alas, how sadly has the church failed in this respect! It is an appalling thought that after nineteen centuries of gospel preaching there are many millions of men and women still sitting in darkness and the shadow of death (Isaiah 9:2). They have never heard the name of Jesus, and know nothing of the redemption which He has purchased by His atoning death on the cross.

The program announced by our Lord has never been modified or repealed. It still constitutes what the Iron Duke (Wellington) called the "marching orders" of the church—orders which have however been very largely ignored by the great bulk of professing Christians. The first six centuries of the present era were characterized by great missionary zeal, when at times whole nations were brought to at least an outward profession of faith in Christ. But the next thousand years, which Rome calls "the ages of faith" but which instructed Christians rightly designate "the dark ages," were marked in great measure by an eclipse of true gospel activity. With the coming of the Protestant Reformation came a new interest in missions, in which the Moravians were the pioneers. Later, within the last century and a half, there has followed a great awakening as to the responsibility of the church to evangelize the regions beyond. Today there is no excuse either for lack of information or lack of zeal as to missionary activity.

There are some who deny that we of the church age are to act at all on this commission as given here, insisting that it was intended for a Jewish testimony in the coming era of the great tribulation. This is fanciful in the extreme. Far more important than any quibbling as to the exact character of this commission is the truth of our responsibility to carry the story of redeeming love to all men everywhere. It is given not alone to those we may think of as official ministers or specially designated missionaries. The commission is given to every believer in the Lord Jesus Christ to make Him known to others and so to win as many precious souls as possible while the day of grace continues. This is the first great business of every member of the church of the living God. All are called to be witnesses, according to their measure. It is ours to "go" (Matthew 28:19), to "pray" (9:38), and to help send out (Acts 13:3) and sustain those who are able to leave home and friends as they hasten forth into distant lands to carry the gospel to other regions beyond (3 John 6-8).

The command to teach, or disciple, all nations, does not mean that it is our responsibility to educate the heathen along secular lines. This may come in as a byproduct of missionary service, but it is not the supreme work of the herald of the cross. It is a lamentable fact that much missionary money has been devoted to founding and maintaining schools and colleges that have turned out bitter enemies of the cross of Christ. Had the same money and energy been devoted to preaching the gospel, the results would have been far different. Schoolteaching is a laudable profession, but it should not be confused with gospel testimony, though it would be a happy and blessed thing if each schoolteacher were also a proclaimer of the glad tidings of grace.

The Lord's instructions never yet have been fully obeyed, and we know that not all the nations will accept the message in this age of grace. But we are commanded to go in the name of the triune God, proclaiming the authority of the risen King and encouraging all men to yield to Him in glad surrender, and so enter into peace and blessing while waiting for His return from Heaven.

The Gospel of Matthew closes with the Lord sending out His messengers. We do not read of Christ's ascension here. This is significant, for it is the King commissioning His ambassadors that the Holy Spirit desired to emphasize. The last we see of Him, He is directing His representatives to go to all nations, calling on men and women everywhere to acknowledge Him as their Savior and become subject to His will.

When the commanding officer speaks, a loyal soldier has but to obey. The "captain of the host of the Lord" (Joshua 5:14) has said, "Go ye!" It is ours to act on His instructions. The blessing of God has always rested in a very special way upon the individual or the church that was missionary-minded. None ever lost out by obedience to our risen Lord's command.

When we say there are plenty of heathen at home to whom we should give our attention rather than to seek the lost in distant lands, we forget that all at home are within easy reach of the gospel, if they are interested in it. Untold myriads are dying in heathen lands, ignorant of the way of life. They have never heard of the Bible or the Savior it reveals.

There were no missionary societies in the early church because the entire body of believers was supposed to be engaged in the great work of evangelizing the world. It was after the church as a whole lost this vision that societies were formed to arouse interest in and forward missionary activity.

Sending out men and women as missionaries who do not themselves have a definite Christian experience is folly of the worst kind.

It is but the blind leading the blind, and both are headed for the ditch (Matthew 15:14). No one is fit to be a missionary abroad who is not a missionary at home. An ocean voyage never made a missionary of anyone. There must be a divinely implanted love for lost souls before one is ready to go in Christ's name to carry His gospel to the heathen world. One of the first evidences of genuine conversion to Christ is the desire to make Him known to others.

It has been asked: What right has anyone to hear the gospel hundreds of times when millions have never heard it once? We may well be exercised as to this, for we are called to be *ambassadors* for Christ. This is the title Paul gave to those who seek to carry out our Lord's instruction as to evangelizing the nations (2 Corinthians 5:20). While our Savior Himself is personally in Heaven, seated on the right hand of the divine Majesty (Hebrews 1:3), we are called to represent Him in this world, going to rebels against the authority of the God of Heaven and earth. We are to plead with them to be reconciled to Him who sent His Son in grace that all men might have life and peace through Him. We are unfaithful representatives indeed if we fail to respond to the command laid on us, and allow our fellow men to perish in their sins unwarned and knowing not the way of life.

A HARMONY OF THE GOSPELS

	Matthew	Mark	Luke	John
Genealogies of Jesus	1:1-17		3:23-38	
The Coming Forerunner			1:5-25	
Annunciation to Mary			1:26-38	
The Magnificat			1:46-56	
Birth of John the Baptist			1:57-80	
Birth of Jesus	1:18-25		2:1-7	
The Message of the Angels			2:8-20	
The Presentation in the Temple			2:21-38	
Visit of the Magi	2:1-12			
Flight into Egypt	2:13-15			
Vengeance of Herod	2:16-23			
The Childhood of Jesus			2:39-52	
John the Baptist's Ministry	3:1-12	1:2-8	3:1-22	1:6-14
John Baptizes Jesus	3:13-17	1:9-11	3:21-22	
Jesus Is Tempted	4:1-11	1:12-13	4:1-13	
The Testimony of John the Baptist				1:15-36
Initial Calling of Disciples				1:35-51
Jesus' First Miracle				2:1-11
First Cleansing of the Temple				2:12-25

	Matthew	Mark	Luke	John
Talk with Nicodemus				3:1-21
John the Baptist's Final Testimony				3:22-36
Woman at the Well				4:1-26
The Conversion of the Samaritans				4:27-42
Jesus Begins Ministry in Galilee	4:12-17			
Healing of Nobleman's Son				4:46-54
Jesus Is Rejected at Nazareth			4:14-30	
Jesus Calls His First Disciples	4:18-25	1:14-20	5:1-11	
Jesus Casts Out Demons		1:21-28	4:31-37	
Jesus Heals Peter's Mother-in-law	8:14-17	1:29-34	4:38-41	
Jesus Cleanses a Leper	8:1-4	1:35-45	5:12-15	
Jesus Heals a Paralytic	9:1-8	2:1-12	5:16-26	
Calling of Matthew	9:9-13	2:13-17	5:27-32	
Healing and Teaching at Pool of Bethesda				5:1-47
Jesus Defends His Disciples	9:14-17	2:18-22	5:33-39	
Defining Sabbath Day Observance	12:1-8	2:23-28	6:1-11	
Jesus Heals on the Sabbath	12:9-21	3:1-6	6:6-11	
Multitudes Healed	12:15-21	3:7-12		
Jesus Ordains the Twelve		3:13-19	6:12-16	
Sermon on the Mount	5:1–7:29		6:17-49	
Jesus Heals the Centurion's Servant	8:5-13		7:1-10	

	Matthew	Mark	Luke	John
Jesus Raises the Widow's Son			7:11-18	
Jesus Testifies to the Greatness of John the Baptist	11:1-19		7:19-35	
Jesus Proclaims Misery on Unrepentant Cities	11:20-24		10:13-15	
Jesus Offers Rest for the Weary	11:25-30			
Jesus Teaches of Forgiveness			7:36-50	
Jesus Confirms His Authority	12:22-30	3:22-27	11:14-28	
The Unpardonable Sin	12:31-37	3:28-30	12:10	
Jesus Condemns Jews' Unbelief	12:38-45		11:29-54	
Jesus Introduces a New Family	12:46-50	3:31-35	8:19-21	
Parables of the Kingdom	13:1-53	4:1-34	8:1-15; 13:18-21	
Power over Creation	8:23-27	4:35-41	8:22-25	
Gadarene Demoniac Healed	8:28-34	5:1-20	8:26-39	
Jairus's Daughter Raised	9:18-19, 23-26	5:21-24, 35-43	8:40-42, 49-56	
Woman with Issue of Blood Healed	9:20-22	5:25-34	8:43-48	
Healing of Blind and Mute	9:27-34			
The Prophet Without Honor	13:54-58	6:1-6		
Jesus Sends Out His Couriers	9:35–10:15	6:7-13	9:1-11	
Warning of Coming Persecution	10:16-23			

	Matthew	Mark	Luke	John
Promise of Care and Comfort	10:24-33			
Warning of Conflict	10:34-39			
Reward for Those who Accept His Couriers	10:40-42			
John the Baptist Murdered	14:1-14	6:14-29	9:7-9	
Five Thousand Fed	14:15-21	6:33-46	9:11-17	6:1-15
Jesus Walks on Water	14:22-36	6:47-52		6:16-21
The Food that Endures				6:22-71
Jesus Condemns Pharisaic Tradition	15:1-20	7:1-23		
Jesus Rewards the Faith of a Gentile Woman	15:21-28	7:24-30		
Jesus Opens Ears of Deaf		7:31-37		
Four Thousand Fed	15:29-39	8:1-9		
Pharisees Demand a Sign	16:1-4	8:10-13		
Jesus Warns His Disciples	16:5-12	8:14-21	12:1-21	
A Blind Man Healed		8:22-26		
Peter's Confession	16:13-20	8:27-30	9:18-21	
Christ Foretells His Death and Resurrection	16:21-26	8:31-37	9:22-25	
Christ Tells of the Coming of His Kingdom	16:27-28	8:38–9:1	9:26-27	
The Transfiguration	17:1-8	9:2-8	9:28-36	
Explanation of the Coming of Elijah	17:9-13	9:9-13		
Demon-Possessed Boy Healed	17:14-21	9:14-29	9:37-43	
Christ Again Foretells His Death and Resurrection	17:22-23	9:30-32	9:44-45	

	Matthew	Mark	Luke	John
Payment of Temple Tax	17:24-27			
Greatest in the Kingdom	18:1-14	9:33-50	9:46-50	
Lessons in Forgiveness	18:15-35		17:3-4	
Attitudes of World toward Christ				7:1-53
Rebuking Intolerance			9:51-56	
Cost of Discipleship	8:19-22		9:57-62	
Woman Taken in Adultery				8:1-11
The Light of the World				8:12-20
Salvation After Death?				8:21-32
Children of the Devil				8:33-47
The Pre-existent Christ				8:48-59
Man Born Blind Healed				9:1-41
The Good Shepherd				10:1-16
The Mission of the Seventy			10:1-20	
The Mystery of the Incarnation			10:21-24	
Parable of the Good Samaritan			10:25-37	
Service and Fellowship			10:38-42	
Teaching on Prayer			11:1-13	
Warning of Danger of Covetousness			12:13-21	
Living Without Anxiety			12:22-34	
Waiting for the Lord's Return			12:35-48	
The Offense of the Cross			12:49-59	
A Call to Repentance			13:1-9	

	Matthew	Mark	Luke	John
Crippled Woman Healed on the Sabbath			13:10-17	
Security of Christ's Sheep				10:17-30
Jesus's Works Testify to His Deity				10:31-42
A Great Crisis			13:22-35	
Jesus Heals Again on the Sabbath			14:1-6	
Parable of the Ambitious Guest			14:7-14	
Parable of the Great Supper			14:15-24	
Counting the Cost			14:25-35	
Lost Ones Found			15:1-32	
Parable of the Unjust Steward			16:1-17	
Teaching on Divorce	19:1-12	10:1-12	16:18	
The Rich Man and Lazarus			16:19-31	
Subjection to Christ			17:1-10	
Ten Lepers Cleansed			17:11-19	
Teaching on Christ's Second Advent			17:20-37	
Persistence in Prayer			18:1-8	
Right Attitude in Prayer			18:9-14	
Raising of Lazarus				11:1-46
One Man to Die				11:47-54
Christ Blesses Children	19:13-15	10:13-16	18:15-17	
Rich Young Ruler	19:16-30	10:17-31	18:18-30	
Parable of the Laborers	20:1-16			

	Matthew	Mark	Luke	John
Third Prediction by Christ of His Death	20:17-19	10:32-34	18:31-34	
Worldly Ambition	20:20-28	10:35-45		
Healing the Blind	20:29-34	10:46-52	18:35-43	
Jesus Meets Zacchaeus			19:1-10	
Parable of the Pounds			19:11-27	
The Triumphal Entry	21:1-11	11:1-11	19:28-44	12:12-19
Second Cleansing of Temple	21:12-16	11:12-19	19:45-48	
Jesus Predicts His Death				12:20-36
Christ Still Rejected				12:37-43
Christ: Not Judge But Savior				12:44-50
Jesus Curses the Fig Tree	21:17-22	11:12-14, 19-26		
Jesus Affirms His Authority	21:23-27	11:27-33	20:1-8	
Parable of the Two Sons	21:28-32			
Parable of the Vineyard	21:33-46	12:1-12	20:9-20	
Parable of the Wedding Feast	22:1-14			
Lesson on Paying Taxes	22:15-22	12:13-17	20:21-26	
Lesson on the Resurrection	22:23-33	12:18-27	20:27-40	
Lesson on the Great Commandment	22:34-40	12:28-34		
Lesson on Jesus' Identity	22:41-46	12:35-37	20:41-44	
Warning against Seeking Earthly Glory	23:1-12	12:38-40		
Woes on Religious Leaders	23:13-39		20:45-47	
Lesson on Giving		12:41-44	21:1-4	

	Matthew	Mark	Luke	John
Characteristics of Present Age	24:1-8	13:1-8	21:5-11	
Signs of Last Days	24:9-14	13:9-13	21:12-19	
Great Tribulation	24:15-28	13:14-23	21:20-24	
Coming of the Son	24:29-31	13:24-27	21:25-28	
The Sign of Christ's Coming	24:32-41	13:28-31	21:29-33	
Our Duty to Watch	24:42-51	13:32-37	21:34-38	
Parable of Ten Virgins	25:1-13			
Parable of Talents	25:14-30			
Sheep and Goats	25:31-46			
Mary's Devotion	26:1-13	14:1-9		12:1-11
Jesus Washes Disciples' Feet				13:1-17
The Last Passover	26:14-25	14:10-21	22:1-14	
Jesus Reveals the Betrayer	26:21-25	14:18-21	22:21-23	13:18-30
The Lord's Supper	26:26-30	14:22-25	22:15-20	
Jesus' Warning	26:31-35	14:27-31	22:24-38	13:31-38
Jesus Comforts His Disciples				14:1-31
Discourse on the Road to Gethsemane				15:1-27
The Work of the Holy Spirit				16:1-33
Jesus Prays for His Followers				17:1-26
Agony in the Garden	26:36-46	14:32-42	22:39-46	
Jesus' Arrest	26:47-56	14:43-50	22:47-53	18:1-11

	Matthew	Mark	Luke	John
Jesus before the Priests	26:57-68	14:53-65	22:63-71	18:12-14, 19-24
Peter's Denial	26:69-75	14:66-72	22:54-62	18:15-18, 25-27
Judas's Remorse	27:1-10			
Pilate's Court	27:11-18	15:1-10	23:1-5, 13-19	18:28-40
Herod's Court			23:6-12	
Pilate's Weakness	27:19-26	15:11-15	23:20-25	19:1-16
The Soldiers' Cruelty	27:27-32	15:16-21		19:1-3
The Crucifixion	27:33-44	15:22-32	23:26-43	19:17-27
Jesus' Death	27:45-56	15:33-41	23:44-49	19:28-37
Jesus' Burial	27:57-66	15:42-47	23:50-56	19:38-42
The Resurrection	28:1-10	16:1-8	24:1-12	
Peter and John at the Empty Tomb				20:1-10
Jesus Appears to Mary		16:9-11		20:11-18
The Road to Emmaus		16:12-13	24:13-35	
The Guard's Report	28:11-15			
Jesus with His Disciples				20:19-31
Miraculous Catch of Fish				21:1-14
Peter Reinstated				21:15-25
Christ's Final Command	28:16-20	16:15-20	24:36-49	
The Ascension		16:19	24:50-53	

AUTHOR BIOGRAPHY

HENRY ALLAN IRONSIDE, one of this century's greatest preachers, was born in Toronto, Canada, on October 14, 1876. He lived his life by faith; his needs at crucial moments were met in the most remarkable ways.

Though his classes stopped with grammar school, his fondness for reading and an incredibly retentive memory put learning to use. His scholarship was well recognized in academic circles with Wheaton College awarding an honorary Litt. D. in 1930 and Bob Jones University an honorary D.D. in 1942. Dr. Ironside was also appointed to the boards of numerous Bible institutes, seminaries, and Christian organizations.

"HAI" lived to preach and he did so widely throughout the United States and abroad. E. Schuyler English, in his biography of Ironside, revealed that during 1948, the year HAI was 72, and in spite of failing eyesight, he "gave 569 addresses, besides participating in many other ways." In his eighteen years at Chicago's Moody Memorial Church, his only pastorate, every Sunday but two had at least one profession of faith in Christ.

H. A. Ironside went to be with the Lord on January 15, 1951. Throughout his ministry, he authored expositions on 51 books of the Bible and through the great clarity of his messages led hundreds of thousands, worldwide, to a knowledge of God's Word. His words are as fresh and meaningful today as when first preached.

The official biography of Dr. Ironside, *H. A. Ironside: Ordained of the Lord*, is available from the publisher.

THE WRITTEN MINISTRY OF
H. A. IRONSIDE

Expositions

Joshua
Ezra
Nehemiah
Esther
Psalms (1-41 only)
Proverbs
Song of Solomon
Isaiah
Jeremiah
Lamentations
Ezekiel
Daniel
The Minor Prophets
Matthew
Mark
Luke
John

Acts
Romans
1 & 2 Corinthians
Galatians
Ephesians
Philippians
Colossians
1 & 2 Thessalonians
1 & 2 Timothy
Titus
Philemon
Hebrews
James
1 & 2 Peter
1,2, & 3 John
Jude
Revelation

Doctrinal Works

Baptism
Death and Afterward
Eternal Security of the Believer
Holiness: The False and
  the True
The Holy Trinity

Letters to a Roman Catholic
  Priest
The Levitical Offerings
Not Wrath But Rapture
Wrongly Dividing the Word
  of Truth

Historical Works

The Four Hundred Silent Years
A Historical Sketch of the Brethren Movement

Other works by the author are brought back into print from time to time. All of this material is available from your local Christian bookstore or from the publisher.

LOIZEAUX

A Heritage of Ministry . . .

Paul and Timothy Loizeaux began their printing and publishing activities in the farming community of Vinton, Iowa, in 1876. Their tools were rudimentary: a hand press, several fonts of loose type, ink, and a small supply of paper. There was certainly no dream of a thriving commercial enterprise. It was merely the means of supplying the literature needs for their own ministries, with the hope that the Lord would grant a wider circulation. It wasn't a business; it was a ministry.

Our Foundation Is the Word of God

We stand without embarrassment on the great fundamentals of the faith: the inspiration and authority of Scripture, the deity and spotless humanity of our Lord Jesus Christ, His atoning sacrifice and resurrection, the indwelling of the Holy Spirit, the unity of the church, the second coming of the Lord, and the eternal destinies of the saved and lost.

Our Mission Is to Help People Understand God's Word

We are not in the entertainment business. We only publish books we believe will be of genuine help to God's people, both through the faithful exposition of Scripture and practical application of its principles to contemporary need.

Faithfulness to the Word and consistency in what we publish have been hallmarks of Loizeaux through four generations. And that means when you see the name Loizeaux on the outside, you can trust what is on the inside. That is our promise to the Lord...and to you.

If Paul and Timothy were to visit us today they would still recognize the work they began in 1876. Because some very important things haven't changed at all...this is still a ministry.